"*The Elephant in the Room* is as wise as it is practical. The 'relational perspective' will change how you think about leadership effectiveness. You'll soon see that the way executives interact with each other is more important to the success of an organization than their qualities as individuals. Drawing from her own consulting practice and accounts of famous work partnerships, Smith provides compelling stories of relationships between leaders—famous and not so famous—that influenced business and government outcomes in profound ways. The inescapable conclusion is that a relationship-based concept of leadership is long overdue."

—**Amy Edmondson**, Novartis Professor of Leadership and Management, Harvard Business School

"It is very rare for someone to write a book of this kind based on real life experience that is both sensitive in human terms but also practical and hard edged."

—**Lord Dennis Stevenson**, banker, former chairman, HBOS plc

"No matter where you are along your professional journey, you'll wish you had read *The Elephant in the Room* earlier. Diana Smith's insights into what made some contemporary and historical business and political relationships succeed and others fail will make you pause and reflect. Most important, her frameworks and insights on what you can do to make your relationships successful will become part of your professional toolkit."

—**Paula A. Sneed**, chairman and CEO, Phelps Prescott Group; retired executive vice president, Kraft Foods Inc.

"This book offers vivid and practical insight into the relationship dynamics central to effective leadership and sustained organizational success."

—**Ashley Unwin**, UK consulting leader, PwC Consulting

"*The Elephant in the Room* shows you how to navigate even the trickiest business relationships. Drawing on stories from decades of research, Smith lays out the skills we all need to develop to succeed as leaders today. An invaluable handbook for anyone seeking to get results through others."

—**Marilyn Paul**, author, *It's Hard to Make a Difference When You Can't Find Your Keys*

"*The Elephant in the Room* reveals priceless insights into what it takes to develop and sustain healthy, productive relationships. A must-read for anyone who wants to be a successful leader."

—**Gerald Chertavian**, founder and CEO, Year Up

"Smith outlines practical strategies for building constructive relationships in a fast-moving business context. A must for leaders as well as HR professionals."

—**Jens R. Jenssen**, senior vice president of people and organization, Statoil

"Leadership is a relationship. And it's the quality of your relationships that will ultimately determine your level of success. No one understands this better than Diana McLain Smith. Her new book, *The Elephant in the Room*, is extraordinary. It's one of the most insightful and discerning examinations of interpersonal relationships at work I've ever read. Diana begins with a revealing and intimate portrait of two corporate executives whose relationship starts as a 'bromance' but eventually sours, and then she moves us to carefully examine our own relationship challenges. *The Elephant in the Room* is not another one of those quick fix, flavor-of-the-month, faddish books that offers pabulum solutions to very challenging problems. It is just the opposite. *The Elephant in the Room* is a very serious book about a very serious issue, and the most significant factor in your success as a leader. Diana blends clinical analysis, compassionate coaching, and practical business advice that lead to those stunning insights, aha moments, and useful information that we always seek but don't find in most books. You'll definitely find them in *The Elephant in the Room*. Buy it, read it, use it."

—**Jim Kouzes**, coauthor, *The Leadership Challenge*, and The Dean's Executive Fellow of Leadership, Leavey School of Business, Santa Clara University

The ELEPHANT in the ROOM

HOW RELATIONSHIPS MAKE OR BREAK THE SUCCESS OF LEADERS AND ORGANIZATIONS

Diana McLain Smith

FOREWORD BY PETER SENGE

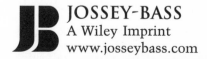

JOSSEY-BASS
A Wiley Imprint
www.josseybass.com

Copyright © 2011 by Diana McLain Smith. All rights reserved.

Published by Jossey-Bass
A Wiley Imprint
989 Market Street, San Francisco, CA 94103-1741—www.josseybass.com

No part of this publication may be reproduced, stored in a retrieval system, or transmitted in any form or by any means, electronic, mechanical, photocopying, recording, scanning, or otherwise, except as permitted under Section 107 or 108 of the 1976 United States Copyright Act, without either the prior written permission of the publisher, or authorization through payment of the appropriate per-copy fee to the Copyright Clearance Center, Inc., 222 Rosewood Drive, Danvers, MA 01923, 978-750-8400, fax 978-646-8600, or on the Web at www.copyright.com. Requests to the publisher for permission should be addressed to the Permissions Department, John Wiley & Sons, Inc., 111 River Street, Hoboken, NJ 07030, 201-748-6011, fax 201-748-6008, or online at www.wiley.com/go/permissions.

Additional credit lines are listed on page 306.

Readers should be aware that Internet Web sites offered as citations and/or sources for further information may have changed or disappeared between the time this was written and when it is read.

Limit of Liability/Disclaimer of Warranty: While the publisher and author have used their best efforts in preparing this book, they make no representations or warranties with respect to the accuracy or completeness of the contents of this book and specifically disclaim any implied warranties of merchantability or fitness for a particular purpose. No warranty may be created or extended by sales representatives or written sales materials. The advice and strategies contained herein may not be suitable for your situation. You should consult with a professional where appropriate. Neither the publisher nor author shall be liable for any loss of profit or any other commercial damages, including but not limited to special, incidental, consequential, or other damages.

Jossey-Bass books and products are available through most bookstores. To contact Jossey-Bass directly call our Customer Care Department within the U.S. at 800-956-7739, outside the U.S. at 317-572-3986, or fax 317-572-4002.

Jossey-Bass also publishes its books in a variety of electronic formats. Some content that appears in print may not be available in electronic books.

Library of Congress Cataloging-in-Publication Data

Smith, Diana McLain.
  The elephant in the room: how relationships make or break the success of leaders and organizations / Diana McLain Smith; foreword by Peter Senge.
    p. cm
  Includes bibliographical references and index.
  ISBN 978-1-118-01542-1 (cloth); ISBN: 978-1-118-08673-5 (ebk);
ISBN: 978-1-118-08674-2 (ebk); ISBN: 978-1-118-08676-6 (ebk)
  1. Leadership. 2. Interpersonal relations. 3. Organizational behavior. I. Title.
  HD57.7.S6473 2011
  658.4'092–dc23

                                                                      2011017896

Printed in the United States of America
FIRST EDITION
HB Printing   10 9 8 7 6 5 4 3 2 1

CONTENTS

FOREWORD   ix
Peter Senge

PART 1   Understanding Relationships   1

1   Present and Unaccounted For   3
2   The Life and Death of a Relationship   17
3   It's a Matter of Perspective   47

PART 2   Strengthening Relationships   67

4   Using the Heat of the Moment   69
5   Mapping Relationships   89
6   Focusing Investments, Managing Costs   119

PART 3   Transforming Relationships   131

7   Navigating Change Over Time   133
8   Disrupting Patterns   143
9   Reframing Each Other   173
10   Revising What You Know   197

Contents

Appendix A: A Guide to Behavioral Repertoires   231

Appendix B: The Ladder of Reflection   243

Notes   255

Bibliography   277

Additional Reading   287

Acknowledgments   291

The Author   295

Index   297

To my brother, Rob, and my husband, Bruce
For being there

FOREWORD

Human beings are social animals. We are not especially big or especially strong. Our ability to survive and evolve has always hinged on our ability to learn collectively, to adapt our ways of living to new circumstances, to innovate. We have deep instincts for kindness and concern for the other. We care about one another, not because we need to but because we want to. As the pioneering biologist Humberto Maturana says, "We are loving animals."

But instincts need to be cultivated. Although relationships have always been the context in which innovation and learning either flourish or founder, challenging work settings demand more than instincts. This becomes evident as soon as conflicts arise. What happens when we face others with "crazy ideas," ideas with which we strongly disagree, even ideas we consider dangerous for the team or organization we are part of? Quickly, good feelings give way to fear, anger, and distrust. In a flicker of an eye, the predisposition toward concern and mutuality becomes competition for whose idea will win out.

Cultivating practical capacity regarding relationships—how they work, develop, and change—requires a consensual body of knowledge. We need practical tools and shared understanding for building relationships that enable innovation and continual learning. We need practices to cultivate our awareness and fluidity in action. We need shared commitment to mutual learning, based on the understanding that this matters, personally and organizationally.

Without common tools and shared language, the nurturing of relationships fades into the background, an organizational bass clef of disregard and disquiet drowned out by the more immediate demands of tasks and results. When this happens, relationships become "the soft stuff," ignored as a domain of strategic significance and conscious capacity-building. Habitual mental and behavioral habits govern. Simple behavioral rules such as "be nice" and "listen politely" substitute for building skills and behavioral repertoires that can prepare us for the difficulties that inevitably come. The results are failed relationships and, often, failed institutions. Diagnoses of what went wrong inevitably focus on strategic errors and operational breakdowns but rarely trace the sources upstream to relationships that failed to generate the deep trust and capacity for mutual inquiry and collective creativity that demanding circumstances required.

For decades Diana Smith has been a leader helping people develop relational intelligence in challenging management contexts. Her insights start with a simple shift in the lens by which we frame difficulties when they arise: *it's not about her or him; it's about us.* Relationships are embedded in webs of interactions. It's a system. But we usually start with the lens of individuals. Starting off on the wrong foot heads us down a path with little leverage for real change.

That said, there is a good reason we impose an individualistic lens on a systemic phenomenon. Most of us simply do not know how to do otherwise.

This leads to the second part of Smith's insight: *there are predictable patterns of growth and change in work relationships, and they can be understood and influenced*.

Smith lays out a conceptual framework that can be used to understand the forces that drive relationships north or south. She also provides a general way for gauging the capacities of key work relationships, along with tried and tested tools for strengthening them. Grounded in years of research and consulting with management and other working teams, Smith's frameworks are complex yet intuitive. Once you understand the basics of her lens and tools and work with them, they will grow into a fundamental element of your leadership practice. This is a big claim. But read on, and see for yourself.

While the issues and lessons here are timeless, never have they been more timely. In a world that is increasingly distributed, interdependent, and multicultural, mastery in the domain of productive work relationships will often be the distinguishing feature of organizations that succeed or fail. A CEO mentor of mine pointed out many years ago that he saw this as the fundamental shift unfolding in leadership and management: "Whereas marketing, manufacturing, technology, and financial sophistication used to distinguish firms, today they are the ticket for admission in global industries. Increasingly, what will set companies apart will be their sophistication in the human domain. What was folklore and untested aphorisms will need to become more systematized, just as has happened in these other fields."

Herein lies a defining challenge of our time. In a world increasingly interconnected by technology, our abilities to understand one another and cultivate the capacity for truly thinking together become ever more critical. To the extent we fail to do so, we will become victims of a great irony, expressed succinctly by a young student recently: "We are more and more connected, and yet we are more and more separate."

Cambridge, Massachusetts   Peter Senge
February 2011

The elephant in the room
A major problem or controversial issue
that is obviously present but avoided
as a subject for discussion
because it is more
comfortable to do so.

—Oxford English
Dictionary

PART 1

Understanding Relationships

The relationship—the pivotal point
on which all else turns—is built
(or undermined) in every interaction.

—Suzanne Clothier[1]

ONE

Present and Unaccounted For

If civilization is to survive, we must cultivate the science
of human relationships.

—FRANKLIN ROOSEVELT, THE DAY BEFORE HE DIED

"Relationships? Get over it!" a leader once told me, looking askance. "We're not married. We just have to work together." Yes, and that's exactly the point, I replied. You do have to work together, and if you don't get your relationships right, a lot can go wrong—both for you and your organization.

Countless examples in the historical record and in my own research suggest that if you don't treat relationships as a strategic asset—and invest accordingly—they can easily become a serious, even fatal liability. Think of Apple in the 1980s. Two years after Steve Jobs hired John Sculley as Apple's CEO, the two had a falling out, the board sided with Sculley, Jobs left, and the company nearly faded into oblivion. "I'm actually convinced that if Steve hadn't come back when he did," John Sculley himself said in a 2010 interview, "Apple would have been history. It would have been gone, absolutely gone."[1]

3

The personal aftermath is harder to discern, since it is less public. But in Jobs and Sculley's occasional post-facto accounts of their breakup, you can see the toll it took on their lives. You can also see, if you look closely, that neither man seems to grasp the role he played in creating a relationship that almost brought down a great company.

In 1995, with Jobs still in exile and Apple struggling to survive, Jobs had this to say about why Apple was doing so poorly: "John Sculley ruined Apple, and he ruined it by bringing a set of values to the top of Apple which were corrupt and corrupted some of the top people who were there, drove out some of the ones who were not corruptible, and brought in more corrupt ones and paid themselves collectively tens of millions of dollars and cared more about their own glory and wealth than they did about what built Apple in the first place—which was making great computers for people to use."[2]

Ten years later, after his triumphant return to Apple, a more sanguine Jobs tells what he calls "a story of love and loss" in a 2005 commencement speech delivered at Stanford University: "I was lucky. I found what I loved to do early in life. Woz and I started Apple in my parents' garage when I was twenty. We worked hard and in ten years, Apple had grown from just the two of us in a garage into a $2 billion company with over 4,000 employees. We'd just released our finest creation, the Macintosh, a year earlier, and I'd just turned thirty, and then I got fired. How can you get fired from a company you started?"

His answer, though brief, says a lot: "Well, as Apple grew, we hired someone who I thought was very talented to run the company with me, and for the first year or so, things went well. But then our visions of the future began to diverge, and eventually we had a falling out. When we did, our board of directors sided with him, and so at thirty, I was out, and very publicly out."

Of what happened next, he says, "What had been the focus of my entire adult life was gone, and it was devastating. I really didn't know what to do for a few months. I felt that I had let the previous generation of entrepreneurs down, that I had dropped the baton as it was being passed to me.... I was a very public failure and I even thought about running away from the Valley. But something slowly began to dawn on me. I still loved what I did. The turn of events at Apple had not changed that one bit. I'd been rejected but I was still in love. And so I decided to start over."[3]

The breakup with Sculley cost Jobs dearly. It was, as he put it, a devastating public failure, from which a lesser man might not have recovered. Still, his answer to the question of how he got fired—their visions diverged; they had a falling out; the board sided with Sculley—displays little insight into *how* their relationship fell apart or why the board felt the need to side with either one of them, but most important: *Why Sculley?*

The point is, there's little here Jobs could use to ensure it wouldn't happen again—if not to him, then to the next generation of entrepreneurs to whom he is passing the baton. While no speech could ever detail the rise and fall of a complicated relationship, this account makes no mention of what we'll see in Chapter Two; namely, that Jobs and Sculley interacted in ways that made it impossible for them to reconcile their differences, brought out the worst in both of them, and led to the choice faced by the board: one or the other had to go, and go quickly, if the company was to survive. What's more, it's not enough simply to say that the board sided with Sculley. *The board felt it had no choice.* Jobs's out-of-control behavior in response to Sculley's increasingly controlling behavior had painted a rather large target on Jobs's chest. By the time the board was forced to choose, they had lost whatever confidence they had in him as a leader.

THE FAR SIDE®   By GARY LARSON

© 1986 FarWorks, Inc. All Rights Reserved/Dist. by Creators Syndicate

The Far Side® by Gary Larson © 1986 FarWorks, Inc. All Rights Reserved. The Far Side® and the Larson® signature are registered trademarks of FarWorks, Inc. Used with permission.

"Bummer of a birthmark, Hal."

In a 2010 article, "Being Steve Jobs' Boss," Sculley also looks back at his life-changing relationship with Jobs. His version of the events, like the man himself, is more cerebral than the one Jobs tells, his feelings harder to make out. Even so, Sculley's account, like Jobs's, is as revealing for what it leaves out as for what it says:

> Looking back, it was a big mistake that I was ever hired as CEO.
> I was not the first choice that Steve wanted to be the CEO. He

was the first choice, but the board wasn't prepared to make him CEO when he was 25, 26 years old. . . . It would have been much more honest if the board had said, "Let's figure out a way for him to be CEO. You could focus on the stuff that you bring, and he focuses on the stuff he brings."

Remember, he was the chairman of the board, the largest shareholder, and he ran the Macintosh division, so he was above me and below me. It was a little bit of a façade, and my guess is we never would have had the breakup if the board had done a better job of thinking through not just how do we get a CEO to come and join the company that Steve will approve of, but how do we make sure we create a situation where this thing is going to be successful over time?[4]

Sculley may be right that Steve was Steve's first choice for CEO and that the board made a mistake in hiring Sculley. They certainly made a mistake in not thinking through how to "create a situation where this thing is going to be successful over time." But then Sculley made the same two mistakes. He agreed to become CEO, and he was the one who put Jobs in charge of the Macintosh division, wedging himself between Jobs-as-boss and Jobs-as-subordinate. Yet to listen to Sculley's account, it's as if he was in the back seat and the board behind the wheel as the firm careened off a cliff.

In earlier accounts, Sculley is a bit more self-scrutinizing. In his 1987 memoir, written while he was riding high as Apple's CEO, he acknowledges that he "created a monster" by giving Steve control of Macintosh. But just as the movie *Frankenstein* focuses on the monster, not the creator, so does Sculley. Nowhere does Sculley entertain the possibility that his cautious, cerebral approach might have evoked more volatility in Jobs, not less, or that his efforts to control Jobs might have evoked less self-control, not more. In the end, Sculley blames the board; Jobs blames Sculley; and neither says much about his own role in creating a relationship that cost them and Apple dearly.

Relationships: Strategic Asset or Liability?

What happened to Jobs and Sculley at Apple may be especially dramatic, but it's not rare. History is awash with accounts of failed relationships among leaders of every stripe. General McChrystal and President Obama; Larry Summers and the Harvard faculty; Carly Fiorina and the Hewlett-Packard board; Michael Ovitz and Michael Eisner at Disney. All the way back to Achilles and Agamemnon on the beaches of Troy, relationships have had the power to create or to destroy enormous amounts of human, social, and economic capital.

But never before have we faced a time when relationships have mattered more. Leaders today must be able to make decisions and take action well and quickly with others with whom they share very little—perhaps not even a time zone. No longer can we work within our own silos without regard for those at work in theirs. No longer can we take the time to send conflicts up the hierarchy instead of settling them ourselves. No longer can we count on like-minded colleagues of the same race, class, culture, or gender to think and act like we do. No longer can we count on slow markets or sloppy competition to make up for the inefficiencies poor relationships create. We face a crisis today not only of leadership but of relationship.

Small wonder so many leadership experts now underscore the importance of relationships. In their best-seller *The Leadership Challenge,* James Kouzes and Barry Posner argued that the success of leaders depends "upon the capacity to build and sustain those human relationships that enable people to get extraordinary things done on a regular basis." In their view, the quality of the relationship between leader and follower is what "matters most when we're engaged in getting extraordinary things done."[5] Leadership experts Ronald Heifetz and Marty Linsky would agree. In their 2002 book *Leadership on the Line,* they claimed that "the nature and quality of the connections human beings have with each other is more important than almost any other factor in determining results."[6] Perhaps that's why for the past fifteen years Daniel Goleman and his colleagues[7] have also given relationships top billing. In 1995, Goleman included relationship management among the core competencies of emotional intelligence,[8] and in 2008, he and Richard Boyatzis went so far as to call for a "more relationship-based construct" for assessing leadership.[9]

These and many other leadership experts today are all pointing in the same direction: to the central role relationships play in a leader's performance and success.[10] Yet when it comes to the relationship dynamics upon which all this performance and success rest, most experts are curiously silent. Even Goleman and Boyatzis's search for a more relationship-based construct culminated in the interpersonal competencies, neural circuitry, and endocrine systems *of individuals.*[11]

No one has yet asked, let alone answered, the question, *What exactly is a relationship such that it can be managed or drive exceptional performance?*

"I'm right there in the room, and no one even acknowledges me."

Relationships: Seemingly Familiar, Strangely Unexplored

Most leaders today can say a lot about organizations and individuals, and about how best to manage and lead them. After over a hundred years of scholarship devoted to individual psychology and organizational behavior, we know plenty about how people and organizations tick, how they develop naturally over time, and how, with focused effort, they change.

But we still know relatively little about relationships. True, in the personal arena, you can find a plethora of popular books and an increasingly robust body of scholarly research that covers a wide range of topics from attraction to social exchange to the maintenance and repair of personal relationships.[12] But very little of this work transfers easily or at all to the organizational world.

An exception is John Gottman's work with couples. Unlike most researchers studying relationships,[13] Gottman doesn't rely on self-reports. Rather, he observes the words and behaviors couples use to discuss their most recent arguments, then catalogues different behaviors in terms of their effects on the relationship. Those behaviors most damaging to relationships are what Gottman calls "The Four Horsemen of the Apocalypse"—criticism, contempt, defensiveness, and stonewalling.[14] After just *three minutes* of an argument, Gottman is able to use his theory to predict with 83 percent accuracy which couples will divorce within six years![15]

Much less can be said about relationships in the organizational arena.[16] While almost all leadership experts acknowledge the importance of relationships, they haven't investigated the nature of relationships themselves, the behavioral patterns underlying them, or their effects.

The same can be said of most leaders. While many believe relationships are important, few can tell you much about the patterns of interaction that define how their most important relationships work (or fail to work). Others view relationships in a purely transactional light, believing what one leader half-jokingly told me: "You hire employees, and then people show up." And still others get so riveted on the other guy—his quirks, motivations, fears, or defenses—they overlook how they themselves might be reinforcing the very behavior they don't like. Almost all of them are convinced that individual people are the source of their woes and that relationships are too soft to be analyzed and too mysterious to be altered.

As it ends up, they're wrong. This book will show that just as people and organizations have an identifiable character based on predictable patterns, so do relationships. These patterns, which with the proper tools can be analyzed and altered, determine how well a relationship works and whether it will make or break a leader's success.

About This Book

The Elephant in the Room explores a terrain with which all leaders are intimately familiar, yet few are able to discuss, let alone consistently master—relationships.[17] It draws on material from public sources, the historical record, and my own clinical research[18] to take a close look at how relationships at the top of organizations work, why they fail, how they affect the performance and growth of leaders and their firms, and how leaders can strengthen or transform those relationships most critical to their success. In so doing, it takes a topic most of us relegate to our personal lives and puts it at the center of our lives as leaders, where it also belongs.

To anticipate what's to come, Chapter Two draws on Steve Jobs and John Sculley's much publicized breakup to show how, over the course of three stages, leaders negotiate and renegotiate not only their formal roles but their informal roles as well. By looking closely at both negotiations, you can see how an informal structure emerges and evolves, and how that structure determines the fate of leaders far more than any formal structure ever could.

Chapter Three explains why some relationships grow stronger over time, while others grow weaker. It uses stories from the historical record and my own practice to identify two perspectives leaders take to the challenges, conflicts, and pressures they face. The most common of these is what I call *the individual perspective*. When leaders take this perspective, they assume that they alone are right, that this is obvious, and that others don't get it because they're either mad or bad. As we'll see, this set of assumptions brings out the worst in people, lies at the root of blame games and waiting games, and causes even good relationships to break down over time. A second perspective is what I call *the relational perspective*. When leaders take this perspective, they assume that everyone sees some things and misses others, that circumstances shape behavior at least as much as people's dispositions do, and that people together can shape and reshape the circumstances they face. These assumptions help leaders bring out the best in each other, so they can work together to create innovative solutions to the challenges they face together.

The second part of the book provides a set of tools and strategies for building relationships strong enough to handle the most intense pressures and the hottest conflicts. Chapter Four tells the story of two leaders who were able to use a conflict in the heat of the moment to strengthen their relationship. By relying on two essential relational capabilities—reflecting and reframing, first alone, then together—they were able to shift perspective and put their differences to work.

Chapter Five then tells the story of an entrepreneurial CEO and her second-in-command to introduce a powerful new lens through which to see and discuss relationship patterns that are affecting your growth and performance. This lens, which I call the *Anatomy Framework*, makes the underlying structure of a relationship visible and discussable, so you can exert greater control over patterns that have been exerting too much control over you. Over time, using this framework will make it easier, even second nature, for you to see things from a relational perspective.

Chapter Six brings this second part of the book to a close by presenting two tools you can use to more systematically assess *when* to invest in *which* relationships. The first tool offers four basic strategies for handling relationships—ignore, separate, manage, or invest—depending on the degree of interdependence between leaders and the importance of a relationship to their growth and performance. The second tool helps you sequence your invest-ments, depending on the odds of success and the impact of a relationship on you and your organization.

The third part of the book demonstrates something most people doubt: that it's possible to fundamentally transform the underlying structure or character of a relationship. To illustrate, it tells an in-depth story of how two leaders at a professional services firm took their relationship from good to great with the help of a coach and a three-stage model of change. Based on the Anatomy Framework in Chapter Five, this change model describes how you can transform relationships—first by interrupting the act-react patterns that define a relationship, then by challenging and changing the interpretations or "frames" that perpetuate those patterns, and finally by revisiting and revising the experiential knowledge and contextual constraints that lock those frames into place.

In writing this book, I had two audiences in mind: those charged with helping leaders—coaches, consultants, HR professionals, faculty at professional schools—and those in leadership positions or aspiring to be. My own use of the ideas and tools presented in this book is based on thirty years of practice; still, my work with leaders, consultants, and academics has convinced me (and them) that these ideas and tools are useful, even powerful, in other people's hands. That's because each one offers a new way of seeing and doing things that will allow you, or those you help, to discuss and navigate even the toughest relationships more effectively.

What This Book Is Not About

This book is not about individual leaders or their styles, personalities, habits, or principles. So you'll find no mention of difficult people or personalities, narcissists or neurotics. If anything, these notions are part of the problem, because they locate the crux of any troubles you face in people's dispositions, rendering you powerless to change what you see.

This isn't to say that people don't have dispositions or that those dispositions don't affect the health of a relationship. It is to say two other things.

First, when someone behaves in ways we don't like, we make a mistake so pervasive cognitive psychologists call it the *fundamental attribution error:* we overattribute the cause of behavior to a person's disposition, and we systematically underestimate the impact situations have on behavior.[19] Second, our tendency to focus on people's dispositions leads us to overlook the power that relationships have to modify or amplify even genetically programmed dispositions. As I'll detail later, recent research on genetics and families transcends the debate over nature versus nurture to show how nature (our genes) works hand-in-hand with nurture (our relationships) to shape the person we become.

The Heart of the Matter

In our shrinking, shifting world of tighter interdependencies and tougher competition, building strong relationships is no longer an elective; it's a requirement. Leaders today must be able to forge relationships that can span divides, withstand constant pressure and uncertainty, help them learn and turn on a dime, inspire trust and confidence in a diverse set of constituents, and make the most of even the hottest conflicts.

That's a tall order—and a new order.

Today's leaders need a new set of ideas and tools to fulfill it. Only then can they acknowledge the elephant in the room, stop it from running amok, and perhaps even invite it to dance.

TWO

The Life and Death of a Relationship

> I now had what the self-help books called baggage, which I would carry around for the rest of my life. The trick was to meet someone with similar baggage, and form a matching set, but how would one go about finding such a person?
>
> —DAVID SEDARIS[1]

More than twenty-five years have passed since Steve Jobs and John Sculley's much-publicized breakup at Apple. Yet it still serves as a cautionary tale. In two short years, their celebrated camaraderie turned into an antagonism so great it escalated hostilities between divisions, put Apple at risk of a takeover, sent Steve Jobs into a twelve-year exile, and destroyed millions in potential revenue. How these leaders went from soul mates to mortal enemies in such a short time shows how relationships, even those touted as a perfect match, can self-destruct under pressure.

When Jobs and Sculley's relationship first fell apart, most people chalked it up to personalities: Jobs was too volatile, Sculley too cautious and controlled. Others pointed to adverse circumstances: the relationship simply wasn't strong enough to survive a precipitous drop in sales.[2] Still others said their chemistry was off: Sculley was too corporate, Jobs too iconoclastic. While each explanation holds merit, they all overlook the most intriguing and instructive aspect of what happened: the way their relationship developed over time.

Only by understanding how relationships form, develop, and die can you see *why* people form ill-fated matches, *why* certain personalities clash, and *why* some relationships break down so quickly and completely under pressure. And only by understanding how relationships form, develop, and die do you stand a chance of altering the course a relationship takes. By looking closely at how the Jobs and Sculley relationship developed over the course of three stages, we can extract timeless lessons about the life and death of a relationship and its impact on the firm.

Stage 1: How a Relationship Forms

When joining an organization, most people spend weeks or even months negotiating everything from job responsibilities to financial rewards to decision rights. Yet if you look closely at these negotiations, you can see another deal also take shape, as people—through their interactions—define the informal terms of their relationship: the emotional responsibilities each person will seek and shirk, the psychological rewards they'll each want to give and get, and the interpersonal rights they'll each claim and relinquish.

It is the interplay between these two deals that sets the foundation of a relationship. By paying attention to both, you're much more likely to get a relationship off to a good start. Conversely, as this chapter shows, when you ignore the informal side of a relationship, you're much more likely to get into trouble and to be stunned and amazed when you do.

The Story: The Perfect Match

When Steve Jobs and John Sculley first met at a January 1983 dinner following a private preview of Apple's new Lisa computer, their mutual attraction was obvious to everyone.[3] One Apple chronicler, Frank Rose, tells the story of that midwinter evening in New York:[4]

> After an hour or so they went downstairs, where Sculley's limousine was waiting to take them to the Four Seasons for dinner. It was a car that seemed as big as an airplane, with a bar and a TV and a driver named Fred, all on call twenty-four hours a day.... They swept down Park to Fifty-Second ... and pulled up at the discretely canopied entrance to the Four Seasons. Sculley led them into the travertine anteroom, up the stairway to the reservations desk, past the enormous Picasso stage curtain, and into the stark opulence of the Pool Room.
>
> Over dinner the unlikely chemistry between Jobs and Sculley became readily apparent. Despite their obvious differences in age and background—Sculley was strictly Ivy League and corporate, having graduated from Brown University and the Wharton School and having spent most of his professional life at Pepsi; Jobs, seventeen years his junior, had dropped out of Oregon's funky little Reed College during his freshman year—they somehow clicked. It was almost as if each tapped something unrealized in the other. There was a cool, crisp professionalism to Sculley that Jobs respected, a utopian fervor to Jobs that Sculley found intriguing. Sculley was a man who knew how to run a multimillion-dollar enterprise. Jobs was a kid who proved he could change the world. Put them together.... [5]

Earlier that same day, the differences between Sculley and Jobs were as apparent as their affection was at dinner. While Jobs was jumping up and down with enthusiasm for his spanking-new product, Sculley held back. *He* was looking at the product through the eyes of a corporate executive at the helm of a traditional company in an industry in which winning depended more on cost efficiencies and marketing than on product innovation. "[Sculley] didn't take to it wholeheartedly," says Rose. "He was cautious. He had reservations. He wasn't sure that this new technology, dazzling as it was, would have much impact at a big corporation like Pepsi, because it didn't have the IBM logo. No one ever got fired, the saying went, for buying an IBM."[6]

To this side of Sculley, Steve Jobs gave little notice. What he saw was a savvy, ingenious marketer, whom he alone described as "very charismatic."[7] After all, Sculley was the one who had revived the Pepsi Generation campaign in the late 1960s, spurring unprecedented growth for the next six years. By 1978, Pepsi Cola was surpassing Coke in sales for the first time in the firm's eighty-year history.[8] Perhaps at Apple, Sculley could do the same thing—invent the Apple generation. That would certainly advance Jobs's vision of changing the world by resetting the balance of power between the individual and the institution. One person, one computer: that was his motto. Since Apple's inception, he'd dreamed of bringing power to the people, as the saying from the 1960s went. Only, he was going to do it by putting an Apple computer in the hands of every person. With Apple cofounder Steve Wozniak gone and CEO Mike Markkula anxious to move on, the decision whether to hire Sculley was largely up to Jobs. And it looked to him as if Sculley had all the right stuff.

Two months later, the deal was done. In April 1983, Sculley accepted the offer to join Apple as its new president[9] and passed up the once-in-a-lifetime opportunity to succeed his mentor, Donald Kendall, as chairman of PepsiCo. To make the jump more palatable, Apple agreed to give the forty-four-year-old Sculley a

$1 million salary along with a promised $1 million bonus, a $1 million severance package (in case things didn't work out),[10] an option to buy 350,000 shares of stock, a $2 million loan to buy a Tudor-style house in the California hills,[11] and $1.3 million for Sculley's Greenwich (Connecticut) home to save him the trouble of selling it.[12]

Although no small amount in 1983, the money isn't what sealed the deal. Nor was it the opportunity to lead a company growing at a breakneck pace. No, what sealed the deal was the bond Sculley and Jobs forged out of their mutual attraction to power. For Sculley, Jobs held the power to change the world; for Jobs, Sculley held the key to corporate power. It was a heady match, says Frank Rose, seducing them and preoccupying everyone else:

> For weeks they had been gazing worshipfully at each other, finishing each other's sentences, parroting each other's thoughts. It was as if they were on a perpetual honeymoon which they had to share with a great many unruly children.... The summer honeymoon between Steve and John was the talk of the company. The two were inseparable. John was listening and learning, and the person he was learning from was Steve.... He seemed so in awe of Steve—his brashness, his charm, his charisma—that he saw everything through Steve's eyes.... But the infatuation wasn't one-sided. It was almost like a father-son relationship in which the two adopted each other.[13]

Theirs wasn't any father-son relationship, however. As Sculley later wrote, "I felt that part of my role was to nurture Steve from a prince to a king, so he would someday be able to run the company he cofounded."[14] That first summer, they were so absorbed with one another that they failed to see what others feared most— that their father-son indulgences might demolish a useful, if delicate, balance of power within the firm. "In the original tri-umvirate," says Rose of Mike Scott as president, Mike Markkula as chairman, and Jobs as visionary, "Jobs's brash enthusiasms had been leavened by Scotty's stern hand and Markkula's persuasive manner.... Sculley's arrival changed all that. John made Steve his partner, not realizing that Steve had never been a partner in running Apple before. Suddenly there were no restraints. Sculley unleashed him, and Steve unleashed was an astonishing spectacle. People began to liken it to Godzilla being let out of his cage."[15]

But Sculley saw no trace of a monster in the hyperkinetic Jobs. He didn't understand there was a reason no one had ever granted Jobs unchecked access to power. Nor did he see what he later came to believe: that Jobs was often "stubborn, uncompromising and downright impossible."[16] What he saw was a prince entitled to inherit a throne. Similarly, Jobs didn't see in Sculley what others saw: a cautious leader unlikely to make the bold moves that came second nature to Jobs. Nor did he see what he later came to believe: that Sculley was preoccupied with control and would never give Jobs the power or support he wanted. All he saw was a powerful, supportive benefactor who would help him realize his dreams.

What the Story Teaches Us

The one characteristic that marks the beginning of all relationships headed for trouble is obliviousness to the informal side of a relationship. Like most executives, those negotiating Sculley's entry into the firm focused on business matters. They discussed ideas for growing the business; they debated how Apple's technology might change the world; they talked roles and responsibilities; they negotiated compensation. In the end, they came up with a deal so full of potential upside and so buffered against downside risk that Sculley couldn't refuse.[17]

What they didn't do was take a look at the nature of the relationship Sculley and Jobs were forming. Sure, everyone could see the two were enamored of each other. But no one questioned why they'd clicked so quickly and so completely. While some found their instant intimacy unsettling and others worried each didn't see the other for the person he really was, no one could say why or do much about it. All they could do was chalk it up to chemistry and leave it at that.

Most of us do the same thing. When people click or clash, we chalk it up to chemistry and leave it at that. But it is possible to identify and analyze the seemingly mysterious ingredients that go into the makings of a relationship. As this book shows throughout, given the right tools, it's possible to understand what happens when a relationship forms, and then to anticipate what might happen next. For now, let's look more closely at what happened with Jobs and Sculley.

Understanding What Happens When a Relationship Forms

We all bring to relationships our own characteristic ways of interacting with others given our *behavioral repertoires.*[18] Built out of experience, these repertoires are organized around key themes such as power, conflict, control, and success. Over time, as we interact with each other, patterns emerge around these themes, and in these patterns you can discern the informal terms of a relationship, including

- The *emotional responsibilities* we'll seek ("I've *gotta* help this guy!") and those we'll shirk ("No way I'm doing that!")— regardless of formal roles.
- The *interpersonal rights* we'll claim ("You can't treat me that way!") and those we'll relinquish ("Don't worry about it")— regardless of any formal deal.

23

- The *psychological rewards* we'll want to get ("Just once I wish she'd give me a pat on the back!") and those we'll be willing to give ("You did a great job")—regardless of financial rewards.

When people first meet, their themes act like DNA, intersecting to give rise to distinctive patterns of interaction. These theme-bound patterns interact with circumstances to shape the way a relationship evolves over time.[19] In the case of Jobs and Sculley, it was their shared preoccupation with power that gave rise to their mutual attraction. Each saw in the other a form of power he coveted.[20] The effusive Jobs saw in the more cerebral Sculley the corporate power he needed to change the world. Dazzled by the limousine, the chauffeur, and the opulence of the Pool Room, Jobs paid little attention to Sculley's more reserved, controlled side. To Jobs, the "charismatic" Sculley may have seemed more thoughtful than controlled, more sophisticated than reserved. And given Sculley's low-key demeanor, it must have been hard to imagine how he'd ever pose much of a threat.[21] As to how Sculley made it to the top of a competitive—some say cutthroat—firm such as Pepsi, Jobs apparently gave little thought.

Similarly, Sculley saw in Jobs a brilliant visionary with the power to change the world. Like Jobs, Sculley paid little attention to the behaviors he later found so unacceptable, even though they were in full evidence right from the start. Jobs's jumping up and down at the unveiling of Lisa, his unpredictable emotional outbursts, his caustic ridicule of Apple's competitors all must have seemed part of an otherwise attractive package—rough edges that could be smoothed out over time. Just how that smoothing out would occur, well, that too was assumed rather than anticipated. All Sculley saw was an opportunity to do more than sell sugared water for the rest of his life.[22] With Jobs at his side, he too was going to change the world.

24

Anticipating What Might Happen Next

Though less noticeable at the outset, two other themes clashed rather than clicked: Jobs's well-known disdain for institutional authority (you could say he built Apple and its products upon this disdain)[23] and Sculley's corporately honed preference for institutional structure and control (to which his tenure at Pepsi was a tribute).[24] According to Rose, Sculley "liked to tinker with structure. Maybe it was his architectural training, maybe just his natural cast of mind, but he was always thinking about how things fit together. Jobs's thinking tended to be more intuitive, emotional, and visionary; Sculley was more a systems man, rational and analytical. Form and process were what interested him."[25]

Had anyone paid attention to these rather fundamental differences, they might have given thought to how they might play out over time. As it was, no one asked what might happen should Sculley impose the kind of corporate controls at Apple he'd imposed at Pepsi. Nor did they ask what might happen should Jobs bristle under that control. Intent on finding a seasoned executive to counterbalance and contain Jobs's more intuitive, even impulsive leadership style, Apple's board didn't think through how all this counterbalancing and containing would occur.

Nor did they anticipate the events their relationship might set in motion or the effect those events would have on the firm's delicate balance of power.

Stage 2: How a Relationship Develops

In the second stage of a relationship's development, people renegotiate their formal and informal roles. As they do, initial impressions give way to more stable interpretations, and people come to know each other for "who they really are." These more stable interpretations—what I call frames—inform people's negotiations about who should do what *and* turn early patterns of interaction into more informal structures. Though hard to discern without the proper tools, these informal structures give relationships their distinctive character.

Those who pay attention to the informal side of a relationship during this stage understand that what they see is what they'll get, so if they don't like what they get, they can always reconsider the way they see and treat each other. Those who ignore the informal side, as Sculley and Jobs did, believe that what they see is the way it is, leading them to feel trapped in a relationship no longer of their choosing.

The Story: The Road to Disillusionment

Six months before Sculley joined Apple, Jobs had gotten approval from Apple's board to build his own factory for the Macintosh and to get it up and running before turning it over to Del Yocam, Apple's VP of manufacturing. Several months after Sculley's arrival, sometime in the fall of 1983, Sculley knew he had a problem: Jobs didn't want to turn manufacturing over to Yocam. Instead Jobs pitched another idea: let Yocam keep the Apple II division and the Dallas factory, and let Jobs keep the Macintosh division and its new Fremont plant.[26]

After some initial concern, Sculley took to the idea. It would allow him to solve two problems at once: Jobs's desire to take operational control of Macintosh, and his own desire to gain greater control of Apple.[27] Jobs would get his chance to run something, and Sculley would have two profit-and-loss centers to manage, the same way Pepsi, Taco Bell, and Pizza Hut were managed at PepsiCo. But Apple wasn't Pepsi, Sculley wasn't Kendall, and Jobs wasn't Sculley.

"It was a mistake," Sculley later wrote. "I became more remote from the business. . . . He really had more knowledge about what was going on in the business than I did because all the information was coming up through the product divisions. They had all the power. The corporate staff basically became an impotent group."[28]

Though later regretted, Sculley's decision made good sense at the time given his relationship with Jobs. It was autumn 1983. Their summer honeymoon was just ending, and they were turning their attention to building "insanely great products" and growing a "phenomenal firm." During that time, Sculley took on the informal task of turning a prince into a king, and now, in an effort to fulfill that role, he was continually coaching, cajoling, and chastising Jobs into behaving properly. All Jobs needed, Scully thought, was the kind of experience a prince can get by running his own province.[29] Besides, for his part, Jobs was acting like an adoring kid, relenting when cajoled, expressing regret when chastised, and repenting each time Sculley asked him to rein in his sometimes rude, occasionally cruel, and always emotional outbursts.

Six months later, Sculley realized his mistake. In his memoir he cites the precise moment when things took a turn for the worse. It was May 1984, only a year into his tenure at Apple. At a celebratory dinner arranged by Jobs as a tribute to his friend and mentor, Sculley stood up to thank the group and to praise Jobs. He began by speaking glowingly of their relationship, saying they'd developed not just a partnership, but a friendship. Then, pausing for effect, he looked across the room at Jobs and declared: "Apple has one leader, Steve and me."

Later on, Sculley would say of these words: "I didn't yet know it, but my statement proved to be a turning point."[30] Within weeks of that dinner, Sculley began to worry that he was losing his grip on the management of the company. He watched with concern as Jobs's power increased after he decided to fold the Lisa product line into the Macintosh group to create two distinct lines of business.[31] He noticed how Jobs was trying to influence all matters of business, not just those related to product development. Even more ominous, Sculley could tell that he was losing purchase on his relationship with Jobs. His coaching, cajoling, and chastising no longer had much effect, if it ever did. While Jobs kept promising to behave, he never seemed to make good on those promises. "For the first time," Sculley wrote, "I felt as if I was losing control."[32]

That feeling only intensified a few months later after a meeting with a group of Xerox executives. When Sculley first arranged the meeting, he knew Jobs had little respect for the company,[33] but he persuaded Jobs that acquiring a firm like Xerox would accelerate Apple's growth and put it within shooting distance of IBM. With images of a defeated IBM dancing in his head, Jobs agreed to the meeting and promised Sculley that he would behave.

It ended up being a promise Jobs couldn't or wouldn't keep. Within minutes, he was telling the Xerox executives, "*You're doing it wrong; you're just doing it completely wrong!*" Sculley recounts what happened next:

> Adams [head of Xerox's computer systems group] bristled, and things went downhill from there. Glavin [vice chairman of Xerox] glanced across the table at me and rolled his eyes.
>
> "Now let's step back and talk about this," I hopelessly interjected.
>
> But Steve couldn't hold back. A pained look appeared on his face as the words came tumbling out of his mouth.
>
> "I really shouldn't say this," he said. "But I'm going to say it. You guys don't have any idea what you're doing."
>
> Within fifteen minutes or so, it was clear we were going to accomplish nothing. So I pulled Bill Glavin aside and suggested that we call off the session and perhaps regroup at a later date.

The meeting quickly ended and Steve and I left the room. I was incredulous.

"Steve," I asked. "Why did you do that? I thought we had an agreement that you were going to control yourself."

"I'm sorry, but I couldn't help myself," he said contritely in a little boy's voice. "I went to Xerox PARC and saw that they had all the great people and they were doing all the great things and they just didn't see it. . . . I just couldn't control myself. I'm sorry."

Steve and I never rescheduled the meeting with Xerox.[34]

Sculley was shaken. For the first time it occurred to him that his efforts might fail, that no matter how much he cajoled or coached, Jobs might not be able to control himself—ever.

During this same time, Jobs's doubts about Sculley were also taking shape. Things weren't going so well for Macintosh. While Apple's profitability was soaring, Mac sales for September were less than two-thirds of what they'd projected. At first, Jobs felt like a failure. Stunned and upset, he walked around, head down, asking those around him what price he'd have to pay for having failed them.[35] It didn't last long. Within days his self-flagellation gave way to blame, most of it aimed at Sculley. Says Rose:

The reason Macintosh wasn't more profitable, Jobs was convinced, was that the company . . . wasn't supporting it. Take distribution. He had gone to Sculley with his vision of 747s loading up computers at the factory gates, but other people were trying to block him on it. . . . He wanted to fire all those people and close down their warehouses and go with Federal Express right away. . . . Sculley was hedging. He wanted to appoint somebody to study it. Jobs saw no need for study.... And so he was beginning to question Sculley's performance. He was beginning to wonder why the CEO he'd picked wasn't providing the leadership he needed.[36]

Jobs *must* have been mystified. Sculley had been his most avid ally, opening doors to corporate power everyone else had kept shut. Now, Sculley was cautioning him *to slow down, to study the problem.* He couldn't believe it. Instead of helping him stave off failure, Sculley was blocking his success! For the first time, he questioned Sculley's more measured, studious approach to leadership. Perhaps Sculley *wasn't* the key to power after all. Perhaps he was just another ineffectual authority who didn't get it and had no right to tell him what to do.

What the Story Teaches Us

Sculley made three fateful decisions during this stage; later on, he regretted all three. First, after creating two separate divisions—one for the Mac, the other for Apple II—he decided to give Jobs operational control of Mac. Next, much to the chagrin of those working on Lisa (Jobs called them "bozos"), he agreed to fold the Lisa line into the Mac division, expanding the division's scope and Jobs's power. Finally, to signal that Jobs did in fact have operational control of the Macintosh division, he changed Jobs's title from vice president to executive vice president. Together, these choices moved Jobs closer to the operations of the company, gave Jobs more formal power, and wedged Sculley between Jobs-as-boss and Jobs-as-subordinate.

When leaders make bad design choices like these, it's often a sign that they're caught in informal structures that make bad choices look smart. Sculley's choices, as bad as they were, flowed logically from the pattern of interaction established during the first stage of their relationship. In this initial pattern, Sculley indulged Jobs without holding him accountable, while Jobs admired Sculley without giving him the power Kendall had given him at Pepsi. Within this relational context, it made sense for Jobs to ask for a division of his own and for Sculley to give it to him.[37] Their informal dealings had led them to see each other in a particular light and to expect certain things from each other, turning their early pattern of interaction into a more enduring structure. Let's take a look at how an informal structure forms and evolves, then consider its effects.

How an Informal Structure Takes Shape

After Sculley put Jobs in charge of Macintosh, he started paying closer attention to the impact Jobs had on him and others. He noticed that "[Jobs] could inspire people, and he could make them sweat. . . . At one moment, he could drain all your self-esteem. At the very next, he could praise you, offering just a few complimentary crumbs that somehow made all the angst worthwhile."[38]

While Sculley understood that this kind of behavior would never be tolerated at Pepsi, he accepted it in Jobs. "Steve was unique," he explained. "People made exceptions for him. They held him to the standard of a young, smart kid; they didn't really view him as an adult.[39]

Besides, Sculley added, "When he looked at me, it was a look of admiration, a what-can-I-learn look that was terribly gripping. In Steve's eyes I couldn't do anything wrong."[40]

Perhaps even more gripping, Sculley saw himself in Jobs: "None of Steve's behavior alarmed me, maybe because I so clearly saw my younger self in him. People had often found me difficult to deal with during my early days at Pepsi, too. I never verbally attacked anyone, but I insisted on only the best from them, as Steve did. So I tried to coach Steve the way Chuck Mangold coached me at Pepsi."

This way of seeing Jobs led Sculley to stop short of holding him accountable for his impact. He figured he could coach and cajole Steve into behaving more constructively.

"You've got to learn to hold back some things," I told him. "All you're going to do is cause a lot of unnecessary frustration, which isn't constructive."

Treating his mentor as an indulgent father figure who could do nothing wrong, Jobs responded by relenting, regretting, and repenting.

"You're right," he said. "I know it. Keep talking to me, you're absolutely right. I know I shouldn't do that."[41]

If you look at what's happened so far, you can see the outlines of a structure emerge. If you were to map or draw a diagram of that structure, it would look something like Figure 2.1.

As the figure shows, Sculley invites and reinforces the very behavior in Jobs that he later finds so unacceptable. By repeatedly making exceptions for Jobs and never holding him accountable, Sculley makes it less likely that Jobs will ever feel the need to control himself. Jobs, in turn, invites and reinforces the very behavior in Sculley he later finds so unacceptable. By refusing to control himself, he makes it more likely that Sculley will feel the need to control him. It doesn't occur to either one of them that Sculley might come to feel so threatened that he will feel the need to reassert his power—at Jobs's and Apple's expense.

These interlocking actions—Sculley making exceptions for Jobs, Jobs refusing to control himself—flow from the way each man *frames* his role in relation to the other. In seeing their roles one way and not another, some actions seem obvious, others irrelevant. *It's these less-conscious informal roles that lock patterns into place, turning them into more stable structures.*

Figure 2.1 An Informal Structure Takes Shape.

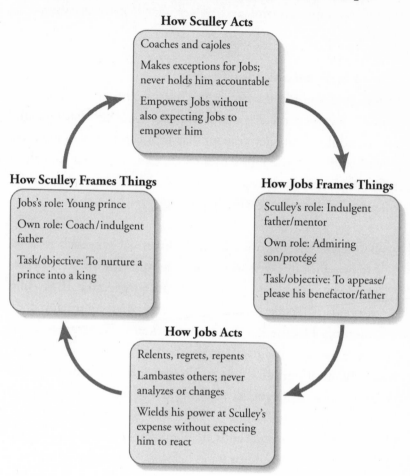

How Sculley Acts

Coaches and cajoles

Makes exceptions for Jobs; never holds him accountable

Empowers Jobs without also expecting Jobs to empower him

How Sculley Frames Things

Jobs's role: Young prince

Own role: Coach/indulgent father

Task/objective: To nurture a prince into a king

How Jobs Frames Things

Sculley's role: Indulgent father/mentor

Own role: Admiring son/protégé

Task/objective: To appease/please his benefactor/father

How Jobs Acts

Relents, regrets, repents

Lambastes others; never analyzes or changes

Wields his power at Sculley's expense without expecting him to react

Unaware of the informal side of their relationship, neither Jobs nor Sculley saw any of this at the time. Only later, when Sculley's decisions end up undermining his control, does Sculley see what he couldn't see then: that he had let power flow unchecked from himself to Jobs. And only later, when Sculley seeks to reassert his power, does Jobs see what he couldn't see then: that Sculley wanted far more control and power than Jobs ever wanted to give him.

How an Informal Structure Evolves

The turning point in the two men's relationship takes place when the two meet with the executives from Xerox. After that meeting, an "incredulous" Sculley realizes that Jobs can't or won't control himself, and a contrite Jobs senses he's in trouble. To see how these shifts occur and how they affect the evolution of their relationship, let's take a closer look at what happened:

- Before the meeting, Sculley takes his usual approach to Jobs, cajoling him into attending the meeting with the Xerox executives by appealing to his ambition to overtake IBM. Jobs responds to Sculley's cajoling by doing what he usually does: relenting. Despite his disrespect for Xerox, he agrees to come to the meeting and to behave himself.
- At the meeting, Jobs violates his agreement by launching into an emotional harangue, accusing the executives of getting it wrong, *all wrong.*
- As soon as the meeting ends, Sculley asks Jobs the same question he'd asked him countless times before, "Why did you do that?" Only, this time he adds in utter frustration, "I thought we had an agreement that you were going to control yourself."
- Sensing Sculley's disappointment and mounting frustration, Jobs appeals for forgiveness, explaining that he *couldn't* control himself, that the folks at Xerox *made* him do it.

This sequence of events marks a subtle but irrevocable shift in how Jobs and Sculley see each other. Jobs's inability to keep his agreements or to take responsibility for his actions signals to Sculley that he may be unable or unwilling to control himself. For the first time, Sculley sees just how unruly a prince Jobs can be, leading him to take on a new role and a new task: that of a disapproving parent, intent on controlling an unruly charge who can't or won't control himself.

At the same time, the frustration permeating Sculley's question signals to Jobs that Sculley wants more than an answer. He wants Jobs—no, he *expects* Jobs—to follow through on his agreements. Sensing this shift, Jobs also takes on a new role and task: that of a contrite little boy intent on eliciting the forgiveness he needs to retain Sculley's indulgence.

By mapping this sequence, we can see why this moment is such a turning point. It marks a fundamental structural shift in their relationship. As Figure 2.2 shows, once Sculley casts Jobs in the role of an unruly prince, he himself must take on a new role—that of a disciplinarian whose task is to *get* Jobs to behave. In that role and with that task, some actions make more sense than others. No longer believing that Jobs can control himself, Sculley stops coaching and cajoling him and starts challenging, confronting, and criticizing him.

Adapting to this shift, Jobs no longer sees Sculley as an indulgent father but as a disapproving one, leading him to take on the role of a contrite little boy intent on retaining Sculley's indulgence. Since his prior actions aren't quite up to this new task, Jobs must adopt new ones, which he does. He stops relenting and repenting and starts apologizing and begging for forgiveness.

Within this structure, the two struggle mightily to get what they want from each other; and when they fail, all they see is what the other person is doing to make matters worse. What they can't see is what the map so clearly shows: *that they're each*

Figure 2.2   An Informal Structure Evolves.

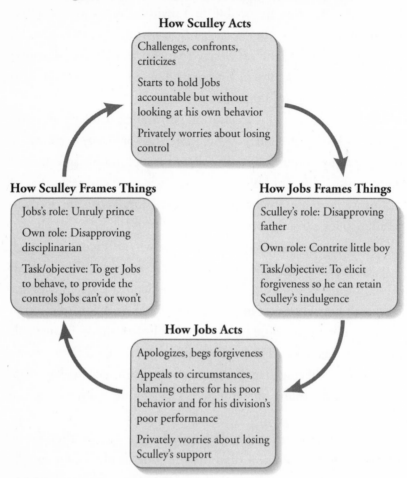

How Sculley Acts

Challenges, confronts, criticizes

Starts to hold Jobs accountable but without looking at his own behavior

Privately worries about losing control

How Sculley Frames Things

Jobs's role: Unruly prince

Own role: Disapproving disciplinarian

Task/objective: To get Jobs to behave, to provide the controls Jobs can't or won't

How Jobs Frames Things

Sculley's role: Disapproving father

Own role: Contrite little boy

Task/objective: To elicit forgiveness so he can retain Sculley's indulgence

How Jobs Acts

Apologizes, begs forgiveness

Appeals to circumstances, blaming others for his poor behavior and for his division's poor performance

Privately worries about losing Sculley's support

eliciting from the other the very responses that trouble them the most. The more critical and controlling Sculley becomes, the more Jobs apologizes, blames others, and appeals to circumstance; and the more Jobs apologizes, blames others, and appeals to circumstance, the more critical and controlling Sculley becomes. By the end of this stage, they're left with nothing but a paradox: the more their relationship develops, the more fragile it becomes.

"It's not enough that we succeed. Cats must also fail."

Stage 3: How a Relationship Dies

As Sculley continues to challenge, confront, and criticize Jobs, an increasingly perplexed Jobs realizes that his apologies will no longer elicit the indulgent responses to which he's grown accustomed. Soon he starts to bristle under Sculley's control, doing what he wants without Sculley's knowledge or approval. This only angers Sculley, who feels less and less able to control Jobs or the organization he's designed.

In this new relational context, the power they originally found so appealing in each other takes on a threatening cast. From here on in, Sculley scurries to gain control of the firm, while Jobs seeks the power he needs to resist, putting them on a direct collision course.

37

When they finally collide under the pressure of a failing business, their relationship breaks down completely and comes to an abrupt end. In this third stage, what seemed impossible at the outset now seems inevitable. Let's take a close look at how it happened.

The Story: Things Fall Apart

By the end of 1984, just after Jobs and Sculley appeared on the cover of *BusinessWeek* as "Apple's Dynamic Duo,"[42] it was clear that Macintosh was in trouble. Sure, it was selling well enough to universities, but it wasn't moving anywhere else.[43] As inventory piled up each day, such people as Debi Coleman, head of manufacturing at Macintosh, and Roy Weaver, vice president in charge of distribution, knew something was wrong.

Those at the very top, however, didn't seem to notice. It didn't seem to occur to them that Apple had been growing not so much because of its insanely great products, or because it was beating the competition, but because the market was growing.[44]

"We had no reason to suspect that our success would not carry us in our race into the next year," Sculley later wrote. "If anything, 1985 seemed to promise as much or even more for us than any other year in the company's history."[45]

Like Sculley, everyone at the top was focusing on the good news: profits for the quarter ending December 28 had leapt almost eightfold to a record $46.1 million. Sales had more than doubled to a record $698.3 million.[46] No one had a clue that Apple's world was about to crumble.[47]

But crumble it did. A critical new product, Macintosh Office, was late. The Macintosh division was at war with the Apple II division. IBM was cutting into Apple II sales with a discounted PCjr. Shipments had slowed. Unsold computers were lining the shelves of Apple dealers. Apple's cofounder and Jobs's longtime friend, Steve Wozniak, was leaving the company for the second and last time, as were many other executives. The press was scrambling for gossip and forecasting the company's demise.

The impact on Sculley and Jobs's relationship wasn't good. As Sculley recalls, "Inside Apple, we were increasingly absorbed by finger-pointing and infighting. The long, meandering chats and intellectual debates about how technology would change the world became far more basic. For the first time since Steve and I had met, we found ourselves entrenched on opposite sides of major issues."[48]

The operative word here is *entrenched*—and not just on the business issues. Their views of each other had also hardened. By this point, Jobs was certain he'd made a mistake in hiring Sculley,[49] and Sculley was equally convinced that he'd created a "monster."[50]

Soon they found themselves agreeing on less and less and fighting more and more.[51] Every time Sculley asked Jobs to account for Macintosh's disappointing results, he would blame Sculley.[52] And every time Jobs told Sculley how to solve the distribution problem, Sculley would tell him to *stay out of it, and let the task force handle it!*[53]

Others around them couldn't help but notice the mounting tension. Increasingly worried, they paid less attention to the business and more attention to the interpersonal chaos swirling around them. And no wonder: Sculley, ordinarily cerebral and controlled, was becoming increasingly upset. In one meeting, after discovering that one of Jobs's direct reports hadn't heard of an upcoming divisional review, he finally blew. "After two years as an emotional cipher," Rose recounts, "[Sculley] suddenly switched to an 'on' state. He was screaming, cursing, pounding the table. He'd scheduled a formal performance review for all the different divisions of the company, and Steve had never told his staff about it? He couldn't believe it. Well, there was going to be one, and if her boss didn't show up for it he would be fired."[54]

Incidents like this began to pile up, distracting everyone within shooting distance. Sculley's administrative assistant threatened to resign, the animosity between the two executives making it impossible to even schedule a meeting. By March, the business was failing fast. Excessive inventory forced them to close all four of their California manufacturing plants for a week. Analysts on Wall Street were cutting their estimates of their earnings. Their stock was in free fall. Rumors of a takeover were everywhere.[55] They were desperate, and it was time to come to Jesus. Rose offers a sobering account of what happened next:

> The beginning of the end came on a rainy night in March, the night John finally confronted Steve. He wasn't eager to go through with it. But Jay Elliot [Apple's VP of HR] had been pushing for a meeting, because he thought it was time that the two of them shared their feelings with each other. For John that meant telling Steve that he was dissatisfied with how he was running Macintosh. . . . Steve and his minions had grown openly contemptuous of, not just of the Apple II division but of corporate Apple as well—'Corportino,' Debi [Coleman] called it. More and more Corportino was being challenged to justify its own existence. This meeting was considerably overdue.[56]

For the next several hours, they "shared their feelings" about the worsening situation:

> John was willing to acknowledge that he hadn't been running things as aggressively as he might have, but he also had to say that Steve hadn't given him the opportunity. Steve was always interfering. That's how the finger-pointing began. Why was Mac in such trouble? Steve claimed it was because John wasn't keeping on top of the inventory situation, wasn't taking care of the distribution issue, wasn't taking charge of finance, wasn't providing the leadership to run the company. John said it was

because the product wasn't right, because they didn't have the software and the office products to make it work. Maybe he had been too far removed from operations, but now he was going to take charge, and he wanted somebody else to run Macintosh.[57]

As often happens at such meetings, the fact that they were finally being honest with each other obfuscated the fact that they were being dishonest with themselves. At no point did either of them explore his own role in creating the situation he found so unacceptable. Instead, they each emphasized the other's shortcomings, and they never entertained the possibility that they were both right: the products *were* late; distribution *was* a disaster; each of them *had* made it harder for the other to succeed. Sculley *was* abdicating leadership; Jobs *was* creating too much divisiveness. In the end, all they could see was what the other guy was doing to screw things up.

After the meeting ended, Sculley stepped out into the rain, convinced he had no choice. "There was nothing else to do," he recalls thinking. "I had to remove Steve as general manager of the Macintosh division." He then adds, "It was a painful decision because I knew the cost was high. Steve would pay the price of a job that he liked; I would pay the price of our friendship because I knew it could never survive this. For days I wracked my mind for an alternative. But I knew I wasn't doing what I was hired to do. My responsibility was to the shareholders, the board, and the employees."[58]

The next two months were consumed with countless meetings—some with the board, some with the executive staff, others with the two of them, either alone or with another executive. In each meeting people tried desperately to redeem the situation. Several, including Sculley, asked Jobs to take on a nonoperational role. Jobs refused, his heart set on leading the operations of the company. Jobs suggested that Sculley become chairman and leave him to run the company. Sculley refused, not wanting to become a figurehead. Jobs then suggested that they divide the firm up, so they could each lead their own separate division. But Sculley no longer had any confidence in Jobs and didn't want to share power with him. With no options left, a depressed but not yet defeated Jobs made a last-ditch effort to come out on top, secretly lobbying the executive staff and the board to throw Sculley out.

His efforts failed. In a meeting held late in May 1985, all but one executive staff member lined up behind Sculley. Later that same week, the board voted to remove Jobs as executive vice president of the Macintosh division. Only Jay Elliot refused. He didn't want to support either one of them; he was going to support Apple. Disgusted, he told them they were both being "self-indulgent with their little power struggle."[59]

It was simply too late, and everyone knew it. Neither Jobs nor Sculley could find a way to make their relationship work. In their minds, no pleas—no matter how impassioned—could alter what had now become a basic "fact." Their relationship was over, and they could find no way to revive it. A few days later, Sculley recounts, he asked Jobs to sign the papers making it official.

"Well," [Steve] said meekly, obviously hurt, "I guess that's it."

"I'm sorry, Steve," I said. "I guess it is."[60]

What the Story Teaches Us

By the time Jobs and Sculley's relationship broke down, their degrees of freedom were so limited they could only imagine one solution: get rid of the other. It never occurred to them that it was the informal structure underlying their relationship—the way they saw and interacted with each other—that was at fault. It never occurred to them that they were both right, that they had both put Apple and their relationship at risk. And it never occurred to them that it would take a lot of work on both their parts to set it right.

But let's say it did occur to them. They would likely have rejected the idea. And who could blame them? They would have had to invest a lot of time and energy to turn around their relationship, and there was no guarantee that that investment would pay off. And then where would they and the firm be? Sculley and Jobs were right. They had no choice. One or the other of them had to go.

And that's exactly the point. When leaders ignore the informal side of their relationships, they're more apt to create relationships that leave them little choice. By the second stage of their relationship, Jobs and Sculley had created a structure that significantly reduced their degrees of freedom; by the third stage, they had none. Let's take a closer look at how this third stage unfolds.

Nearing the End

By the time Sculley and Jobs reach this third stage in their relationship, they have moved from idolizing to demonizing each other. At this point Sculley no longer sees Jobs as the rightful heir to Apple's throne, but as a "monster,"[61] unable to stay out of things and incapable of controlling himself.[62] For his part, Jobs no longer sees Sculley as an indulgent, supportive mentor committed to his vision, but as an ineffectual manager, intent on controlling him and undermining the values that had made Apple great.[63]

Seeing each other in this more toxic light, Jobs and Sculley treat each other accordingly: either fighting or distancing. Unable to agree on much of anything, they blame each other for their troubles and outright refuse to do what the other no longer requests but demands.[64] This new structure leads their relationship to take on a whole new look and feel—that of mortal enemies locked in a fight to the death. By mapping the relationship at this third stage (see Figure 2.3), you can see just how toxic the structure underlying it has grown.

43

Figure 2.3   An Informal Structure Grows Toxic.

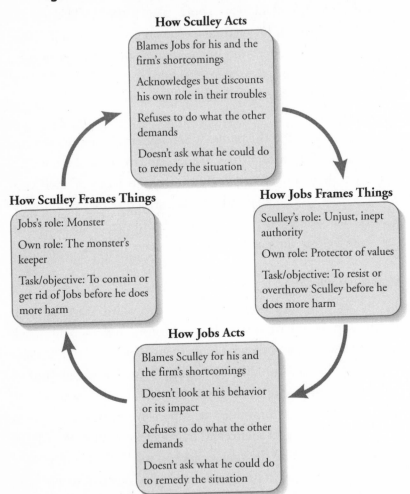

How Sculley Acts

Blames Jobs for his and the firm's shortcomings

Acknowledges but discounts his own role in their troubles

Refuses to do what the other demands

Doesn't ask what he could do to remedy the situation

How Sculley Frames Things

Jobs's role: Monster

Own role: The monster's keeper

Task/objective: To contain or get rid of Jobs before he does more harm

How Jobs Frames Things

Sculley's role: Unjust, inept authority

Own role: Protector of values

Task/objective: To resist or overthrow Sculley before he does more harm

How Jobs Acts

Blames Sculley for his and the firm's shortcomings

Doesn't look at his behavior or its impact

Refuses to do what the other demands

Doesn't ask what he could do to remedy the situation

Sealing Their Fate

Not until the very end do Sculley and Jobs sit down to discuss their relationship, and by then, it's too late. At no point in their come-to-Jesus discussion does either of them ask about or seek to understand the behavior that bothered them so much. Nor do they show any interest in understanding their own roles, how their relationship went wrong, or how they might set it right. By the meeting's end, Jobs leaves more convinced than ever that hiring Sculley was the biggest mistake of his life, and Sculley leaves confirmed in his belief that he has no choice but to go to the board with his ultimatum: remove Jobs as the head of Macintosh, or he'll resign.

A few days later, the board removes Jobs. Afterward, the two men cast about for roles they can both live with, but neither can imagine any that would work given the state of their relationship. It doesn't occur to anyone, except perhaps Jay Elliot,[65] that it is their relationship—not their roles—that needs redesigning. And so it is that Jobs goes into exile, Apple goes into decline, and their relationship comes to an end. Even now, more than twenty-five years later, all they seem to have taken from their relationship is the same thing David Sedaris took from his: what those self-help books call baggage.[66]

KEY POINTS

All relationships develop at a formal and informal level. At a formal level people define and redefine their formal roles, including responsibilities, decision rights, and rewards. At an informal level people define and redefine their informal roles: the emotional responsibilities they'll seek and shirk, the interpersonal rights they'll claim and relinquish, and the psychological rewards they'll want to give and get.

All relationships evolve over a series of stages, as people adapt to each other and the circumstances around them. Some adaptations are better than others. Jobs and Sculley's adaptations generated vicious cycles that gave rise to structures that reduced their degrees of freedom until they had none left. In two action-packed years, they moved from idolizing to demonizing each other, acting in ways that brought out the worst in each other. By the time they discussed their troubles, their views were so entrenched they were impervious to change, making it impossible for them to create a different future. In the end, they *had* to call it quits.

It need not be this way. As the next chapters show, with the right perspective and tools, it's possible to see, map, and change the informal side of a relationship so it grows stronger, not weaker, over time.

THREE

It's a Matter of Perspective

There's only three things for sure: Taxes, death, and trouble.

—MARVIN GAYE

So prevalent are relationship troubles that most of us merely accept them as the way things are. A *Time* magazine article in 2002 went so far as to say, "Until recently, being driven mad by others and driving others mad was known as life."[1] The article, titled "I'm OK. You're OK. We're not OK," questioned whether it was wise to include "relational disorders" in the newest edition of a diagnostic manual. What would happen, the columnist asked, to notions of personal responsibility? How could anyone ever be held accountable for anything? After all, you can fire or sue a person, but not a relationship. Besides, he concluded, relationship troubles are simply a fact of life. You're better off keeping your eye on individuals where responsibility can be clearly assigned and appropriately taken.

I doubt many people would disagree. There's already enough blame in organizations without adding another excuse: "It wasn't me. My relationship made me do it." But taking a relational perspective doesn't preempt people from taking responsibility.

Paradoxically, as I'll show in this chapter, just the opposite happens. When people think in relational terms, *they are more willing and able to take responsibility for their part in any problems or difficulties.*

To illustrate, this chapter introduces two perspectives that leaders might take to any differences, challenges, or troubles they face. The more common is what I call the individual perspective, based on the assumptions that there is one right answer, people either get it or don't get it, and when they don't, their dispositions are largely to blame. When leaders hold this perspective, their relationships grow weaker over time and many break down altogether.

Less common is what I call the relational perspective, based on the assumptions that different people will see different things, that solid common ground can only be found after exploring basic differences, and that the strength of a relationship will determine how well and how quickly people can put their differences to work. Leaders who take this perspective are able to use the heat of the moment to forge stronger relationships.

Let's take a look at each perspective, then consider both in light of some recent research on relationships.

The Individual Perspective

Recall what happened to John Sculley and Steve Jobs. At play in how they handled their troubles is the same set of assumptions. When sales at Apple plummeted, Jobs blamed Sculley for not solving Apple's distribution problems fast enough; Sculley blamed Jobs for getting Macintosh Office to market late. Both assumed only one of them could be right, and both set out to convince the other that it was himself.

As Apple's situation deteriorated and the two were unable to convince each other of anything, they began accusing each other of behaving in ways that were making matters worse: Jobs said Sculley was failing to provide enough leadership; Sculley said Jobs was meddling in things that were none of his business. Again, neither could imagine how they could both be right; each assumed the other alone was at fault.

This shared assumption riveted each man's attention on what the other person was doing and turned his attention away from what he himself was doing to reinforce the very behavior he blamed for their troubles. As a result, each assumed that the other was acting the way he was, not because of what he himself was doing, but because of the other's disposition: the other guy was either *mad* (stubborn, unable to control himself) or *bad* (corrupt, cares only about wealth and glory).

We see this time and time again (see Table 3.1). The assumptions that "you alone are responsible" and "you are either mad or bad" lead people to locate the cause of problems *in* individuals and *outside* their own influence. In the case of Jobs and Sculley, this

Table 3.1 The Individual Perspective.

	Core Assumptions
The Issues (The Substance)	There is only one right answer or view.
	Any rational person can see that my view is right and yours is wrong.
	Your view is unreasonable; you just don't get it.
The People (The Relationship)	Since you don't get it, you must be either mad or bad.
	You alone are responsible.
	You must change for our relationship to work.
	Until you change, it isn't worth investing in our relationship.

led each man to feel as if he had no choice but to go to the board and ask for the other's removal.

In the end, all we're left with is a paradox. The more Jobs and Sculley tried to get the other to take responsibility, the less responsibility each man took, and the more each man blamed the other.

Though especially dramatic in its results, this paradox is not unique to Apple. You can see it at work in organizations every day: the more people try to get others to take individual responsibility, the less individual responsibility they take.

Why? One possible answer can be found by looking closely at an interaction I witnessed a number of years ago at a pharmaceutical company I'll call Clear Inc.[2] The interaction unfolded when two executives at a struggling division got into a debate over who was to blame for the division's poor performance. It started when Peter Naughton, the division's new CEO, confronted Tom Bedford, the division's VP of research and development. Listen in as Naughton launches the debate:

NAUGHTON: So now the question is: To what extent is R&D going to make the really difficult choices? Because one thing is clear: we can't just keep adding and adding costs to R&D.

BEDFORD: We'll start looking at that next month. But actually, I think we've got to revisit [corporate's] strategy first. Our competitors see a very different future than the one corporate imagines for us. *That's* the big problem. They're spending fortunes and putting down bigger bets than we're able to—

NAUGHTON: [Interrupting] Hang on a second! If we're honest about this, our problem is that we were late waking up to what we might, could, and should do. There *is* an issue, but the issue is, *we were late.* Many of these

50

questions should have been tackled *three years ago.*
They weren't. It was simply, "Oh, let's toss another
three million into the annual R&D budget." That's
hardly a strategic answer.

Notice what happens in this opening exchange, in which
Naughton defines and Bedford accepts the terms of the debate:
who's to blame for the division's woes. Naughton says it's the
division; Bedford says it's corporate.[3] Now what? With the two
immediately at an impasse, Naughton raises the stakes with an
appeal to honesty—"If we're honest about this, our problem is
that we were late"—as if his view is the only honest view to take.
Although this could easily put Bedford in a bind (either admit
blame or appear dishonest), Bedford forges on, undeterred:

BEDFORD: [Looking down, shaking his head] I'm not complaining. I'm—
NAUGHTON: [Interrupting] We can't just chalk it up to corporate
isn't supporting us.
BEDFORD: [Looking up, raising his voice] But there's no criticism
in my statement!

But notice: there clearly is criticism in Bedford's statement.
He's just said that they need to revisit corporate's strategy, because
their competitors see a very different future than the one corporate
imagines for them. To him, "That's the big problem." So what
would lead Bedford to deny that he's criticizing corporate when
he's clearly doing so? One possibility is that it allows him to appear
honest (he's not criticizing or blaming anyone) while still not
accepting blame himself. Naughton doesn't buy it:

NAUGHTON: [Emphatically] You're saying, "It's not our fault in
R&D. If only corporate would open their eyes, they

would have seen all this." But if you look at how long it's taken us, *you can't blame corporate*—

BEDFORD: And if *you* look at the history of this business, we all know where blame can be placed, and it is on many heads [glares at Naughton].

Barred from blaming corporate yet unwilling to blame himself, Bedford eludes Naughton's grasp once again, this time by placing blame on many unnamed heads. This move, which reveals the hopeless nature of their debate, prompts Naughton to deny having launched it in the first place.

NAUGHTON: [Sighing] I wasn't trying to assign blame. I'm *merely* stating the reason the organization is behind is because *we've* been late.

BEDFORD: And I'm *merely* saying that we've been late because we have yet to convince our corporate masters that the future is different than the one they see.

Now we have Bedford and Naughton both placing blame, while claiming they're not: they're merely "stating" this or "saying" that. This joint denial makes it much harder to continue placing blame, which leaves Naughton no choice: he must close down the debate.

NAUGHTON: Then let it start here [jabbing the table with his index finger]. We haven't convinced ourselves yet. *We're* the ones who need to figure out what we'll invest in and what we'll cease to do. Until we do that, we can't possibly make a compelling case for support. [Putting his papers aside] Next item?

With this declaration of where responsibility must lie—and it's *not* on many heads—Naughton has the last word, but he convinces no one, least of all Bedford. As you can see from their exchange, the more Naughton pushes, the less responsibility Bedford takes—and not just for the division's failure: he won't even take responsibility for not taking responsibility!

THE FAR SIDE®   By GARY LARSON

© 1981 FarWorks, Inc. All Rights Reserved/Dist. by Creators Syndicate

The Far Side® by Gary Larson © 1981 FarWorks, Inc. All Rights Reserved. The Far Side® and the Larson® signature are registered trademarks of FarWorks, Inc. Used with permission.

These are the games we play to navigate around assumptions that make it hard to say what we think, because what we think is so problematic.

The basic problem is this: when we assume that one person is responsible for outcomes we don't like, and that this person is either mad or bad for causing them, all we do is compel that person to defend himself and fill in the part of the picture that, nine times out of ten, is missing. If that person then also assumes that only one person (or side) is at fault, as is usually the case, the best he can do is throw the blame right back at us.

Unless people seek to understand how they are both contributing to outcomes no one likes, they will be forever caught in the same paradoxical game in which the more individual responsibility is sought, the less individual responsibility is found.

So what's the alternative? As unlikely as it may seem, the glimmers of one can be found in Bedford's notion of blame falling on many heads. What makes this notion problematic isn't that there are many heads, but that the heads are unnamed and the purpose is to blame, not to understand. But what if Bedford and Naughton had sought to understand how the heads of *both* corporate and division had contributed to results neither liked? Perhaps they would have discovered how their waiting for the other to act had made it harder for either to do what they needed to do to improve the division's performance. That is, with the division waiting for corporate to place bigger bets before focusing, and corporate waiting for the division to focus before placing bigger bets, and neither of them looking at their joint responsibility, they together created an impasse that prevented them from improving the division's performance.

Most leaders I know believe deeply in taking personal responsibility for their actions and results, and they recognize how self-defeating it is to place blame on others. And most are acutely aware of when those around them are doing it.[4] But very few are aware of when they themselves are doing the very same thing. When it comes to themselves, many leaders truly believe that others are largely responsible for the circumstances they face, and as a result, truly believe that they have little choice but to act the way they do.

Only in the interactions of the most mature leaders do you see a different perspective based on a different set of assumptions. These assumptions, which constitute what I call the *relational perspective*, focus on mutual responsibility and stress the importance of relationships. The next section shows what these assumptions look like in action.

The Relational Perspective

At the beginning of World War II, when Winston Churchill and Franklin Roosevelt first came together to form an alliance against Hitler, they were a study in contrasts: Roosevelt, secretive; Churchill, transparent. Roosevelt, calculated and at times manipulative; Churchill, expressive and at times impulsive. Roosevelt, intent on keeping the United States out of the war; Churchill, equally intent on bringing the United States into the war. Roosevelt, a constant critic of colonialism; Churchill, a steadfast defender of the British colonial empire. Roosevelt, convinced that a leader ought to keep his ear to the ground of popular opinion; Churchill, equally convinced that a leader ought to get out in front and shape popular opinion. The two couldn't have been more different in personality, interests, or beliefs. And yet over the course of the war, as Jon Meacham recounts in *Franklin and Winston*, they were able to forge an alliance based on a common purpose and what Meacham calls an "epic friendship."

Of the many things they did to build that friendship, one thing Meacham mentions stands out: "They always kept the mission— and their relationship—in mind, understanding that statecraft is an intrinsically imperfect and often frustrating endeavor."[5]

When it came to their mission, Roosevelt and Churchill saw and cared about very different things, triggering disagreements over a wide range of topics. How they handled these disagreements is striking. Instead of discounting each other's views or assuming the other just didn't get it, they engaged in hours of debate, seeking to persuade and to understand. If their interests or beliefs clashed, they didn't denigrate the other's interests or beliefs; they took them into account and sought to address them whenever they could. And if either of them did things to make matters worse, more often than not they looked to the other's circumstances, not his character, to understand why, and they repeatedly offered a helping hand.

This way of handling their differences became apparent early on, when Churchill repeatedly petitioned Roosevelt to enter the war and Roosevelt just as repeatedly refused. With 90 percent of Americans opposed to the war, Roosevelt sought every way possible to support Britain short of sending troops. It wasn't enough. France quickly fell, Britain alone was left fighting the Nazis, and Roosevelt came under attack in the British Parliament for refusing to enter the war.

The one person who came to his defense was Churchill. "[America has] promised fullest aid in materials, munitions," Churchill began at a closed session of Parliament on June 20, 1940. Calling the aid a "tribute to Roosevelt," he then alluded to America's upcoming presidential election, saying, "All depends upon our resolute bearing until Election issues are settled there. If we can do so, I cannot doubt a whole English-speaking world will be in line together."[6]

That Churchill defended Roosevelt at all is interesting enough. But how he did so is especially instructive. Given Churchill's political pressures and beliefs, it would have been easy for him to join in Britain's outrage or to accuse Roosevelt of being a slave to public opinion. But he didn't. Instead he pointed to the circumstances that impinged on Roosevelt's choices, and instead of pressing Roosevelt to deliver something he couldn't practically do, he made it easier for Roosevelt, believing that this would be more likely to bring them in line after the election.

Roosevelt took a similar approach after the fall of Singapore, the jewel of the British empire. It was a devastating blow for Britain, and in an effort to soften it, Churchill gave a radio address in which, among other things, he referred to American sea power as having been "dashed to the ground" at Pearl Harbor. Washington's inner circles were aghast, and a number of them went running to Roosevelt to complain that Churchill had just blamed the U.S. Navy for the fall of Singapore.

Roosevelt, who waved away their complaints with a curt, "Winston had to say *something*," responded by picking up a pen and writing Churchill a note. "I realize how the fall of Singapore has affected you and the British people," he began. "It gives the well-known backseat drivers a field day.... I hope you will be of good heart in these trying weeks because I am very sure that you have the great confidence of the masses of the British people. I want you to know that I think of you often and I know you will not hesitate to ask me if there is anything you think I can do."

When it came to their relationship, neither Roosevelt nor Churchill expected they would always get along—nor did they. But because they understood that their relationship would have a decisive impact on the success or failure of their mission, they gave it the same strategic attention they gave every other aspect of the war. All told, they met nine times between 1941 and 1945 in a range of different locales from Canada to Casablanca to Iran. In between, they exchanged countless wires, letters, and phone calls on everything from their families' well-being to their flagging spirits to matters of war.

It all began with a letter—sent eight days after Hitler invaded Poland on September 1, 1939, nine months before Churchill became prime minister, and two years before the United States entered the war. Knowing that Churchill had just been appointed First Lord of the Admiralty, Roosevelt wrote,

My dear Churchill,

It is because you and I occupied similar positions in the World War that I want you to know how glad I am that you are back again in the Admiralty. Your problems are, I realize, complicated by new factors but the essential is not very different. What I want you and the Prime Minister to know is that I shall at all times welcome it if you will keep me in touch personally with anything you want me to know about.

Roosevelt ended the letter in keeping with remarks about "the importance of personal relationships among allied nations" that he'd made at a dinner during World War I where he'd first met Churchill: "I am glad you did the Marlboro volumes before this thing started—and I much enjoyed reading them."[7]

Once Churchill became prime minister, the two men went to great lengths to meet face-to-face. In August 1941, four months before the Japanese attacked Pearl Harbor and six weeks after Germany invaded the Soviet Union, they traveled by ship in secret and at great risk to Placentia Bay, Newfoundland. There, aboard their two vessels, through days of talking, drinking, and smoking together, they forged a common bond and a common purpose. Roosevelt's speechwriter, Robert Sherwood, wrote of their meeting:

They were two men in the same line of business—politico-military leadership on a global scale—and theirs was a very limited field and the few who achieve it seldom have opportunities for getting together with fellow craftsmen in the same trade to compare notes and talk shop. They appraised each other through the practiced eyes of professionals and from this appraisal resulted a degree of admiration and sympathetic understanding of each other's professional problems that lesser craftsmen could not have achieved . . . they had a wonderful capacity to stimulate and refresh each other.[8]

Churchill left their initial encounter believing that Roosevelt's "heart seemed to respond to many of the impulses that stirred my own," while Roosevelt's son, Elliot, observed, "My experience of [my father] in the past had been that he had dominated every gathering he was part of; not because he insisted on it so much as that it always seemed his natural due. Tonight, Father listened." Naval aide-de-camp Commander C. R. "Tommy" Thompson said the same of Roosevelt: "I had never met a person of the President's distinction who showed such apparently real interest in one's own replies to his questions."[9]

During the religious services held upon the *Prince of Wales*—which Roosevelt called the "keynote" of their meeting—Churchill could see their common purpose in evidence: "When I look upon the densely-packed congregation of fighting men of the same language, the same faith, of the same fundamental laws and the same ideals, and now to a large extent of the same interests, and certainly in different degrees facing the same dangers, it swept across me that here was the only hope, but also the sure hope, of saving the world from measureless degradation."[10]

Churchill's hope notwithstanding, it was during this first visit that basic differences also emerged. "The two disagreed," Meacham recounts, "and would for the rest of the war, about colonialism . . . setting the stage for a long-running source of tension between the two men."[11] And this was not their only source of tension—or their most difficult one.

As the war neared its end, Roosevelt and Churchill disagreed vehemently over how to handle Premier Josef Stalin and the Soviet

Union. In their first three-way meeting, Roosevelt sought to charm and placate the premier in hopes of securing his support for a United Nations, while Churchill took a tougher stand, fearing that if they did not, they would face Soviet aggression after the war. Though Churchill would eventually prove prescient, at that meeting, it was Churchill, not Stalin, who played the odd man out.

Unsurprisingly, during this time of constant tension, their relationship grew more contentious. In a steady stream of cable traffic, the two fought over how best to end the war and structure the peace. With Churchill intent on protecting Britain's post-war place, and Roosevelt just as intent on advancing America's post-war interests, the two men argued fiercely. In their last fight, this one over whether they should try to beat the Soviets to Berlin, the two failed to reach agreement. In the end, Churchill conceded.[12] Afterward he wrote Roosevelt a note to reassure him that there were no hard feelings: "I regard the matter as closed," he wrote, "and to prove my sincerity I will use one of my very few Latin quotations, '*Amantium irae amoris integratio est.*'" Translation: "Lovers' quarrels always go with true love."[13] A week later, their friendship came to an end with Roosevelt's death.

Of that friendship, Meacham writes, "For all the tensions, and there were many . . . there was a personal bond at work that, though often tested, held them together."[14] I would argue that the strength of that bond was a product of the way they saw and handled their most fundamental differences. When disagreements broke out and pressures mounted, they sought to understand how the other thought and ticked. And while neither man hesitated to advance his own views or interests, they were equally quick to ask about the other's and to listen with genuine interest. As a result, no matter how frustrated they became, they never reduced each other to a caricature. Instead they built an ever more nuanced and subtle understanding of—and appreciation for—each other as people and for each other's views and beliefs.[15]

Most important and most unusual, despite the many competing demands on their time and the geographic distance between them, they took great pains throughout the war to invest in their relationship. More than anything else, this investment—and their mutual willingness to make it—allowed them to find common ground in the face of basic differences and to withstand the vast uncertainties and pressures of war.

Throughout, the two leaders illustrate a perspective built on a set of assumptions many leaders espouse but few enact (see Table 3.2). This perspective, which I call the relational perspective, is based on a core belief best expressed by Karl Popper: "While differing widely in the various little bits we know, in our infinite ignorance we are all equal." This basic belief leads people to

Table 3.2   The Relational Perspective.

	Core Assumptions
The Substance (The Issues)	Each of us sees things the other misses.
	Reasonable people can reasonably disagree.
	Complex, ambiguous tasks are inherently frustrating.
The People (The Relationship)	Relationships upon which success depends are a strategic asset in need of continual investment.
	We are both responsible for ensuring the strength of our relationship.
	Solid common ground can be found only after exploring basic differences.
	We're doing the best we can under the circumstances and need each other's help to do better.

assume that we all see things others miss, that disagreements are inevitable and valuable, that those disagreements will at times cause frustration, and that people will be better off if they help each other build relationships that can handle those differences well, especially under pressure.

Reality Check: The Power of Relationships

What happened to Jobs and Sculley at Apple and to Naughton and Bedford at Clear Inc. is an all-too-common occurrence. In both cases, each man assumed that he alone was right, that the other just didn't get it, and that the other's disposition was at fault: he was either mad or bad.

Whether aware of it or not—usually not—all of us tend to ascribe behavior we don't like to people's dispositions, and we assume those dispositions are impervious to change.

We're wrong, it turns out, on both counts.

All of us are exquisitely sensitive to experience and to circumstance.[16] For decades now, one psychology experiment after another has shown that situations have far greater sway over people's behavior than we think. Yet the belief that behavior is determined by disposition is so pervasive that psychologists call it the *fundamental attribution error.*

Even more intriguing is recent research conducted by genetic and family researchers. A number of them are discovering that our relationships have the power to either amplify or modify even genetically based predispositions. Take, for example, a twelve-year study of 720 adolescents led by family psychiatrist David Reiss. It found that relationships within a family affect whether and how strongly genes underlying complex behavior get expressed.

"Many genetic factors, powerful as they may be," says Reiss, "exert their influence only through the good offices of the family."[17] Some parental responses to genetic proclivities—say, toward shyness or antisocial behavior—exaggerate traits, while others mute them.

"Our proposal," says Reiss, "is not simply that the environment has a general and non-specific facilitative or preparatory role in the behavioral expression of genetic influences, but rather that specific family processes may have distinctive and necessary roles in the actual mechanisms of genetic expression."[18] In other words, to have any effect, genes must be turned on, and relationships are the finger that flips the switch.

To illustrate how, *Newsweek* writer Sharon Begley asks us to consider how rats behave. (*Actual* rats, that is—not the people with whom we wish we didn't work.) Citing McGill University professor Michael Meaney's study, Begley explains how the interaction between genes and environment accounts for much of the variance among the responses of baby rats to stress:

> As soon as their wriggly little pups are born, rat mothers lick and groom them, but like mothers of other species they vary in how obsessive they are about getting every one of their offspring's hairs in place. Pups whose mothers treat them like living lollipops grow up different from pups of less devoted mothers: particular genes in the pups' brains are turned on "high." These brain genes play a pivotal role in behavior. With the genes turned up full blast, the rats churn out fewer stress hormones and, as adults, are more resistant to stress. . . . These rats don't startle as easily, are less fearful in the face of novel situations and braver when they have to explore an open field.[19]

Behavioral geneticist Kenneth Kendler of the Medical College of Virginia has found the same thing among humans.

> Family is like a catapult. Kids with a difficult temperament can be managed and set on a good course, or their innate tendencies can be magnified by the family and catapulted into a conduct disorder.... A child with a difficult temperament—irritability, aggressiveness—brings on parents' harsh discipline, verbal abuse, anger, hostility and relentless criticism. That seems to exacerbate the child's innate bad side, which only makes parents even more negative, on and on in a vicious cycle until the adolescent loses all sense of responsibility and academic focus.[20]

What's more, the power of relationships to shape behavior doesn't stop in childhood. If we're wired to do anything, it seems, we're wired to learn. "Learning is not the antithesis of innateness," says Gary Marcus in *The Birth of the Mind*.[21] "The reason animals can learn is that they can alter their nervous systems based on external experience. And the reason they can do that is that *experience itself can modify the expression of genes*."[22]

Reams of research suggest that the brain continues to change in response to experience. Even adult brains are proving more mutable than most people think.[23] Indeed, it's looking more and more that *our genes are continually working together with our environments— and most important, our relationships—to define and redefine who we are by structuring and restructuring our brains.*

All this research adds up to one important conclusion: our assumptions about individuals are quite simply wrong. Even so-called "difficult" people aren't innately or irrevocably mad or bad. The relationships we build with others have the power to bring out the best or the worst in all of us. It's the relationship we should be focusing on, not on individuals alone and in isolation.

The next chapter shows you how.

KEY POINTS

Troubles—challenges, conflicts, pressures, failures, mistakes—are inevitable. How we see and handle them with others is a matter of choice, even if made unconsciously or automatically. When people take an individual perspective, they assume they alone are right, that this is obvious, and that others don't get it because they are either mad or bad. This perspective leads to blaming and waiting games that erode personal responsibility and tear at the threads of even good relationships. In contrast, when people take a relational perspective, they assume that others see things they miss, that reasonable people can disagree, and that it's important that people work together to build relationships strong enough to weather the troubles they will face.

Despite its cultural dominance, the individual perspective is based on assumptions that scientists of different stripes are increasingly calling into question. Cognitive psychologists have shown again and again that our circumstances shape our behavior at least as much as our dispositions, and more recently, family psychologists and geneticists are finding that relationships are the most powerful circumstance of all, amplifying or muting even genetically programmed predispositions.

While many leaders can see the value of taking a relational perspective, most find it hard to do in the heat of the moment. The next chapters provide a set of tools that will help you shift perspective even when things get hot.

PART 2

Strengthening Relationships

I don't like that man. I must get to know him better.

—Abraham Lincoln[1]

FOUR

Using the Heat
of the Moment

As conflict—difference—is here in the world, as we cannot
avoid it, . . . Instead of condemning it, we should set it to
work for us.

——MARY PARKER FOLLETT, 1925

I n the chaos just after Abraham Lincoln was shot, Secretary
of War Edwin Stanton mistakenly rushed to the house of the
wounded secretary of state, William Seward. There he found blood
splattered from the first floor to the third, but no president.[1]
Next he ran to the boardinghouse near Ford's Theatre, where he
found Lincoln lying unconscious on a narrow bed, and where the
surgeon general quietly told him the president would not recover.
Of what happened next, historian Charles Flood writes, "Stanton,
a man who never displayed his emotions, began sobbing loudly, his
shoulders convulsively shaking for several minutes."[2] For months
afterward, Stanton's grief was uncontrollable. "At the mention of
Mr. Lincoln's name," recalled one witness, "he would break down
and weep bitterly."[3]

It had not always been so between the two men. Long before
President Lincoln asked Edwin Stanton to replace the incompetent

Simon Cameron as secretary of war, and long before Stanton accepted, Stanton said of the young lawyer from Illinois, loud enough for Lincoln to hear, "He does not know anything and can do you no good."[4] Lincoln's election to the presidency did not change Stanton's low opinion. A month into Lincoln's first term, Stanton wrote a friend and former cabinet secretary, asking him to sell Stanton's government bonds, "There is no settled principle or line of action—no token of any intelligent understanding by Lincoln. Bluster & bravado alternates with timosity & despair—recklessness and helplessness by turns rule the hour."[5]

Despite Stanton's contempt, Lincoln decided to appoint him to the War Department post, convinced he was the best man for the job. Not everyone shared Lincoln's view. Upon hearing the news, Congressman Henry Dawes of Massachusetts dropped by the White House to tell Lincoln that some folks feared that Stanton might run away with the whole concern. Lincoln thought about that for a moment, then replied, "We may have to treat him as they are sometimes obliged to treat a Methodist minister I know of out West. He gets wrought up to so high a pitch of excitement in his prayers and exhortations that they are obliged to put bricks in his pockets to keep him down. We may be obliged to serve Stanton in the same way, but I guess we'll let him jump a while first."[6]

Over the next three years, Lincoln would walk over to the War Office and join Stanton in the telegraph room, where Stanton would jump and Lincoln would stretch out on the sofa as telegraphs arrived from the field, sometimes for hours on end late into the night.[7] It was in this room that the two worked through their differences and stemmed the tide of Union failures—first as adversaries, then as partners, and finally, improbably, as friends.

Forging relationships strong enough to withstand pressures and conflicts is as difficult as it is critical. But it is not impossible, nor is it simply a matter of chemistry. Most strong relationships, like the one between Stanton and Lincoln, must be forged in the face of differences that seem insurmountable in the heat of the moment, but that prove—upon reflection—to be the very thing that save the day and make the relationship work.

This chapter shows how two contemporary leaders in a professional services firm used the heat of the moment to forge a relationship strong enough to meet the demands they faced. It describes how two relational capabilities—reflecting and reframing; first alone, then together—helped these leaders shift perspective, so they could strengthen their relationship over time in much the same way Abraham Lincoln and Edwin Stanton strengthened theirs.[8]

Founding Friends

Twenty-five years ago, a band of friends fresh out of business school set out to build an elite professional services firm. They were convinced that by wedding stellar client service to innovative new content, they could surpass other players currently dominating the industry. At the same time, they were committed to building a firm that put into practice ideals many firms espouse but few enact. They wanted to demonstrate—not just state—an uncompromising commitment to excellence, innovation, colleagueship, learning, and professional growth. For the founders of Merrimac,[9] these ideals weren't mere niceties. They were essential to attracting and retaining the best talent and the best clients in an industry growing more competitive by the year.

Over the next eighteen months, the firm catapulted to success. Revenues in the first year exceeded expectations; its reputation for quality spread; it attracted exceptional talent; and its client list included some of the best companies in the world. Before the founders knew it, they were off and running, growing so quickly they could scarcely keep up.

Soon it became clear that the very pace of their growth was letting loose a stream of controversial issues, one right after the other: how the firm should be run, whom they should hire, how rewards should be allocated, who should be accountable for what, how decisions should get made and by whom. As people took different sides on each of these issues, tensions erupted and threatened to stretch the group to the breaking point.

At first, not wanting to jeopardize their success, everyone papered over their differences. But as time went on and problems festered, a kind of cold war set in, with people forming adversarial coalitions behind the scenes and working hard to disguise their growing animosity whenever they met. Before long, colleagueship broke down, almost no one was telling the truth, and learning came to a halt. Only two years into the life of the firm, they ran the risk of falling apart. Though revenues remained solid and product

"All those in favor say 'Aye.'"
"Aye."   *"Aye."*   *"Aye."*
        "Aye."   *"Aye."*

quality high, the environment around them was growing more toxic by the month.

In the midst of their third year, a dismayed but determined CEO, Dan Gavin, decided to get help. After doing some research, he asked a highly regarded organizational consultant to help him and his cohorts look at what had happened and advise them on what to do next. Today, many still credit that work with getting them through the first crisis in the life of the firm. More than that, they credit it with establishing the shared belief that, as leaders, they were mutually responsible for the kinds of relationships they created and for working through any tensions or conflicts that arose among them. While some founders believed this more than others did, it gave the group enough common ground to turn their collective attention to growing the firm.

On that common ground, they grew quickly. They went after and served some of the best firms in the world. They opened offices on almost every continent on the globe, and they launched and acquired new businesses. They went from a firm of 150 professionals to over 1,000, and they swelled their ranks every summer with eager young talent from top schools. By the late 1990s, they were bursting at the seams. They had taken a single company and grown it into a group of businesses. Now, with far more people, geographies, and businesses than leaders to manage them, they encountered their second developmental crisis: there just weren't enough leaders to go around.

Bringing the Next Generation Along

Even with excellent staff support, the founder-heavy executive team couldn't keep up with the pace of growth. The sheer scope and complexity of the business was fast outstripping their ability to manage the firm's operations. At an informal level, the firm's overdependence on Dan Gavin was wearing thin. Ever since the firm's inception, Dan had become the indispensable hub in the wheel of relationships that propelled the firm forward. No one knew more about people's lives or offered more motivation or inspiration. Now, with the number of people in the firm multiplying by the day, that wheel was slowing down, and the bonds of affection holding it together were starting to fray. It was time to take a few risks and bring the next generation of leaders along.

That's probably why Dan took to the idea of Luke Turner leading FastStart, one of the firm's newer businesses. For many years Dan had seen great leadership potential in Luke's grasp of people and in his even-keeled response to business crises. As Luke's mentor, Dan had spent many an evening talking with Luke about his long-range goals, encouraging him to aim high and to take big risks. Over the years Dan's encouragement had endeared him to Luke, who admired Dan's quick, incisive intellect and felt indebted to Dan for his many kindnesses. Over the years, their personal regard for each other had turned the two of them into friends.

The more Dan mulled over the idea of Luke leading FastStart, the more he liked the idea. The fledgling unit needed a leader to bring costs under control and to spur growth, and Luke needed leadership experience to grow professionally. It all made sense.

Though it took some selling to the firm's new board—some were as wary of new leaders as they were of new businesses—Dan convinced them to go along. True, Luke had never had profit-and-loss responsibility for a business unit, Dan told them, but few outside the founder's group had. If they were going to keep growing, he argued, they would need to take some risks on people. With some reservation, the board agreed.

Things Heat Up

A year after Luke took the helm, FastStart's results looked promising. In twelve months, Luke had successfully managed to cut unnecessary costs, reduce overhead, increase people's motivation, and improve revenue growth. Halfway into the second year, however, growth started to level off, and Dan began to worry. Ever sensitive to board politics, Dan knew that Luke and the new business were still politically vulnerable, as was he for having convinced the board to bet on Luke. Growing increasingly worried that the inexperienced Luke wasn't moving fast enough to remedy the situation, Dan sent what Luke later called a "flaming" voice mail a week before the next board meeting:

> Luke, we've got a problem. You're not making decisions fast enough. You're being too bureaucratic and making too many decisions by committee. It's slowing down the whole company! I don't know whether you're risk-averse or just anxious, but it's a problem. Last year, you and I convinced the board to invest in your business unit and they bought it. Now you're not delivering. I'm going to a board meeting in a week, and I have no fucking idea what I'm going to tell them. They expect results, and we've got none to speak of. The sooner we can connect on this the better. [Click.]

As soon as Luke got Dan's message, he felt "mad as hell." This wasn't the first time he'd received this kind of message from Dan. Long at the center of the firm, Dan would disappear for months, focusing on one part of the business only to show up in another, using his laser-like attention to uncover problems. Ever anxious to see those problems solved, Dan would ask what people were doing—sometimes patiently, other times not. Right now, Dan was looking mighty impatient, and unfairly so from Luke's point of view.

How dare you say we're not moving fast enough?! Luke thought to himself. *We've done a lot—built a leadership team, launched new programs, improved profitability. And no thanks to you, I might add. I'm all for moving fast, but let's get real about what's going on here. If you returned my calls, I'd be glad to move faster.*

Cooling Down

Increasingly furious, Luke reached for the "respond" button with every intention of blasting Dan for sending such a negative message. But then, just as his finger touched the button, he stopped himself.

Wait a second, he thought. *What am I doing? This isn't going to accomplish anything.*

In his mind's eye, he fast-forwarded in time and imagined what would happen next: *If I retaliate in kind, Dan will only dig in further and nothing will get done, and then Dan will be right; we will be moving too slowly.*

Realizing how quickly his reactions could become part of the problem, Luke mulled over the year from Dan's perspective. *It would be better if he weren't so negative about our progress,* he thought, *but I can see how from his point of view we are moving too slowly.*

Luke again reached for the "respond" button, this time in a more temperate state of mind. "I'm with you," he told Dan. "I agree we need to move faster. I'll make sure we meet soon to talk about it. I have some thoughts on how I might speed things up, and I'd like to get yours."

When Dan heard Luke's response, he quickly relaxed. Ever since sending the voice mail, he'd worried that Luke might get so defensive it would slow things down further. Now, listening to Luke's message, he felt instant relief, prompting him to wonder why he'd gotten so overwrought and sent such an intemperate voice mail in the first place. *If anything,* he thought, *it was a bit hysterical.* Feeling chagrined, he took a moment to reflect on the source of his agitation.

The next day, Dan reflected with Luke on what had happened: "My voice mail made me realize that I have a sentimental as well as a practical interest in your taking on more leadership in the firm. When I see you including a lot of people in your decision making, I get anxious it's going to slow you down and undermine your credibility. But I feel like I can't say anything, because I don't want to be seen as hovering, which of course I'm prone to do, since I'm so invested in your success. Hence the hysteria."

By recounting his dilemma, Dan helped Luke see that his hysteria had sprung from his feeling caught between an interest in Luke's success and a desire not to hover. This revelation gave Luke what he needed to help. "Actually, there was a part of the message that was very helpful," Luke told him. "Although you were rumbling me, you were very clear about what you needed. I'd have to be an idiot not to get it. 'Dan wants to go faster,' I thought. 'I want to go faster too. Let's go fast together.'"

If anything, Luke's problem wasn't that Dan was hovering, as Dan worried. It was that he waited so long to express his concerns that all Dan could do was focus on the negative. This made sense to Dan, and it helped relax the dilemma that was keeping him from voicing his worries until they reached a fevered pitch.

At this point, the two struck a new deal: Dan agreed to raise his concerns earlier, while Luke agreed to make it easier by asking if he had any. They were now free to turn their attention to how they might speed up progress. Here Luke agreed to modify his decision-making process, while Dan agreed to modify his tendency to go silent. Most important, in the weeks following the meeting, neither of them simply sat back and watched to see if the other guy changed. Quite the contrary, they helped each other out by reflecting on how they were doing and looking together for ways to do better.

No Easy Answers

Luke and Dan were not alone in their experience. As other leaders outside the founding group stepped into leadership roles, they took on as part of their responsibilities the obligation to make their relationships work. This helped them immeasurably a year later, when a combination of industry forces and firm choices conspired to slow Merrimac's growth. Figuring out which factors and what choices were causing the problem put the firm's leaders squarely at odds. Some believed the firm's strategy was at fault; others believed that they'd allowed "peripheral" investments to take their eye off of the core business; and still others thought that too much control had been left in the hands of too few for too long and that lingering dysfunctions among the founders had led revenues to lag and costs to rise.

At the same time, tensions within and among generations emerged over the future of the firm. Many people thought it was past time to decide what the firm wanted to be when it grew up. Did they want to remain a private company or to go public? And how should they divide the rewards of their successes? Should they offer liquidity to the older generation or more stock to the younger ones? With no easy answers in sight and different people's interests at odds, resolution eluded them for months, raising fundamental doubts about the future of the firm and about one another.

Whether the people in those relationships will be able to use what happened to grow as leaders and as partners, the jury is still out. Meanwhile I can say this: they stand a better chance than most. The next section explains why.

When Things Get Hot

When President John F. Kennedy learned that Soviet Premier Nikita Khrushchev was secretly installing missiles in Cuba, his first reaction was, "He can't do that to me!" He then added, "I guess we're going to have to bomb them!"[10]

In the heat of the moment, cooler heads rarely prevail. The very phrase, *in the heat of the moment,* suggests why. You're *in* the moment, unable to gain perspective on it. Your emotions are heating up and overwhelming your ability to think. And the moment itself, well, it's going by *really fast.* Before you know it, your automatic responses are kicking in and your self-control is petering out.

This is especially true when you're dealing with what Amy Edmondson and I call *hot topics* (see Table 4.1).[11] When you're dealing with hot topics, the stakes are high; the facts are either in dispute or difficult to access; the level of certainty is low;[12] and people's goals or interests are clashing. Before you know it, everyone's hot buttons are being pushed and the discussion turns emotional. In contrast, *cool topics* rarely trigger us, because they're fairly easy to resolve. The stakes are low to moderate; the facts aren't too difficult to access; the level of certainty is

Table 4.1 Cool Versus Hot Topics.

Cool Topics	Hot Topics
Data are accessible and objective.	Data are inaccessible or in dispute.
Competing interpretations are easy to test.	Competing interpretations are hard to test.
Certainty is high.	Certainty is low.
Stakes are relatively low.	Stakes are very high.
Goals, values, beliefs, and interests are largely shared.	Goals, values, beliefs, and interests are in conflict.
The discussion is fact-based, reasoned, and collegial.	The discussion is value-laden, emotional, and adversarial.

fairly high; and people's goals and interests are aligned, making agreement easier to reach and discussions more rational and collegial.[13]

Leaders confront hot topics every day. This means they must continually manage their emotional reactions, so they don't distort their judgment or cripple their decision making. How well leaders do this depends in large part on how quickly they can shift out of what psychologists Janet Metcalfe and Walter Mischel call the brain's *hot system*—that part of the brain where our hot buttons live—and into the brain's *cool system*. According to Metcalfe and Mischel, these two systems process events in very different ways, our hot system leading us to react quickly and impulsively, our cool system helping us think more rationally and thoughtfully about events (see Table 4.2).[14]

My clinical research suggests that two relational capabilities—reflecting and reframing; first alone, then together—help leaders shift systems, so they can regain perspective and use their conflicts to strengthen their relationships.

Table 4.2   Hot and Cool Systems.

Hot System	Cool System
Emotional	Cognitive
"Go"	"Know"
Simple	Complex
Reflexive	Reflective
Fast	Slow
Develops early	Develops late
Accentuated by stress	Attenuated by stress

Source: Based on J. Metcalfe and W. Mischel, "A Hot/Cool System Analysis of Delay of Gratification."

Reflecting and Reframing—First Alone, Then Together

There's a whole host of cultural and cognitive reasons why people take an individual perspective to the challenges and differences they face.[15] But one important reason has to do with the difficulty people have shifting out of their brains' hot systems and into their cool systems when dealing with hot topics.

My research suggests that by using a tool called the Ladder of Reflection to reflect and reframe—first alone, then together—leaders can help each other shift systems and perspectives (see Figure 4.1). In fact, if my clinical work is any indication, I suspect that, with time and practice, these two relational capabilities develop our cool system and our access to it, so we can shift

Figure 4.1 Using the Ladder of Reflection.

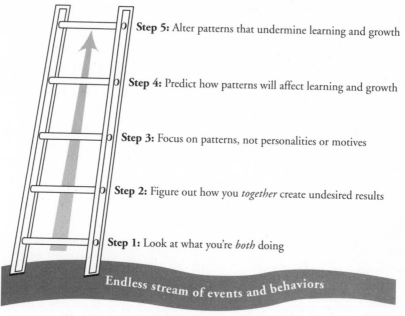

Step 5: Alter patterns that undermine learning and growth

Step 4: Predict how patterns will affect learning and growth

Step 3: Focus on patterns, not personalities or motives

Step 2: Figure out how you *together* create undesired results

Step 1: Look at what you're *both* doing

Endless stream of events and behaviors

Note: See Appendix B for detail on the Ladder of Reflection.

81

perspective more quickly and easily, even in the heat of the moment.[16]

To see what these two relational capabilities look like in action, let's look at what Dan and Luke did over the course of six steps, then consider the implications for shifting systems and gaining perspective.

- *Step One:* Though mad as hell, Luke stops himself before hitting the "respond" button to blast Dan for being so negative. What stops him is the ability to imagine what will happen next if he "goes" and acts on his first-blush reaction. In a matter of seconds, he "knows" that Dan will only dig in further; he knows that he (Luke) will do the same; and he knows that *nothing will get done.* The reason Luke knows these things is that he and Dan have spent time reflecting together on the patterns of interaction that get in their way. Chief among them is the pattern depicted in Figure 4.2, in which they dig in their heels and fail to convince each other of anything, except perhaps their unreasonableness. Some version of this map, one of several mental representations stored in Luke and Dan's collective cool system, springs to mind just as Luke reaches for the "respond" button, stopping him in his tracks.

- *Step Two:* As soon as Luke retrieves some version of this map, he's able to get the distance he needs to reframe what's happening from a more relational perspective.[17] No longer caught up in the moment, he's able to look back at what happened from the outside. While he had originally seen Dan's voice mail in purely stimulus-response terms—Dan *made* me angry—he's now able to entertain the idea that he might have played a role in Dan's upset. While he still doesn't like Dan's negativity, he no longer sees it as a product of Dan's personality

Figure 4.2   Recognizing an Unproductive Pattern.

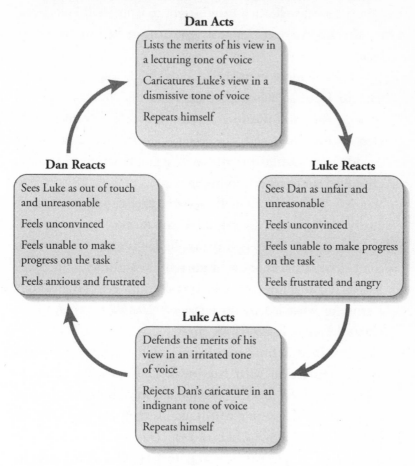

alone, and he no longer sees himself as a victim of it. As we'll see later, this shift sets the stage for their reflecting together.

- *Step Three:* No longer as emotionally triggered, Luke is able to use the Ladder of Reflection to look at Dan's assertions about his decision-making pace in a cooler light.[18] This allows him to reassess his decision-making pace in light of Dan's concerns. While he still objects to Dan's caricatures of him as "bureaucratic" and "risk averse," he recognizes that he needs the board's support. If the board thinks he's going too slowly, as Dan suggests, well, then Dan is right to worry and Luke needs to take his concerns seriously, no matter how he conveyed them.

- *Step Four:* A more even-keeled Luke sends a temperate voice mail to Dan, signaling that he hears his concerns without agreeing with his caricatures of him (Luke). The former recalls Dan to his better self; the latter suggests that Luke won't collude with Dan at his worst. The combination of the two prompts Dan to reflect on his "hysteria."

- *Step Five:* As a more thoughtful Dan reflects, he doesn't try to justify his "hysteria" by making a case for how "bureaucratic" or "risk averse" Luke is. Instead, he looks at himself, and he comes to see that his practical and sentimental interest in Luke's success is competing with a desire not to hover. This gives him a sense of what led to his behavior: *Unable to contain or to express his anxieties, he finally blew!*

- *Step Six:* In this final step in the sequence, Dan and Luke together reflect on what happened. Dan goes first. Here he doesn't apologize for his behavior and leave it at that. Instead he shares his reflections with Luke so they can explore them together. This allows Luke to help Dan see that his fear of hovering is misplaced: he wants to hear Dan's concerns; he even finds them helpful. The only thing he finds problematic is Dan's negativity, which Luke can now trace to Dan's censoring concerns until they build up to the point of hysteria. This joint reflection leads them to see the situation and each other in a new light, allowing them to address their concerns more quickly and effectively next time.

By reflecting and reframing—first alone, then together—Dan and Luke were able to shift perspective and use their conflict to strengthen their relationship. These two capabilities worked hand in hand, allowing them to use their emotions to puzzle through what happened together. As they did so, they were able to learn from what happened and to build their collective cool system by adding another map to it (see Figure 4.3). This gives them a

Figure 4.3 Creating a More Productive Pattern.

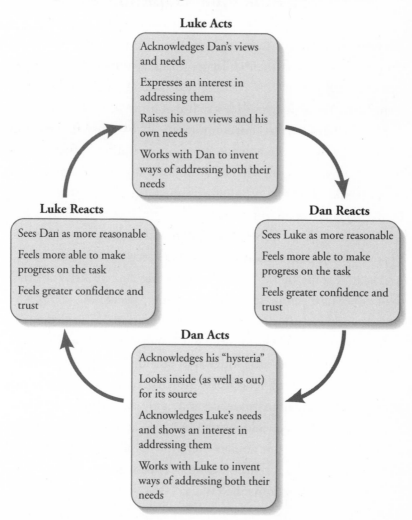

Luke Acts

Acknowledges Dan's views and needs

Expresses an interest in addressing them

Raises his own views and his own needs

Works with Dan to invent ways of addressing both their needs

Dan Reacts

Sees Luke as more reasonable

Feels more able to make progress on the task

Feels greater confidence and trust

Dan Acts

Acknowledges his "hysteria"

Looks inside (as well as out) for its source

Acknowledges Luke's needs and shows an interest in addressing them

Works with Luke to invent ways of addressing both their needs

Luke Reacts

Sees Dan as more reasonable

Feels more able to make progress on the task

Feels greater confidence and trust

roadmap they can use next time. Connected to what happened and focused on their interactions, it reframes what happened from a relational perspective so they can each see what they need to do to build a relationship strong enough to take the heat.

Reflecting and Reframing as Core Relational Capabilities

Recently, as I rode a train to New York, I sat across from three people talking about their colleagues back at the office. The most common reflection? "He (or she) just doesn't get it." They then went on to speculate why. "He's so full of himself." "He's missing a chip in his brain." "She's not committed." The woman in the group occasionally offered up an alternative interpretation, reframing the men's more disparaging views: "He's just a shy analytic type. Give him a break." The others politely listened, then went back to their own less generous interpretations.

The thing is, not all reflecting and reframing helps us cool down or strengthens our relationships. Some reflection—like the kind I overheard on the train—escalates ill feeling and weakens our ties. This is because people spend all their time speculating about why someone is the way he or she is. These speculations, informed by the individual perspective introduced in Chapter Four, locate the cause of any troubles inside individuals and outside anyone's influence.

I call this type of reflection "armchair reflection." Divorced from events, difficult to influence, and rarely shared with the person in question, it fails to yield insights anyone can use to change what they see. If anything, it renders everyone helpless, because no one dares to discuss their reflections for fear of making things worse. It's hard to imagine someone saying, "Gee, Frank, the problem is you just don't get it, because you're missing a chip in your brain." So, of course, Frank gets no chance to learn, or to say how he sees things, or to point out what's missing from the picture—not a chip, but all the things the other person is doing to reinforce the very behavior he or she doesn't like. This type of reflection only accelerates already downward-spinning spirals.

The same can be said for most efforts to reframe people in a more constructive light. The idea that Frank is a shy analytic type may be true, but it suggests the best we can do is give him a break. There is little to be done here, nothing to be learned. Yet countless tools such as Myers-Briggs take exactly this tack.[19] "The other person isn't mad (missing a chip) or bad (full of himself)," these tools suggest. "He's simply different. He's an introvert, while you're an extrovert. He's someone who judges events, while you're someone who perceives them."

So far, so good. Reframing people's differences in these more descriptive, less toxic ways makes it much more likely that people can discuss their difficulties and give each other the benefit of the doubt—at least for a few weeks. But because these instruments say nothing about how to manage differences in the heat of the moment, this generosity of spirit eventually peters out, as people struggle and fail to find a way to put their differences to work.

The point is, knowing someone is different doesn't tell you how to deal with someone who is different. Without some way of seeing how you are managing your differences, you can't do much to alter the relational patterns that are wreaking havoc. As a result, those patterns escalate, as do people's emotions, making it harder to cool down or gain the perspective needed to see or alter the patterns. In the end, everyone not only feels stuck, they *are* stuck.

KEY POINTS

Armchair reflection is so abstract, speculative, and categorical that it kills curiosity and locks interpretations into place. Similarly, instruments that reframe people's differences in a less toxic light offer no guidance on how to manage those differences in the heat of the moment.

To regain your cool and shift perspective, it helps to ground your reflections in what actually happened by using a tool such as the Ladder of Reflection (1) to explore what each of you did to contribute to a situation neither of you liked and (2) to imagine what each of you might do differently going forward.

By reflecting and reframing in this way—first alone, then together—Luke and Dan were able to cool down enough to invent a way forward and to strengthen their relationship. Over time this helped them build their cool systems and their access to them, so they could cool down even more quickly.

FIVE

Mapping Relationships

> Some key part of human activity—whether it is something
> as simple as pounding out a Morse code message or as
> complex as being married to someone—has an
> identifiable and stable pattern.
>
> —MALCOLM GLADWELL[1]

When a relationship isn't going well, most of us become so riveted on the other person—on divining his motives or avoiding his impact—that we don't look at what we're each doing to create a relationship that neither of us wants. In the end, we feel as if we have little choice: end the relationship or settle for one that doesn't work.

To improve a relationship, people need to look not only at each other but at the repetitious patterns that define the anatomy or structure of a relationship. Only then can people see what they otherwise find so hard to imagine: that they're not nearly as helpless or constrained as they think they are.

There's just one problem; it's not so easy to see these patterns. In fact, there's a good reason why we focus on others. It's much easier to notice what others are doing than to see what we're doing to evoke or reinforce their behavior. To discern patterns, you need a tool that will allow you to see things you can't easily see, much as a microscope allows you to see microbes. The framework introduced in this chapter is one such tool (see Figure 5.1 later in this chapter). By directing attention to the behavioral patterns that define relationships, this framework helps people see each other in a more relational light, so they stop waiting for others to change and start working together to strengthen their relationships.

To illustrate, I tell the story of what happened to a divisional CEO and her next-in-command, then look at the events of their relationship through the relational lens the framework provides.

The Story: Dangerous Times at SafetyNet

Three years ago, Christina Bellanti was a woman on a mission. When she first joined Secureware,[2] a software company that sells security products for computer networks, it was as CEO of the firm's largest but worst-performing division, SafetyNet. A tall, energetic woman in her early forties, Chris was the quintessential entrepreneur, utterly convinced that she could turn around the division's flagging performance and establish it as the industry leader in security products worldwide. She was right. Eighteen months later SafetyNet was one of the most profitable divisions in the firm, and Chris was setting her sights on becoming the industry leader.

She had only one problem. She needed a second-in-command who could help her grow the division more quickly than ever. Always on the lookout for emerging young talent, she thought she'd spotted the right stuff in Peter Thompson, a brilliant project manager in his early thirties from another division. Over the course of a year, Peter had been assigned to several projects in Chris's division. While working together with her, Peter had come to admire Chris's charismatic leadership and passion for SafetyNet's products, while Chris had come to respect Peter's unusually sharp intelligence and dedication. After their third project together, Chris thought Peter might just be the guy who could help her turn SafetyNet into a world-class firm.

The Beginning of a Beautiful Friendship

When Chris first broached the possibility of Peter joining her as the division's COO, Peter agreed to meet with her to explore the opportunity further. Over two dinners that went late into the night, Peter, intrigued but noncommittal, sat back and listened as Chris regaled him with stories about SafetyNet's recent success and talked about her vision for its future.

Peter was impressed. Chris had all the effusiveness, passion, and vision that his own CEO lacked, and her division was growing faster than any other in the company. Even better, this could be his chance to move into a real leadership position.

At the end of their third dinner, they relaxed back into their chairs, as the waiter handed them each a snifter of cognac. "I need a partner," Chris said, leaning forward as if to confide in Peter. "I need someone who shares my vision and has the technical savvy to help me turn it into a reality." Pausing for a moment, she then added, "I feel in my gut that that partner is you."

Peter felt flattered but cautious. He wanted to make sure that this really was the leadership opportunity he was looking for. Leaning back in his chair, he asked what kinds of opportunities the new role would offer: Would he have free rein in managing the top team? How much time and counsel would Chris give him? How would decisions get made? Would he be able to influence them?

The more they talked, the better the match looked. Chris felt confident that she could rely on Peter's calm demeanor and analytic sharps to complement her own less systematic and more intuitive approach, while Peter thought he had a lot to learn about leadership from Chris.

After an hour, Peter broke into a warm smile, and by the evening's end, they'd sealed the deal. Peter agreed to manage the top team and help drive the division's growth; Chris agreed to coach Peter on his leadership and to help him realize his ambitions within the firm.

As they left the restaurant and stepped into the night, Chris quipped, "I think this is the beginning of a beautiful friendship."

The Plot Thickens

A few months after Peter joined the division, a small incident occurred that signaled a subtle but important shift in their relationship. Earlier that day Chris and Peter had decided to call a meeting of the division's top team to discuss the sales numbers Peter had delivered to Chris that morning. Everyone filed into the conference room with coffee in hand, relaxed and joking—everyone, that is, except Peter, who knew Chris was disappointed in the numbers. Quiet and tense, Peter took his seat, looking over at Chris, who was busy rifling through a pile of spreadsheets. As Peter waited for her to start the meeting, as she usually did, Chris continued to sort through the spreadsheets, ignoring him.

After a few moments, Peter turned to Chris. "So how would you like to proceed?"

Looking up for the first time, Chris shot back, "Rather than ask me, why don't you take the lead and tell us how you'd like to proceed?"

Surprised and embarrassed, Peter took a moment to compose himself, then went ahead and proposed an agenda. An hour and a half later, the meeting ended with no one giving much notice to how it began—except for Peter and Chris, that is. They both knew something out of the ordinary had just happened, but they weren't quite sure what it was or what it meant.

Later on, Peter said of the incident, "In the overall scheme of things what Chris did wasn't a big deal. But it *was* mystifying and embarrassing to be confronted that way in front of the group." What happened next? "I let it go. But I did have this lingering doubt: it wasn't the first time I'd seen Chris overreact; it was just the first time she'd directed it at me."

Looking back, Chris said of the same incident, "It was a bad day. Just as people were taking their seats, I noticed an error in the numbers Peter had given me, and I was checking to see if it would affect the overall picture. The whole time, I could feel Peter looking at me, expecting me to start the meeting, when I've been waiting for him to step up and lead the meetings as the COO. In that moment, I found his passivity especially irritating, and I let it show. I don't like it, but there it is."

After the meeting a somewhat sheepish Chris approached David, the head of sales, to ask if she'd been too harsh on Peter. In a measured tone, David said circumspectly, "Let's put it this way: I wouldn't have felt so good if you had done that to me."

"No, I guess not," Chris said, then turned to go in search of Peter.

A few minutes later she found him standing by the coffee machine in the corporate kitchen. "Look, I'm sorry about this morning," she said. Then, in a mildly accusatory tone, she added, "I feel uncomfortable when people defer to me. I really want you to step up and take more leadership. I respect your opinion, and I want to hear it. But I feel like you're always asking questions and waiting for me to take the lead. I really want you to start taking more initiative."

Relieved by the apology, Peter decided to overlook the implied criticism. "I understand. No problem," he replied. "I'll try to weigh in more." What he didn't say was that he had an uneasy feeling. He wasn't so sure how Chris would react if he took her up on her request and exercised more leadership.

Though the next few months went by without major incident, the truce they struck wasn't wholly satisfying, either. More cautious about asking Chris for advice or testing his ideas with her, Peter wasn't learning as much. And Chris, who continued to tease opinions out of an even more hesitant Peter, got the uncomfortable feeling that, while technically sharp, Peter might turn into more of a burden than a partner who could take initiative.

The Plot Sickens

Several months later, at another team meeting, Chris and Peter grew convinced that things had taken a turn for the worse. Right before that meeting, Chris was upset to learn from her lead engineer, Donna Petersen, that their most important new product, due for release in a month, might have a serious defect. Only a week earlier Chris had met with Secureware's CEO, Katie Lang, to assure her that Netsafe was on track and the delivery date on schedule. A lot was riding on this product, Lang reminded her, from commercial success to people's reputations—"yours and mine included," she added. Supremely confident, Chris had just reassured her that there was nothing to worry about. Everything was going according to plan.

Now, as she took her seat at the conference table, it looked like everything was going to hell. Netsafe's delivery date was at risk, and the product itself might be a bust. Anxious to get to the bottom of the problem, Chris turned to Donna. "Tell me exactly what you found."

"Well, it's not exactly clear," Donna began, then went on to describe in great technical detail how she'd uncovered the problem. As Chris listened, she tapped her pencil on the table, all the while wishing that Donna would hurry up, get to the point, and tell her whether the problem could be fixed and by when.

Peter, a software engineer by training, wasn't in such a hurry. As he listened to Donna's account, he found himself thinking, *This just doesn't sound right. It just doesn't add up to a major glitch.* He wanted to know more. "Donna, I'm curious about something," he said, coming in as she was finishing up. "Under what conditions does this problem actually occur?"

"Hang on a second," Chris interrupted. "Curiosity aside, I'd like to know if we can have *any faith* in what we've been telling people about this product?!"

Not sure what to say or to whom, a startled Donna froze while others looked furtively over at Peter, then down at the table. No one, including Peter, said a word.

Frustrated by the silence, Chris came in again. "Well, Donna, you're closest to it. What do you think? Can we have *any faith* in this product?"

After a moment's pause, Donna began, "Perhaps if we target the home market—"

"But we're not!" Chris interrupted. "We're targeting the corporate market!"

Donna glanced down at her hands, as the rest of the team looked over at Peter, who was now so angry he could hardly speak. "Maybe I'm missing something," he finally said, his voice trembling. "But even if we can't fix it, doesn't it still meet current standards for the corporate market?"

Opening her mouth in exaggerated disbelief, Chris thought, *Is he serious? Settle for current standards when we've promoted Netsafe as the next big breakthrough?* Her frustration curdling into anger, she stood up, collected her papers, and turned to leave the room.

"I'm not going to tell people this product represents a breakthrough until I know that's the case! We've invested a lot of time and money in developing this software, and I want to know if it's going to deliver to our customers what we said it's going to deliver! Peter, I want you to get back to me tomorrow morning on what you plan to do about this."

As she left the room, Chris felt defeated. *God almighty! Peter just doesn't get it. You can't be an industry leader with products that meet current standards. What can he possibly be thinking? He's way too detached and passive to take this business to the next level.*

Peter said nothing as he filed out of the room with the rest of the team, but he was furious: *What an emotional tyrant! Her volatility is going to destroy the entire team's morale. These outbursts have got to stop!* Still, he was painfully aware that the division's future depended on this product. Putting his anger aside, he went to find Donna.

For the next six days and nights, the two of them worked with the engineering team until they finally located the problem and discovered a way to fix it. When Peter told Chris the good news, she offered only a cursory thanks, which he accepted with a nod.

The following day, an exhausted Peter met David, the head of sales, for lunch. "No offense, pal," David said, pulling out a chair for Peter as he arrived, "but you look horrible."

"I've got no idea what she thinks she's doing," Peter said as he sat down. "But whatever it is, it isn't working. She's really pissing me off!"

David raised his eyebrows, but said nothing in the hope that Peter might say more.

"I can't just sit back, David, and let her moods dictate. She's browbeating the whole team! I've got to do something." Then shaking his head, he added, "*We've* got to do something."

"I couldn't agree more," David said. "Her outbursts are impossible. She's totally unprofessional. But what are we supposed to do? The woman's a *nut*." For the next hour, they commiserated, telling each other stories about how difficult Chris was.

By the end of lunch, they knew something had to be done, but they didn't know what it was, and so the next few months passed as the previous few had. Every time Chris did something that struck Peter and David as more emotional than the situation warranted, they'd get together and vent their frustration.

Meanwhile, back at the office, Chris also knew something had to be done. Increasingly isolated, she felt more and more burdened by responsibilities she now had to shoulder alone. *I guess if you want a friend, you should get a dog*, she told herself. *I'd hoped Peter would help me lead the division, not sit around waiting for me to tell him what to do. He's behaving like such a kid; I can't rely on him to do anything.* The only way to keep her enthusiasm above the watermark, she concluded, was to look outside the division for collaborators she could count on.

Nearing the End

Six months later a series of incidents brought things to a head. The division, under CEO Katie Lang's increasing scrutiny, had recently committed to a strategy that required unprecedented discipline and focus, something Chris was finding more difficult by the day. At almost every meeting of the leadership team, Chris would talk about the next new project they should pursue, while Peter would think, *Is she serious?! We can't take this on! It's clearly off strategy, and it makes absolutely no economic sense.*

Convinced that expressing any doubts would only set Chris off, Peter kept them to himself. Instead, each time Chris raised an idea, he'd work hard to gently steer her away from it. "I'm confused," he would say. "Maybe I'm missing something, but this opportunity doesn't look like it's on strategy, at least not to me." Or: "Yes, we could do that, but I don't think we have anybody available right now to pursue it." Or when really pressed: "I'm not sure this is something we can do right now, given our capacity constraints. But let me look into it, and perhaps we can talk later on." Only they never did.

Chris got the message loud and clear despite Peter's efforts. *He thinks this is a bad idea but isn't telling me. What a wimp!* Too discouraged for words, Chris's only response was a pouting silence, which Peter took as further evidence of her emotional instability. *Is she actually sulking?* he'd ask himself as he'd watch discouragement cross Chris's face. *All I did was suggest that we might not be able to do every project that pops into her head. What a nut!*

Now after almost every meeting Peter would seek David out, and in an effort to shore up his flagging spirits, he'd vent into his ear. "The team's getting spread too thin," he'd say. "We're not going to be able to deliver against our objectives if this keeps up."

David, who could always be counted on to commiserate, finally told Peter. "Look, Chris isn't going to be happy unless she's doing something new that takes her outside the division. If you raise this with her, she'll just get angry. There's nothing you can do. Leave it alone, or look for something else. That's what I'm doing."

Two months later, after David announced his departure, Peter had had enough. He knew a tough conversation was long overdue, but he'd always had some reason to put off what now seemed inevitable. No longer seeing any other choice, he walked toward Chris's office.

"What's up?" Chris asked, signaling with her hand for him to take a seat, as she hung up her phone. Then, turning her back to Peter to check her email, she asked, "How goes it?"

Peter cleared his throat. "Not so good. For the past few weeks, I've been giving my job here a lot of thought, and I think it may be time for me to move on. I don't think I've been that effective leading the team, and I'm not sure there's much more for me to learn or do here."

Chris sighed audibly. "I can't say I'm terribly surprised." Then turning to face Peter, she asked, "Have you made up your mind?"

"Pretty much," Peter hedged. "I'm certainly leaning in that direction. But maybe we should talk about it before deciding what makes sense."

"If you feel it would help," Chris offered, with little confidence it would. "I've got to run now. But why don't we put some time aside early next week to talk about it."

"I'm looking for a 'yes man', who can say 'no' without sounding negative."

The Anatomy of a Relationship

After talking about it, Chris and Peter decided that they wanted to do more than just air their grievances. They wanted to look at how they'd gotten into trouble to see whether they could get out. For years, Lang and others at the top of Secureware had invested in their relationships, and they'd encouraged their division heads to do the same. At Lang's suggestion, they asked for my help, and the next week, the three of us sat down to take a look at what had happened. As I listened to each of their accounts, I used the Anatomy Framework to make sense of what I heard (see Figure 5.1 and the sidebar "About the Anatomy Framework").[3] That framework helped us uncover and map the four elements that combined to give their relationship its distinctive character. The following pages illustrate what we learned, starting with their interlocking actions and reactions.

Figure 5.1   The Anatomy Framework.

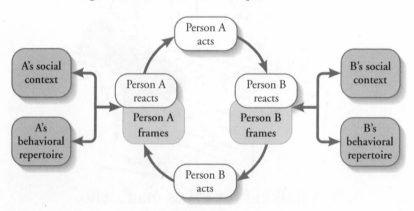

About the Anatomy Framework

All relationships have an informal structure that emerges over time out of repetitious patterns. Four interlocking elements make up that structure.

1. *Actions and Reactions.* Patterns form out of people's intersecting actions and reactions. Actions refer to what someone actually says and does, while reactions refer to what someone thinks and feels in response to what the other person says and does. Each person's actions evoke reactions in the other, leading that person to act one way and not another (see the white boxes in the diagram and the way they reinforce each other).

2. *Frames.* Frames lead patterns to repeat until they form a more enduring informal structure. Frames refer to our spontaneous interpretations of ourselves in relation to others and the goals we set as a result. Frames make some actions seem obvious, others impractical (see the gray boxes behind "Person A Reacts" and "Person B Reacts").

3. *Social Contexts.* Social contexts form the contextual backdrop against which some triggering event occurs, prompting the need to respond. They include things such as our formal roles, resource constraints, time pressures, and historical events. Our contexts filter what we see, and along with our repertoires, shape how we frame each other (see the gray boxes with the two-way arrows

running into "A Frames Situation" and "B Frames Situation").

4. *Behavioral Repertoires.* Behavioral repertoires define the range of responses people have at their disposal for framing and acting in different social contexts, once triggered by some event (again, see the gray boxes with the two-way arrows running into "A Frames Situation" and "B Frames Situation"). Our repertoires include both a stock of *experiential knowledge* and a set of *interpretive strategies* for making sense of situations, events, and people. As the arrows suggest, people's behavioral repertoires both shape and are shaped by their *social contexts.* Together the two govern the way people frame situations, leading them to react and act some ways and not others.

These four elements combine to give a relationship its distinctive character, one we intuitively recognize but have difficulty seeing or changing. While our frames and actions are the engine that propels a relationship forward, our social contexts and our behavioral repertoires provide the fuel for that engine and set the direction of a relationship.

Interlocking Actions and Reactions

If you look closely enough at Peter and Chris's interactions, you can see that those interactions formed a pattern right from the start. When they first met over dinner, Chris's talk and body language filled the space around her. She leaned forward; she regaled Peter with one story after another about SafetyNet's success; she made sweeping claims about the division's future; she waxed enthusiastic about what a powerful partnership they'd make; and she asked Peter very little about what he wanted or what he thought.

Peter's talk and body language stood in stark contrast. He reserved judgment; he leaned back; he asked Chris about the COO role without ever expressing his own preferences; he listened to her answers in silence; he analyzed what she said quietly; and the few times he responded, he chose his words with great care. If Chris's actions filled up the space around her, Peter's created a vacuum.

This basic pattern of interaction, established in their first dinner and reestablished in the room with me, escalated over the next year and a half. In each of the incidents that followed, their actions and reactions reinforced each other: Chris's emotional declarations filling the space, with Peter's analytic quiet making it easier for Chris to do so. At first, this was no big deal. If anything, they considered their differences an asset. Only under pressure—when their differences clashed and no longer seemed so benign—did doubt emerge and, later on, despair set in.

Looking at What Happened

In the first incident, disappointing sales numbers, coupled with the pressures of time, combine to put Peter's "calm demeanor" and Chris's "passion" on a collision course that culminates in Chris's snapping and Peter's surprise and embarrassment. For the first time, Chris and Peter get the uneasy feeling that the very characteristics they'd found so attractive in the other might actually become a problem.

The second incident moves the relationship into a more ominous zone. Anxious to fix a defect jeopardizing an important new product, Chris is shocked by Peter's "curiosity" and lack of urgency. Worried that neither he nor Donna will come up with an answer quickly enough, Chris engineers an interpersonal takeover, determining who talks about what when. In response, Peter gets so furious he fears losing his temper. Cautiously entering the conversation, he takes pains to qualify his challenge ("Maybe I'm missing something") and to couch his views as a question ("Doesn't it still meet current standards for the corporate market?"). But all this does is suggest to Chris that she's the only one truly concerned about the defect, leading her to get angry and leave. Afterward, the two search out solace elsewhere, Chris going outside the division and Peter turning to David. This last move, designed to relieve their upset, only alienates them further.

By the time the final series of incidents occurs, they're so far apart that they resort to game playing: Peter repeatedly challenges Chris's initiatives while acting as if he's not, and Chris speaks volumes through her uncharacteristic silences. In the end, when Peter finally goes to Chris, they can only halfheartedly agree to seek advice on whether to call it quits.

Analyzing What Happened

After Peter and Chris recounted their versions of the events, it was clear that they each saw only half the picture—the very half the other didn't see: Peter was acutely aware of what Chris was doing and how it made him feel or react, just as Chris was acutely aware of what Peter was doing and how that made her feel or react. But neither Peter nor Chris was aware of what the other was feeling or of what they themselves were doing to evoke it. It's this *asymmetrical awareness* that leads interactions to take on a life of their own, independent of the people who create them.[4] People quite literally lose sight of their own role and see no way to affect what they do see.

To help them see what they couldn't easily see on their own, we used their accounts to map how their actions were triggering

Figure 5.2 Interlocking Actions and Reactions.

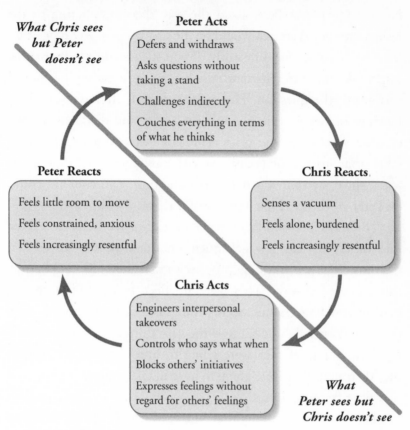

What Chris sees but Peter doesn't see

Peter Acts

Defers and withdraws

Asks questions without taking a stand

Challenges indirectly

Couches everything in terms of what he thinks

Peter Reacts

Feels little room to move

Feels constrained, anxious

Feels increasingly resentful

Chris Reacts

Senses a vacuum

Feels alone, burdened

Feels increasingly resentful

Chris Acts

Engineers interpersonal takeovers

Controls who says what when

Blocks others' initiatives

Expresses feelings without regard for others' feelings

What Peter sees but Chris doesn't see

reactions in each other that reinforced the very behavior they didn't like. As the map shown in Figure 5.2 made evident, the two of them together were unwittingly conspiring to create and maintain a pattern neither wanted nor intended.

What they couldn't yet see or understand is why *this* pattern took shape and not another. To answer that question, we had to peel the onion back further, looking at how they framed each other and the situation such that some actions seemed obvious, while others never entered their minds.

Interlocking Frames

Neither Chris nor Peter liked the way they were acting or the results they got. Yet each would be the first to resist any suggestion that she or he behave differently. If you suggested to Peter that he might take more initiative or raise his concerns earlier, he'd say it was out of the question. He *couldn't* do that. It was impossible. Chris would erupt, things would get worse, and the team and the division would pay the price. Similarly, were you to suggest to Chris that instead of taking over, she ask more of Peter or the team, she'd say *that* was out of the question. You couldn't count on Peter when the chips were down. He was a wimp, a kid.

The way Chris and Peter made sense of each other—or *framed* each other, as I call it—held such emotional power and created such insidious self-fulfilling prophecies that they just couldn't see things any other way.[5] They were, in effect, being held captive by their interlocking frames. Seeing things one way and not another, they could only do one thing—the very thing that reinforced the other's framing. If they were going to break free of the pattern they'd created, they were going to have to take a closer look at how they were framing things.

This, however, is anything but easy. We're all so skilled at framing that we don't go through some methodical step-by-step analytic process. Rather, we size things up in a matter of milliseconds without giving it a moment's thought. So quick is this process that we don't experience it as first thought, then feeling. Instead, everything happens all at once. What we see, feel, and think all flows together to create a unified experience of a particular moment. If we could slow this process down, though, and look at it as it unfolds, we'd see that we're always selecting some things for attention while ignoring others, and we're always organizing these things into some story line that tells us what's going on and what we should do about it.

To uncover how Chris and Peter were framing things, I used their in-the-moment reactions to look at how they were framing: (1) the different situations they faced; (2) themselves in relation to others in those situations; and (3) the goals or tasks they felt compelled to pursue as a result. By taking each in turn, we were able to see how their frames intersected, turning an early pattern of interaction into a more enduring structure.[6]

Framing the Situation

As Chris saw it, when push came to shove she couldn't rely on Peter or on the team. *Look at the way they handled the product defect*, she'd say. *They acted as if nothing was wrong. They just don't get it!* Every one of Chris's accounts focused on the ways in which people had let her down when she needed them most: the product was a mess, the division was in trouble, her reputation was at stake, and *no one but her cared!* This way of framing the situation left Chris in a tough spot: with the division at risk and her team unreliable, taking over wasn't only reasonable, it was a practical necessity.

Though Peter made different things out of the "same" situation, his framing was equally compelling, at least to him. What stood out most for Peter was the situation's volatility and the potential for his team or him to get hurt. When Chris took over the discussion of the product defect, Peter fastened his attention on Chris's emotionally wrought interruptions and noticed how they were immediately followed by the team's silences and averted glances. Assuming the former caused the latter, it never occurred to Peter that Chris might also be feeling vulnerable, or that the team's silences might also be contributing to Chris's upset. Seeing the situation as volatile, even dangerous, Peter was also in a tough spot: the only thing he could do—at least in his mind—was avoid an explosion.

Framing Their Roles in Relation to Each Other

Though we each think of ourselves as having a unified "self," we actually possess a large stock of what psychologists call "self-concepts."[7] While some of these are more stable and central to our identity than others, all of them are exquisitely sensitive to circumstance.[8] Take the young up-and-comer who casts himself in a slightly deferential role with a boss he admires, and you'll soon see this same young man puffing out his chest with his own admiring subordinate. In each case, he assumes for himself—and assigns to others—a role to play, always doing one in relation to the other, given the situation he sees.

Peter and Chris are no different. *Each of them assumed a role relative to the one they assigned to the other.* In the same moment that Peter cast Chris in the role of an emotional tyrant—with the power to determine what happened in a volatile situation—he took on the role of a threatened subject, whose fate lay in her hands. Someone else might have created an altogether different role relationship, one that had nothing to do with either volatility or power. As it was, the role Peter assumed and assigned to Chris gave him little choice but to retreat, which encouraged Chris to see herself as the only one who could make things turn out right.

And that's exactly how she saw it. Preoccupied with others' unreliability in a threatening situation, Chris took on the role of the only adult among a bunch of recalcitrant kids. This way of seeing herself in relation to Peter and the team left her little choice but to fill the many voids she saw. Yet this only heightened her sense of burden—first fueling, then justifying her outbursts, which only encouraged Peter to cast her in the role of an emotional tyrant. And so on it went.

Framing Goals[9]

Once we frame a situation and our role relative to others, some goals spring to mind, while others would never occur to us.[10] In most complex social situations, it's not uncommon for several goals to come to mind all at once, some of them clashing. Hence the adage, he wants to have his cake and eat it too. When conflicting goals spring to mind, we usually feel caught, at which point the best we can do is find or craft a strategy that satisfies each goal well enough to get by.

Such was the case with Peter and Chris. We might reasonably conclude from what Peter felt, thought, and did that his primary goal was to protect himself from intense conflict and emotion. This goal, which followed from his framing of the situation and his role relative to others, inclined Peter to keep his head down and to lie low. But if you look closely enough, you'll see that Peter also had another goal: protecting his team. He saw how quiet the team got, how they looked to him when Chris got upset. This secondary goal, unlike the first, inclined Peter to jump in, so he could help the team out. Thus faced with two conflicting goals—to protect himself *and* to protect his team—Peter could only do those things that would help him do a little of both.

That's why, instead of withdrawing or making suggestions directly, Peter asked questions to steer Chris in the "right" direction ("Might it make sense if we did this?"). And instead of staying completely silent or directly challenging Chris, he qualified anything she could possibly construe as a disagreement ("I may be missing something but . . ."). And instead of exploding or stifling his feelings, Peter couched them in intellectual or practical terms and cast them as a question ("But even if we can't fix it, doesn't it still meet current standards for the corporate market?"). Though designed to protect himself and his team—albeit unconsciously—each action had the unintended effect of confirming Chris's view of Peter as a wimp, which only prompted Chris to act more, not less, volatile.

We might surmise from what Chris thought, felt, and did that her primary goal was to reduce her reliance on others by taking control. This goal, which followed from her framing of the situation and her role relative to others, inclined Chris to be hypervigilant about others' reliability and to take over whenever she got the slightest hint of it. But just as Peter had a secondary goal, so did Chris: she wanted to avoid alienating anyone so they didn't become even more unreliable than they already were.

That's why, instead of asking the group for help or exploring their apparent lack of concern, she engineered interpersonal takeovers, telling this person to be quiet, that person to talk ("Hang on a second," she'd say, interrupting. "I'd like to hear from . . . "). And instead of pointing out their lack of initiative or asking them to take more, she imposed her own view ("But that's not who we're targeting!"). And instead of expressing her upset directly or helping others understand why she was upset, she went outside the division for support and expressed her feelings only indirectly through her tone of voice ("I'm not going to tell people that this product represents a breakthrough until I know that's the case!"). Although Chris relied on these actions to take situations where she wanted them to go, they also took her in a direction she regretted: the more control she took, the more alienated others felt, making them act less, not more, reliably.

Implications

People aren't unidimensional, even if they sometimes seem so in our minds. Everyone has better or worse sides; everyone does their best to satisfy multiple goals—many of which conflict, most of which lie outside their awareness, and all of which follow from their framing of a situation.

The way Chris and Peter framed things made it harder for them to be at their best or to bring out the best in the other. Worse, because they were equally convinced that what they saw was the way it was, they didn't realize that two other factors were also at play, shaping what they saw and how they saw it. These factors—their *social contexts* and their *behavioral repertoires*—make matters of interpretation look like matters of fact, locking frames into place. Let's take a look at each one of these factors and at how, left unnoticed, they conspire to seal the fate of any relationship.

Social Contexts

All events take place within a larger social context—those things outside ourselves we must take into account, even if only peripherally, when interacting with others: limited resources, formal roles, organizational history, physical arrangements, formal structures, cultural norms, corporate politics. It's against this backdrop that events occur, prompting us to frame what's happening so we can act. In Chris and Peter's case, the two of them operated in a social context with both distinct and overlapping aspects. As Table 5.1 illustrates, those aspects that were distinct (shaded in gray) influenced how they saw those aspects that overlapped.

Consider the defect incident. Both Chris and Peter had to move quickly to solve a complex technical problem before it cost them the division's future and, by extension, their own. Both of them had a lot at stake. But what they had at stake differed, as did what they saw.

As divisional CEO, Chris was formally and ultimately accountable for the division's performance, which Secureware's CEO, Katie Lang, had just reminded her of a week earlier when she warned Chris that the future of the firm, not to mention their reputations,

Table 5.1 Peter and Chris's Social Contexts.

	Peter's Context	Chris's Context
Current Role	SafetyNet's COO	SafetyNet's CEO
Accountabilities	Accountable to Chris for managing the team and getting products to market on time	Accountable to Lang, Secureware's CEO, for her division's overall performance
Historical Role	Engineer	Manager
Closest Contacts	SafetyNet's top team, David, other subordinates, Chris	Secureware's CEO, customers, division heads, subordinates, Peter
What's at Stake	Division's performance, his job, the team's morale and performance	Division's performance, her job, SafetyNet's and her reputation
Politics	Highly charged: A lot of dissatisfaction within the division	Highly charged: A lot of competition among divisions
Nature of Problems	Ambiguous, technically complex	
Level of Uncertainty	High: Causes and consequences of the technical problems are unknown	
Interpersonal Context	Significant stylistic differences, distant and emotionally charged	
Time	A lot of time pressure, product's due date in jeopardy	

was riding on this product. During that meeting, Chris had reassured Lang that everything was fine. But now it looked as if it were anything but. Worse, by the time the second incident occurred, Chris's relationship with Peter had deteriorated so much that when she looked around the table that day, she saw no one with whom to confide her worries. All she saw was a COO whose quiet curiosity stood in stark contrast to her own anxieties. For fifteen minutes, she listened to Donna's detailed technical account of the defect, though nothing in her current or prior roles helped her understand the implications. Yet that's exactly what this situation was requiring her to do.

Peter, who was operating in a slightly different context, couldn't help but see the "same" meeting differently. As COO, he'd had very little contact with Lang, and none at all the previous week. In his role, Peter was accountable for managing the top team and for helping them get their products to market on time. He had to exercise this accountability in the context of a relationship with a boss whose actions were affecting the team's morale, a team that was looking to him. He noticed how tense people got every time Chris interceded; he saw the anxiety on their faces. And when he discussed what he saw with David, David only confirmed his views. What's more, when Donna launched into her technical account of the defect, unlike Chris, Peter was able to listen not only as a manager but also as a software engineer. He had no problem grasping the details in her account or in spotting gaps. But absolutely nothing in his past or current roles had prepared him to exercise leadership in the face of such emotional and political complexity. Yet that is exactly what this situation was calling upon him to do.

Once Peter and Chris saw Table 5.1, they were able to see for the first time that each of them was struggling with somewhat different demands and responding to somewhat different constraints. While that helped them empathize more, they would need more than empathy to break free of their interlocking frames. They'd need to understand what predisposed them to see things the way they did within those contexts.

Behavioral Repertoires

When it comes to framing, no one starts from scratch. Like the rest of us, Peter and Chris had built out of experience a large store of *experiential knowledge* with which to make sense of what was happening and a set of *interpretive strategies* with which to apply and revise that knowledge. Together the two make up their *behavioral repertoires,* the range of interpretations and actions they have at their disposal in any social situation.

Like all behavioral repertoires, theirs were organized around a limited number of *key themes*—conflict, authority, success, loss, competence—each of them forged out of emotionally salient and often unsettling events. Now every time Peter and Chris encounter each other, they have to navigate their repertoires, looking for the right explanation here or the appropriate action there. Trouble is, since these repertoires operate largely outside their awareness, Peter and Chris are unable to see, revise, or expand them fast enough to respond effectively to each other or to the circumstances around them.

To help them navigate their repertoires more intelligently and to expand them more quickly, we used "A Guide to Behavioral Repertoires" (see Appendix A). With this guide, we were able to identify the interlocking themes and experiential knowledge they each brought to their relationship.

In Peter's case, we discovered that his relationship with Chris touched on two themes: conflict and emotion. Around these themes, Peter had developed a large stock of experiential knowledge—including theories, stories, values, and practical strategies. This knowledge allowed him to handle even the most threatening situations without giving them much thought. With the use of his theories, he recognized and categorized Chris's behavior as "volatile" and explained it in terms of her "nutty" personality. With the use of his stories, he fashioned a role for himself and gave one to others, all the while imagining what a more or less happy ending might look like. With the use of his value system, he took pride in his emotional restraint and condemned those, like Chris, who got upset. And with the use of his practical strategies, he found a number of ways to avoid conflict and dampen emotion.

What Peter's repertoire lacked, however, was a way of understanding conflict and emotion that underscored the upside of each. Although quick to concede that conflicts can generate learning, Peter had no way of explaining it and no strategies for making it happen. As a result, he couldn't see or handle conflicts any differently *even if he'd wanted to.* He also lacked a value system nuanced enough to distinguish between "good" and "bad" ways of approaching conflict and emotion—ways that, by his own standards, would cause "better" or "worse" things to occur. Similarly, his practical knowledge was full of action strategies for avoiding negative emotion, but he had no strategies for doing these things without making matters worse, and none that told him how to harness conflict or regulate emotion so it stayed in a productive range. When it came to making something good out of an emotionally laden conflict, he was quite literally at a loss.

Just as Peter came to see the themes at play in his responses to Chris, so Chris came to see what was at stake with Peter. Over the course of our work together, Chris identified two themes— reliability and control—around which she'd developed at least as much knowledge as Peter had around emotion and conflict. Around these two themes, Chris had a wide range of theories, stories, values, and strategies to draw on. But as comprehensive as this experiential knowledge was, much of it was geared toward a single end: avoiding dependence and ensuring control. As a result, whenever Chris thought things were spiraling out of control or people were letting her down, her first and last instinct was to take over. As you might expect, this limited her repertoire and prevented her from responding flexibly enough to handle Peter (or others) effectively. Only when she saw these limits and their associated costs did she reexamine what she "knew" about control and reliability—first with Peter, then with others.

A New Story to Tell

When Peter and Chris first recounted what had happened, they each focused on one side of the story—their own. Only by bringing their two perspectives together could they see how their relationship worked, and only by seeing how their relationship worked could they understand how they had each created and sustained it.

Once they took this step, they decided to conduct a series of practical experiments to see if they could improve their relationship. In a surprising but necessary twist, Peter went first, taking the initiative to fill the vacuum he'd created in the past. This in itself was a useful disruption: it went against the grain of their historical pattern in which Chris constantly initiated and Peter either followed or subverted her lead. For the move to succeed, however, Chris had to respond in kind: instead of undermining or discounting Peter's efforts for fear of being let down, she had to learn to put her concerns to work by helping Peter to help her in those moments.

A year later, the two of them had a very different story to tell. Instead of feeling trapped by their relationship, they had come to see it as a context for growth—one in which they could experiment more freely and explore the results of those experiments more openly. Not only did this accelerate their growth as leaders, it improved the morale and functioning of the top team so much that they were able to pick up the pace of growth in their division.

KEY POINTS

Underlying all relationships is an informal structure that emerges over time out of repetitious patterns of interaction. This structure includes four interlocking elements: actions, frames, contexts, and repertoires. If our interlocking frames and actions are the engine that drives the way people interact, their social contexts and behavioral repertoires, provide the fuel that keeps that engine running.

By using the Anatomy Framework to map the structure of their relationship, Chris and Peter could stand outside of it and see what they couldn't see from the inside: their roles in creating a relationship they didn't like or intend to create. This allowed them to take a relational perspective to their differences, which in turn allowed them to build a relationship strong enough to withstand the fast pace and constant uncertainties of an entrepreneurial venture.

Of course, no leader can invest equally in all relationships. Leaders must make choices. The next chapter offers two tools to help you make those choices more wisely.

SIX

Focusing Investments, Managing Costs

That's pretty much how I feel about relationships. They're
totally irrational, crazy, and absurd. But I guess we keep
going through it because most of us need the eggs.

—WOODY ALLEN, *ANNIE HALL*

At the end of *Annie Hall,* the classic 1977 film about relationships, Woody Allen tells an old joke about a guy who goes
to a psychiatrist and says, "Doc, my brother's crazy. He thinks
he's a chicken." Horrified, the doctor asks why he hasn't already
committed him. "I would," the guy answers, "but I need the eggs."

The point is, as difficult as relationships can be, we need what
they give us, even if it's all in our heads. And there's no getting
around it. While relationships give us many things, from a sense of
connection to much-needed political support, they also take effort.
Sometimes, lots of effort.

But not all relationships require the same amount of effort, or
the same kind. Those relationships operating along organizational
fault lines—interfaces where coordination is as essential as it
is difficult—require the most continuous investment. Because
leaders at these interfaces will have different beliefs, competing

interests, and clashing goals, their relationships must be strong enough to handle even the hottest conflicts. Other relationships require less effort, and more often than not, their costs can be managed through other means.

This chapter offers two tools you can use to figure out when and how to invest in which relationships: "The Investment Matrix" and "The Sequencing Matrix." Together these two tools will help you think more strategically and practically about all your relationships.

The Investment Matrix

Too many relationships at the top of organizations leave leaders feeling anxious, frustrated, and depleted, rather than energized, confident, and supported. The result? What *BusinessWeek* journalist Michelle Conlin calls "a new frontier in productivity: emotional inefficiency, which includes all that bickering, backstabbing, and ridiculous playing for approval that are a mark of the modern workplace."[1] Much of that bickering and backstabbing is a direct result of failed relationships. All told, those failures create huge organizational costs: people withhold or distort information; the right information doesn't get to the right people on time; constant quibbling and quarreling slows everything down; products fail to make it to market on time; key decisions either don't get made or get made poorly.

Just as businesses require focused investment, so do relationships. Yet somehow, when it comes to relationships, many of us never quite seem to get around to it. Under the pressures of time and the relentless demands of work, our relationships take on a transactional cast with little to no attention given to the people in front of us, or to how we're interacting with them—at least not until the relationship runs into trouble. Only then do we feel compelled to invest large swaths of time finding some way either to fix the relationship or to dissolve it.

Still, no leader can invest in all relationships all the time. We all have to make choices, sometimes hard choices. In making those choices, it helps to think of relationships along two dimensions: how important the relationship is, and the degree of interdependence between the people. When both are high, leaders should treat the relationship like a strategic asset and invest accordingly.

The Investment Matrix builds on these distinctions (see Figure 6.1). The basic idea is to invest only in those relationships that are highly important *and* highly interdependent.

Figure 6.1   The Investment Matrix.

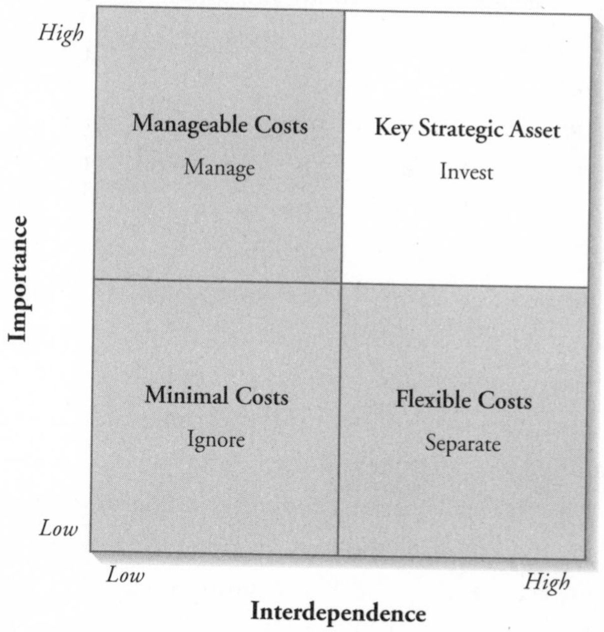

Importance

While all relationships are important at some level—to our well-being, our self-esteem, our sense of connection—not all relationships will impact our growth and performance in the same way or to the same degree. You can assess the importance of a relationship in this special sense along three dimensions[2]—*strategic*, *symbolic*, and *developmental:*

- *Strategic:* To what extent are the people in the relationship especially qualified to fulfill a strategically critical role? The more vital people's talents, knowledge, or experience are to a role critical to the success of the firm, the harder it is to replace them or to redefine the role. The head of R&D, who knows the business and technology better than anyone else, and the head of sales, who personally holds all the important customer relationships, are both important to the success of a firm. Replacing them, if they don't get along, is neither easy nor wise.

- *Symbolic:* To what extent do organizational members look to the people in the relationship, or to the relationship itself, for meaning, guidance, or a sense of purpose? The more symbolically important a relationship is, the faster events related to that relationship will travel throughout the organization, shaping the way people interpret things, including the future, the firm's strategy, and leadership's commitment to it. At one firm, people further down in the organization looked to the head of product design and the head of sales to assess whether the firm was really serious about becoming more commercial, as their new strategy espoused. Every time these two executives fought, the word spread like wildfire, even when their fights occurred behind closed doors.

- *Developmental:* To what extent is the relationship helping or hurting the success or potential of the leaders in the relationship? When a relationship brings out the worst in people, as was the case with John Sculley and Steve Jobs (see Chapters One and Two), it amplifies and magnifies each leader's liabilities, makes it hard for either to grow or learn, and puts their leadership at risk as a result. But if that relationship can be turned into a context for each leader's growth, as Part Three illustrates, then the relationship can accelerate the development of both leaders, each leader needing to realize his or her potential for the relationship and their leadership to succeed.

Interdependence

The more interdependent people are, the stronger their relationships need to be. This is because people must rely on their relationships, not just formal mechanisms, to get things done and to resolve conflicts along the way.[3]

To assess the degree of interdependence, and thus the demands a relationship will have to meet, you need to consider three factors: *information, coordination,* and *decision making.* Each one poses a question and imposes a demand:

- *Information:* To what extent do people's formal roles require them to share information quickly and fully to accomplish key tasks? In thinking through the formal design of an organization, experts have long considered information the key design variable. All things being equal, the more people need to exchange information, the more interdependent their formal roles need to be, so they can get the right information at the right time to get the right things done in a timely fashion.[4] My research suggests that what highly interdependent formal roles

123

offer in terms of information flow, informal relationships can quickly take away, if neglected. If informal relationships don't facilitate the flow of reliable information, including sensitive information or what organizational scholar Chris Argyris calls "undiscussables,"[5] they will undermine the intent of formal roles.

- *Coordination:* To what extent do people in a relationship need to coordinate key activities to get things done? The more people need to coordinate, the more a relationship must encourage cooperation by making it easier to navigate situations in which the need to cooperate to achieve joint goals collides with the need to compete for limited resources. Almost all leaders operate in mixed-motive relationships, which make coordination both desirable and difficult. If a relationship can't handle the ambivalence and conflicts intrinsic to these relationships, it will make it hard to coordinate anything.

- *Decision Making:* To what extent do people in a relationship need to be involved in the same decisions? The more people need to be involved, the more their relationship must facilitate the negotiation of differences, even fundamental ones. If both people in a relationship have significant decision rights, then they need to build a relationship that will make it easier, not harder, to understand, appreciate, and creatively negotiate their different interests and needs on an ongoing basis.

Segment-Specific Strategies

The Investment Matrix identifies four different strategies for handling relationships, depending on their degree of importance and interdependence: *ignore, separate, manage,* or *invest.* The following list explains what each strategy entails and the circumstances under which using it makes the most sense:

- *Ignore.* If two or more people don't depend much on each other and their relationships aren't strategically important, you can ignore these relationships because any costs they incur will be minimal. But beware of fooling yourself into thinking a relationship isn't important when it truly is. If you downplay or ignore the ill effects of any relationship critical to a firm's success, it will take a toll sooner or later on the firm's effectiveness.

- *Separate.* If people's roles are highly interdependent but the people in them aren't vital to the role (that is, they're not uniquely qualified to fulfill it), structural separation may be the best way to handle relationship problems that resist resolution. This could mean transferring or promoting one of the people into a new role, or creating a new structure that reduces interdependence, or even firing one or the other person. As long as you view this strategy as one of several to be used only under these circumstances, it can be used well and fairly. But this strategy rarely works if you overuse it, imposing structural separations willy-nilly for fear of dealing directly with the informal relationship. That only leads to wacky structural arrangements or personnel decisions that harm a firm's performance.

- *Manage.* If people are vital to their roles but the roles themselves aren't that interdependent, any relationship costs should be manageable through diplomacy, insulating people, or protecting one or the other person in the relationship. When applied well and appropriately, this approach can reduce the impact of the occasional relationship snafu. But if you use this strategy to manage the ill effects of a highly interdependent relationship, you'll soon run into trouble, because those effects will be so frequent and so widespread that it will become more costly to manage them than to change them.

125

- *Invest.* This approach makes sense when people are vital to their roles *and* their success cannot be achieved without depending on one another. When importance and interdependence are high, it's much harder to ignore a relationship, to manage its ill effects, or to separate people structurally. Under these conditions, it's best to invest the time, energy, and money in strengthening or changing these relationships, so they can meet the challenges they'll face.

The Sequencing Matrix

Once you've identified those relationships most in need of investment, you can use the Sequencing Matrix to make different types of investments over time (see Figure 6.2).

Figure 6.2   The Sequencing Matrix.

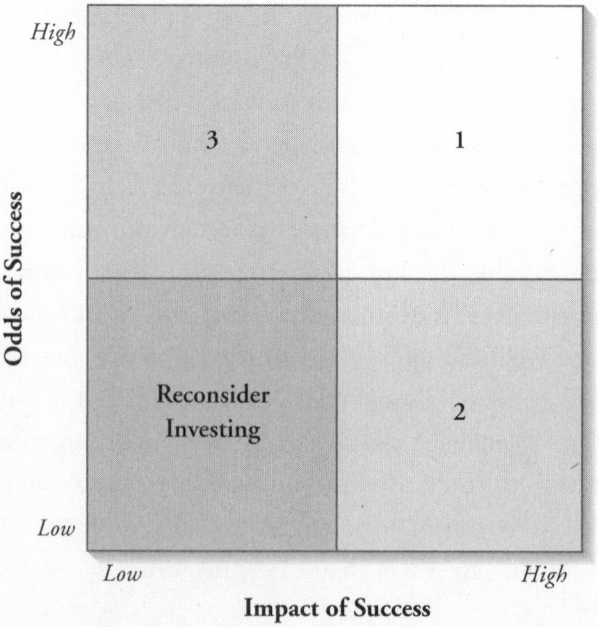

As the chapters in Part Three will illustrate, it's best to start with high-impact relationships that stand the best chance of succeeding. In assessing impact, you can assess a relationship along two dimensions:

- *Impact on People's Leadership:* To what extent will changes in the relationship free up leaders to do their jobs more easily and effectively? The more the relationship prevents people from doing key jobs well, the sooner changes should be made. To what extent will the people in the relationship be more effective and fulfilled as leaders? The more people's relationships are making them look ineffective as leaders or undercutting their sense of well-being, the sooner changes should be made.

- *Impact on the Business:* To what extent will changes in the relationship make it easier for people to make decisions and take actions together more quickly and wisely? The more people's differences are harming critical decisions or the pace with which they get taken, the sooner changes should be made.

In terms of the odds of success, you can assess a relationship along three dimensions:

- *Motivation:* To what extent do the people in the relationship see important benefits for themselves and the firm? The more benefits they see, the more willing they'll be to change.

- *Readiness:* To what extent are the people in the relationship willing and able to invest their time and energy *relative to other things*? The less hampered they are by business crises, whether self-imposed or created by circumstance, the more able and willing people will be to invest their time and energy.

- *Difficulty:* To what extent do the people in the relationship think it's possible that they played some role in creating circumstances they don't like? The more aware people are of themselves and their impact, the more willing and able they will be to change.

B. Smaller

"O.K., if you can't see your way to giving me a pay raise, how about giving Parkerson a pay cut?"

Keep in mind that odds can and should be changed. So while you're focusing on relationships in the first cell (see Figure 6.2), you might turn your attention to increasing the odds of success for those in the second cell—say, by pointing out the changes people in the first cell are making. Soon afterward, you might launch some type of programmatic intervention for people in the third cell. Although less customized, well-designed programs can prepare people for more significant investments later by increasing their awareness of themselves and their role in relationships.

The fourth and last cell is a bit odd. By definition, this matrix focuses only on those relationships you consider worthy of investment. So, in theory, no one should show up in this cell. But chances are, when pressed to choose among the chosen, some will show up here. If so, you might reconsider whether these relationships are worth the investment.

KEY POINTS

All relationships require effort. But not all relationships require the same amount or kind of effort. When people's roles are highly interdependent and the people in them are highly important to the success of the firm, you should invest in making their relationships strong enough to handle the conflicts and pressures they will inevitably face. You can handle all other relationships by managing their costs, separating the people, or simply ignoring them.

PART 3

Transforming Relationships

*By accepting the prescribed ritual
. . . [a person becomes] a player in
the game, thus making it possible
for the game to go on, for it to exist in
the first place.*

—Václav Havel[1]

SEVEN

Navigating Change Over Time

There are no safe paths in this part of the world. Remember you are over the Edge of the Wild now, and in for all sorts of fun wherever you go. Stick to the forest track, keep your spirits up, hope for the best, and with a tremendous slice of luck you *may* come out some day.

—THE WIZARD GANDALF IN J.R.R. TOLKIEN'S *THE HOBBIT*

When people wait for the other person in a relationship to change, they're usually in for a long wait. Odds are, that person is also waiting for them. Think of the leader who keeps looking to her second-in-command to take more initiative so that she doesn't have to tell him what to do, while he keeps looking to her to stop controlling things so that he can take more initiative. Each one waits for the other to make the first move.

The answer to this waiting game isn't the one you usually hear: "Stop trying to change others and change yourself." No, the answer is *to change the relationship*. Relationship patterns—like the one in which one person controls, the other defers—discourage people from taking the emotional and political risks they need to take in order to learn and grow. Indeed, if there's one thing people caught in these patterns can agree on, it's that these patterns aren't serving either one of them. If they can see a way out, they'll be far more likely to try new things, and once they get started, each person's changes will pave the way for the other's.

Like any change, none of this happens overnight, and all of it takes effort. But that alone isn't what usually discourages people. Rather, it's three common mistakes that make the effort seem harder and less promising than it need be.

- *We set unrealistic expectations.* If we assume, as many people do, that it's possible for people to make changes quickly and with little effort, we're apt to despair and give up before giving the effort a true test. Relationship change is like any significant change: it's more like a marathon than a sprint. That means it takes time, it can be hard, and at some point, you're bound to hit the relational equivalent of Heartbreak Hill. If you want to make it to the finish line, use the guidelines later in this chapter to pace yourself and assess how you're doing.

- *We don't anticipate barriers or help each other overcome them.* We assume that if people want to change, they *will* change, and relatively quickly. We fail to understand that ingrained behaviors lie largely outside people's awareness and conscious control, and that people will need our help in seeing and interrupting them. Expect ups and downs. Sometimes the other person will screw up; or you yourself may not always have the time to invest; or conflicts may make it hard to find common ground. When the going gets tough, don't give up. Find out how you can help the other person make it easier for you, and ask her or him to do the same.

- *We miscalculate the effort's costs and benefits.* In assessing whether to invest in changing a relationship, many of us over-look or downplay the time we're already spending on the relationship—strategizing, venting, ruminating, avoiding, and so on. All this time-consuming, energy-draining relationship work never seems to make it onto the balance sheet. The best question to ask isn't whether you want to spend time changing a relationship, but whether you want to spend time perpetuating it or changing it.

The following principles and practices will help you counter these mistakes, so you can navigate change over time and make it worth your while. To bring them to life, the next three chapters show how two partners at a professional services firm took their relationship from good to great by putting these principles into practice.

Principle 1: Use Dual Vision to Set Your Sights

Many change efforts, whether designed for people or for organizations, swing back and forth between two poles. Some promise more change than they can deliver in a short time: personal transformation in a couple of days or cultural transformation in a couple of months. Others aspire for far too little: a meager handful of insights after months of analysis. Similarly, some change efforts focus only on practical results—"We'll cut costs! Beat the competition! Save time and money!"—while others speak only to existential aspirations: "You'll have a sense of purpose! You'll be fulfilled! You'll feel more connected!" For people to be motivated enough to invest over time, they need to set goals that are ambitious and realistic on the one hand, and practically important and personally meaningful on the other.

Practice 1: Be Ambitious *and* Realistic
Most people won't invest in an endeavor that doesn't promise much or that promises a lot but doesn't say how it will deliver.

For change to be worth trying, people need to understand how a series of smaller, more modest goals will eventually add up to bigger and bolder ones. That means you need some model of change that says how one goal, once met, will pave the way for the next. The three-stage model summarized in Table 7.1 and illustrated in the next three chapters is one example. As you can see from the table, the model specifies the objectives or goals of each stage, the steps you need to take to meet them, and the results you can expect to see. With this kind of roadmap in hand, people can see where they're headed and how they'll get there. As a result, they'll be more likely to go along for the ride and better able to decide whether they want to go the whole distance or stop at some point along the way.

Practice 2: Set Goals That Are Practically Important and Personally Meaningful

Most people have a simultaneous interest in practical outcomes (making decisions, increasing revenues, keeping their jobs) and in existential outcomes (a sense of efficacy, connection, meaning, and self-respect). But it's not at all uncommon to hear people argue over which is more important—one person clamoring for meaning, the other for practical results; the first shouting, "Get a life!" and the second shouting, "Get over yourself!" Even so, unless you set goals that speak to both practical matters and existential concerns, most people will end up feeling great but as if they haven't accomplished much, or they'll feel as if they've accomplished a lot but it won't mean much. To sustain change, goals must be practically important *and* personally meaningful.

Table 7.1 A Three-Stage Model of Relationship Change.[2]

Stage	Objectives	Steps	Results
Stage 1: Disrupt	• To disrupt patterns of interaction that are getting in your way • To make your relationship more amenable to change	1. Assess the relationship 2. Map patterns of interaction 3. Design action experiments	• Able to disrupt patterns of interaction that trouble or puzzle you, making it easier to imagine a better future • Willing and able to try new things • Fall back into old patterns under *moderate* stress
Stage 2: Reframe	• To create more flexible patterns of interaction • To accelerate the pace of growth and change	1. Freeze frame 2. Invent new frames 3. Design frame experiments	• Able to use upsetting moments to understand each other better • Operate more freely within the relationship, picking up the pace of change and decision making • Still prone to fall back into old patterns but only under *high* stress
Stage 3: Revise	• To reset the relationship's foundation so changes last • To make growth and change sustainable	1. Revisit past events 2. Restructure outdated knowledge 3. Return to the future	• Able to respond more flexibly and effectively to each other and to the challenges you together face • Able to treat relationships as a context for your own and the firm's growth • Able to recoup when you fall back into old patterns even under extreme stress

Principle 2: Build Resilience While Taking Stock

Most people don't expect a change effort to be perfect, but they do expect observable, meaningful progress. If they can't see that progress, get confused over whether it's real, or get unduly thrown by setbacks, they'll grow discouraged and stop trying. To keep people motivated, you need to take stock of progress and use any setbacks to build resilience over time. You can accomplish this by assessing your progress in ways that build confidence and by putting setbacks, mistakes, and failures to work.

Practice 1: Build Confidence by Assessing Progress

In assessing progress, people tend to make one of two mistakes: either they look at how far they have to go and ignore how far they've come, or they look at how far they've come and overlook how far they have to go. It's the old tendency to see the glass as half empty or half full. Either way, people end up disappointed and find it hard to sustain the effort.

To avoid either mistake, you need metrics connected to some model of change, so you can see how far you've come and how far you have to go. When it comes to improving relationships, the most useful metrics specify the results that you need to see at each stage to be confident that you're making good headway. As the story in the next three chapters illustrates, this means going beyond global evaluations—"We're doing great!" or "We're doing horribly!"—and looking at what people are actually thinking, feeling, and doing.

Practice 2: Put Setbacks, Mistakes, and Failures to Work

Nothing kills motivation more than lambasting people for the inevitable setbacks, mistakes, or failures that accompany any effort to improve a relationship. That's why reflecting and reframing are so important (see Chapter Four). Anytime something goes wrong or someone gets upset, great! That's grist for the mill: take a look at what it has to teach you.

Of course, all of us aspire to learn from mistakes and believe it's important. But it can be terrifically hard to do when embarrassed, angry, or disappointed. Even the most mature people lose their cool from time to time. The last thing you need is to feel embarrassed about being embarrassed, or angry about being angry, or disappointed about being disappointed! Instead of suppressing reactions, use them in much the same way you use mistakes. Learn from them. After all, reacting poorly to mistakes is simply another mistake. Once you lower the bar on what's acceptable to explore, you can use all of it, no matter what it is, to speed up the pace of change.

Principle 3: Put the Fun Back in the Dysfunctional

You can't improve a relationship without exploring delicate issues or taking some emotional risks. At times the endeavor may feel so weighty you'll want to take a pass. To lighten things up, look for opportunities to laugh at the unlaughable, and if you're running out of hope, create it.

Practice 1: Laugh at the Unlaughable

Improving a relationship is challenging enough without making it too earnest or grim. To withstand the tumultuous feelings that accompany any change effort, you have to have fun, you have to laugh, you have to enjoy yourself. If it's all drudgery, you won't stick with it. Besides, if you look hard enough, you can find comic relief in any circumstance. If you can't, then create it. As long as it's not at someone else's expense, laughter can leaven even the heaviest moment.[3]

Practice 2: Create Hope

Hope is the lifeblood of change. It makes people far more resilient in the face of setbacks and far more likely to invest in turning things around.[4] As important as it is, it's astounding how many people work so hard to stamp it out, mostly for fear of being disappointed.

"Why can't you be more like Hutchinson?
You don't hear him complaining."

Not wanting to feel let down, they counsel themselves and others to expect little and to hope for less, and as a result, that's just what they get: little and less.

Since a relationship's prospects are inherently ambiguous, there's nothing to stop you from creating hope by casting those prospects in a positive light, at least provisionally. Even if it stretches your imagination beyond the breaking point, you're still better off *acting* as if you're hopeful. As you'll see in the next three chapters, people are much more likely to create a positive, self-fulfilling prophecy by acting hopeful. When you act *as if* good things might follow, you're more apt to create the circumstances that justify and fulfill that hope. And remember, you can always stop hoping. But it's awfully hard to jump-start hope once pessimism sets in.

KEY POINTS

When people wait for the other person in a relationship to change, they're in for a long wait. To improve a relationship, you need to focus on *changing the relationship,* not just yourself or the other person. By changing the relationship patterns that discourage risk taking, you can accelerate individual change. Relationship change is more sustainable, even fun and fulfilling, if you avoid three common mistakes: setting unrealistic expectations, failing to anticipate barriers, and miscalculating the effort's costs and benefits. You can counter these mistakes and navigate change successfully by following three principles and their associated practices: setting your sights using dual vision; building resilience while taking stock; and putting the fun back in the dysfunctional. Putting these principles into practice generates the motivation and energy needed to sustain change over the long haul. The next three chapters will show you how.

141

EIGHT

Disrupting Patterns

> When life gets creative, it has a tendency to gravitate toward
> certain recurring patterns, whether those patterns are
> emergent and self-organizing, or whether they
> are deliberately crafted by human agents.
>
> —STEVE JOHNSON[1]

When a relationship critical to a firm's success could put that success at risk, it may be time for a change. Fifteen years into their relationship, Dan Gavin and Stu Fine suspected their time had come. For two years, the firm's top leadership had been transforming Merrimac[2] from a professional services firm into a group of businesses that combined these services with innovative new products. CEO Gavin was now looking to Stu, the firm's marketing expert, to launch the firm's first product business. As one of the firm's most respected thought leaders, Stu had driven much of the firm's innovation, and he welcomed the chance to ensure that those innovations took root. At the same time, Dan and Stu both recognized that this new challenge would put a lot more pressure on their relationship. Stu knew he'd have to partner more closely with Dan, while Dan knew he'd have to rely more heavily on Stu. Whether their relationship was up to these

143

tasks, neither could say for sure. To find out, they took three steps with my help:

Step 1: Assess the relationship

Step 2: Map patterns of interaction

Step 3: Design action experiments

As straightforward as these steps may seem, people face a funny kind of paradox before taking even the first one: *they know each other so well, they no longer know each other at all.* All they see are the caricatures in their heads—*he's so sensitive, she's so competitive.* The very efficiency these caricatures give, they also take away because they make a person's underlying complexity—sure to emerge under stress—harder to understand or to handle. That's why, early on, the single most important thing people can do is *slow down and take a closer look at each other and at how their relationship works.* As you'll soon see, this helps people figure out where their relationship is up to the challenges it will face, and where it's not.

Step 1: Assess the Relationship

By conventional standards, most people—including Dan and Stu—would probably say their relationship was doing fine. They felt a good deal of trust; they were committed to making their relationship work; they didn't expect their interactions to be conflict-free; they shared an interest in producing results; and they thought accountability was essential to achieving those results.[3] All things considered, many might say, if it ain't broke, don't fix it.

STEPS TOWARD CHANGE	
Stage 1: Disrupt	Assess the Relationship
	Map Patterns of Interaction
	Design Action Experiments
Stage 2: Reframe	Freeze Frame
	Invent New Frames
	Design Frame Experiments
Stage 3: Revise	Revisit Past Events
	Restructure Outdated Knowledge
	Return to the Future

But as with more and more leaders today, Dan and Stu's standards were anything but conventional: they were far more interested in achieving excellence than in fixing things. The fact that they felt good about their relationship didn't tell them much. What they wanted to know was whether their relationship was strong enough to withstand the pressures they were about to face. To find out, they assessed how well their relationship was likely to handle two kinds of pressures: those bearing down on them from outside, and those bubbling up from within.

Assessing Outside Pressures: Demands + Constraints

Until now, Dan and Stu had built their relationship around their mutual love of ideas and their mutual respect for each other's talents. Although they interacted a lot, their fates had never been intertwined. But that context was now shifting, as Dan looked to Stu to help him implement the firm's group strategy by turning his marketing team into a separate business.

Table 8.1 Outside Pressures on Stu and Dan.

Demands	Constraints
Stu was charged with launching and leading a new business.	Stu had no experience launching or leading a new business.
Dan would have to help Stu launch the business and develop into a general manager.	Dan's expertise was largely intuitive, making it hard to transfer quickly.
They would have to depend on each other for their success like never before.	Failure would be costly. As the first unit to be launched, it would serve as a model for others.
They would have to confront and negotiate differences they could avoid in the past.	Their negotiating styles were quite different. Dan relished good debates; Stu hated them.
They would have to move fast if the group strategy was going to look credible.	Business-building takes time, especially when you're building people's capabilities at the same time.

Like any new strategic challenge, this one posed its own set of demands and constraints (see Table 8.1).[4] On the demand side, Stu had to launch and lead a new business as quickly as possible; on the constraint side, his lack of experience was bound to affect how well and how quickly he did either. This, in turn, placed a demand on Dan: he would have to help Stu launch the business and develop into a general manager; on the constraint side, Dan's expertise was highly complex and largely intuitive, making it hard to transfer to others.

Demands and constraints invariably combine to create pressures that turn the heat up on relationships. When people don't take stock of those pressures, they're much more likely to turn against each other; conversely, when they do take stock, they're much more likely to turn together toward the challenges they face.

By starting here, we increased the odds of Dan and Stu working together instead of at cross-purposes.

Assessing Inside Pressures: Hopes + Worries

To their relationship, Dan and Stu brought both hopes and worries (see Table 8.2). On the one hand, Stu worried that their relationship might grow stale if they didn't invest in improving it. On the other hand, Dan hoped that the decision to invest in their relationship might serve as a model for others. Both hoped that in the course of improving their relationship, they'd accelerate their own development: Dan wanting to change the way his anxiety comes out as anger, Stu wanting to handle tough disagreements more effectively, especially with CEOs. Last but not least, they both hoped the other would change those things that worried them the most: Stu's anxieties and sensitive zones; Dan's debating in ways that shut Stu down.

There's a healthy dose of self-interest in all this. It's as if they're thinking what most people think at this stage: *By investing in this relationship, perhaps the other guy will be less of a pain in the ass, and I'll be better off.*

That kind of thinking is what makes change worthwhile; without it, all you have is some vague notion of improving a relationship for its own sake. That's never enough. To make change of any significance, people need to have skin in the game; Dan and Stu's answers in Table 8.2 suggest they have some. What they say next suggests they have plenty.

Assessing a Relationship's Assets and Liabilities

When assessing a relationship, it helps to take stock of a relationship's assets and liabilities relative to the pressures that relationship is likely to face (see Table 8.3). This way people not only anticipate what might cause them difficulty under pressure, they also identify the assets they can use to deal with any difficulties that do arise.

Table 8.2 Dan and Stu's Inside Pressures.

	What Dan Said	What Stu Said
The Relationship	I want to turbocharge our relationship, move it from a good relationship to an excellent one.	Our relationship is important to me. Right now, it's at risk of going stale.
	I'd like to make this relationship a model for investing in the top people in the firm.	I want to take what is a good relationship and turn it into an excellent one.
The Other Person	I'd like to help Stu with leadership issues that get in his way, like getting anxious about taking on new, controversial, or challenging tasks, and getting too upset when people touch on his sensitive zones.	I'd like to help Dan learn how to be more definitive and prescriptive without getting into the kind of debate behavior that can undermine his effectiveness and shut me and others down.
Themselves	I believe this work will help me reflect on and improve my own behavior.	I want to learn how to put myself in a CEO's shoes, so I can understand how they think about things and what they find more or less helpful.
	I know my anxiety often comes out as anger, which is not particularly constructive. So getting rid of that would be a good idea.	I want to learn how to have constructive, tough disagreements without either shutting down or assuming too much responsibility.

Table 8.3   The Relationship's Assets and Liabilities.

	What Dan Said	**What Stu Said**
Assets	I have genuine respect for Stu's character, integrity, and intellect.	I have a lot of time and patience for Dan. I'm extremely grateful to him for his support, counsel, and understanding over the years.
	I believe his heart is in the right place in terms of fun, family, and our relationship.	I think Dan genuinely cares about me and doesn't just consider me an important economic engine.
	I believe Stu is capable of change and dedicated to learning, and that he can be more helpful to me than most people can.	My faith in Dan's caring for me gives me courage and confidence to acknowledge and challenge some of my behaviors in his presence. I'm eager to change, and I don't think I can do it by myself.
		I also believe that our relationship is important to Merrimac. There are economic incentives to make this work.
Liabilities	It can be difficult to communicate with Stu in short-cycle time; it can take a long time to get things moving.	There's a history of one-way learning in our relationship. I go to Dan with my thinking about a problem, and Dan then pronounces.
	There are things I do or say that have unintended effects on Stu.	

(*continued*)

Table 8.3   The Relationship's Assets and Liabilities.

(*Continued*)

	What Dan Said	What Stu Said
Liabilities (*continued*)	Sometimes without realizing it I raise Stu's anxiety level, hurt his feelings, or cause him to tune out.	Dan talks about situations, not about himself. I don't know or understand Dan very well, out of my own naiveté, lack of curiosity, or his "boss persona."
	There's something about our relationship to which Stu tends to overreact.	As we work to change our patterns, I may come to resent the patterns more and not know how to talk to Dan about it well.
		Finally, we've fallen into a habit of joking about each other in stereotypical terms, which can also cause difficulties.

In taking stock of their assets, Dan and Stu recounted with ease all they had going for them, including a shared belief in their good intentions, mutual respect, a sense of caring, and confidence that they would learn from whatever risks they took.

But when it came to their liabilities, they struggled. Like most people, they could point to symptoms, but not their cause. Dan knew it was difficult to communicate in short-cycle time with Stu, but he couldn't figure out why; he sensed that Stu overreacted to something in their relationship, but he didn't know what it was; he knew his behavior had unintended effects on Stu, but he didn't know what those effects were or what he did to create them. And despite Stu's professed confidence and trust in Dan, it troubled him that he didn't know Dan that well and that their relationship wasn't more reciprocal; he worried that their stereotyping, even in jest, might cause difficulty; and he could see how unnamed patterns, left intact, might breed resentment.

As is often the case at this point, Dan and Stu's assessment of their liabilities wasn't of much help. They sensed things—things that troubled them—but they couldn't give those things a name or explain their existence, let alone change them. Since this would inevitably put their success at risk, I helped them map those interactions that concerned them most.

TAKING ACTION
How to Assess Your Own Relationships

Now that you've seen how we assessed Dan and Stu's relationship, here's what you can do to assess your own.

- Identify a relationship that could make or break your success or that of your unit or organization.
- Invite that person to join you in assessing the ways in which your relationship is making it easier *and* harder for each of you to succeed.
- Focus your attention not just on each other but on your relationship.
- Create a shared list of the challenges you'll have to master together and the pressures they'll generate for each of you.
- Jointly assess the relationship's assets and liabilities relative to those challenges and pressures.

If, based on the assessment, you both want to invest further, proceed to Step 2. If you had trouble taking Step 1, get help before proceeding.

Step 2: Map Patterns of Interaction

This second step zeroes in on interactions that shed light on the concerns Dan and Stu raised in their assessment. To take this step, we used a tool I call the Ladder of Reflection to do three things: capture key interactions, describe them in concrete terms, and map the patterns underlying them (see Chapter Four, Figure 4.1, and Appendix B). This section describes how we took this step, so you can map any interactions that puzzle or trouble you.

	STEPS TOWARD CHANGE	
	Assess the Relationship	
Stage 1: Disrupt	Map Patterns of Interaction	
	Design Action Experiments	
	Freeze Frame	
Stage 2: Reframe	Invent New Frames	
	Design Frame Experiments	
	Revisit Past Events	
Stage 3: Revise	Restructure Outdated Knowledge	
	Return to the Future	

Capturing Interactions

We already know from Dan and Stu's assessment that Dan is concerned about the amount of time it takes to communicate with Stu, his effect on Stu, and what he calls Stu's overreactions. We also know from Stu that the one-way nature of his relationship with Dan worries him, as does Dan's tendency to pronounce and to debate. To understand what they're doing to give rise to these concerns, we recorded their meetings as they went about their work together, and we waited until one of them illustrated his concerns.[5]

It didn't take long.

Shortly after starting our work together, Dan and Stu confronted an issue that immediately put them at odds: how to negotiate a deal with a valued leader by the name of Hal Goldstein so he'd be motivated to stay and help launch Focuspoint, Stu's new marketing business.

As Stu told it, he and Hal had reached an impasse on Hal's salary. In hopes of getting help from Dan, he recounted their negotiations to date and the concerns Hal had expressed.

After listening, Dan was convinced that their impasse didn't revolve around salary at all. Instead, he thought Hal was worried about becoming a "wage slave" whose salary would be forever tethered to the time he spent working rather than the value he created. On the basis of that view, Dan suggested that Stu promise Hal ownership in the new venture. But Stu, who was deeply wary of making promises he couldn't keep, didn't want to go in that direction. Without a legal structure in place, and with little understanding of how the ownership structure would work, Stu didn't trust that he or Dan would be able to deliver the goods. Let's listen in as they discuss what to do about Hal:[6]

DAN: One of the things I hear Hal saying is, "Wage slave! Wage slave! Wage slave!" If he said anything like that to me, I'd take out a venture-capital model and promise him some ownership in the firm, assuming he sticks around. And if it's cash now he wants, I'd tell him he can trade some of that ownership for cash now.

STU: I don't want to go there.

DAN: Why not? He has to be adult about his decisions.

STU: Dan. Dan. I don't have the same degree of certainty you do that there are going to be shares.

DAN: Why wouldn't you, Stu?

STU: Because it depends on what goes on in your head and other things I don't know anything about.

DAN: I have a high degree of certainty. So if it depends on what's going on in my head, I have a high degree of certainty.

STU: I'm making a representation to somebody else about what's in your head. I'm uncomfortable about that.

DAN: But in this case, to the extent my certainty fails to pan out over time, it can only benefit him. You're giving him money now for something that might not exist.

STU: To be blunt, Dan, there are things you've said were going to happen which haven't happened, like, "There may be different kinds of directors" and things like that. So I'm very leery, because I know people will latch on to things. And, I'm bad at this stuff already, Dan!

DAN: [Looking and sounding annoyed] But Stu—

STU: [Putting up his hand up to form a stop sign] I'm just saying that, for me, if it doesn't happen, recouping will take me a century! I don't want to go there!

DAN: [Leaning forward] But, Stu—

STU: [Hand still up] I'm sorry. I'm a coward, but at least I know I'm a coward!

It's not every day you come across someone who makes an apologetic appeal to cowardice as a way out of a conflict. It's so self-deprecating it's disarming, which of course it's meant to be— which isn't to say that Stu is *consciously* trying to disarm Dan. Quite the contrary, he doesn't have to try. His response is so habitual—so intrinsic to his behavioral repertoire[7]—that it comes naturally. All he needs is the proper cue, which Dan's relentless persistence gives him. By the end of the exchange, all Stu wants is for Dan to back off, prompting him to do what he usually does under those circumstances: apologize and appeal to a character flaw—in this case, cowardice—after which Stu and Dan reach the same kind of impasse Stu reached with Hal.

Not good.

This brief exchange exemplifies one of the patterns that get Dan and Stu into trouble. It's a classic. While the particulars may vary—one day they may talk about Hal, the next about products—the pattern itself will remain the same, repeating over and over again until they disrupt it, which they won't be able to do until they can describe it.

"You're a partner now, Cosgrove. Partners don't do self-deprecation."

Describing Interactions

When people look at interactions like the one between Dan and Stu, the first things that usually spring to mind are evaluations: "That went nowhere!" or "That was weird!" That's only natural. But it's not enough: it won't help you change what you see. To change patterns, you first have to see them, which means you have to describe what's happening in concrete terms, so they can connect your description to their behavior.[8] To do that, you must look closely at each step in an interaction and ask, *What is this person actually doing?*

By asking this question, you focus attention on people's behavior instead of their motives. (See Appendix B for more on this distinction.) In other words, instead of speculating about what people are *trying* to do, you simply observe what they *are* doing. There's a reason for this. If you focus on motives—what people are *trying* to do—before describing what they *are* doing, you'll come up with speculations that are quite disconnected from actual behavior. This causes two problems. First, people won't be able to see the behaviors you think they need to change, making it less likely they'll change them. And second, they may wonder whether your speculations say more about you than them, leading them to discount your views. Although there *is* a time and a place for understanding what people are trying to do, it's not now but in the next stage.

To be most useful, descriptions should help people see what they're doing to contribute to those patterns that concern them the most. Take Dan's opening move, when he tells Stu:

> One of the things I hear Hal saying is, "Wage slave! Wage slave! Wage slave!" If he said anything like that to me, I'd take out a venture-capital model. He'd get some ownership in the firm, assuming he sticks around. And if it's cash now that he wants, I'd tell him he can trade some of that ownership for cash.

Different observers will inevitably describe this statement in different ways, which raises the question, Which description should you choose? For all practical purposes, the answer is pretty simple: the one that suits your purposes best. Our purpose here is to understand what Dan and Stu are doing to give rise to the concerns they each have about their relationship. Here you might recall that Stu is concerned about their one-way dynamic. "I go to Dan with my thinking about a problem, and Dan then pronounces" (see Table 8.3). Well, right here, we have a great example of what that pronouncing looks like in action: we might describe Dan's opening statement as *pronouncing what he thinks the right answer is*. By describing Dan's statement this way, we help Stu see the behaviors that concern him, while helping Dan see what he does to create the mystifying "unintended effects" he has on Stu (see Table 8.3).

Moving to the next step in the interaction, Stu responds to Dan's pronouncement: "I don't want to go there." Looking at this statement, you might reasonably say that Stu *rejects Dan's answer*. But notice: it's not any old rejection. Stu doesn't say why he rejects Dan's suggestion, nor does he build on it by saying what might make it more appealing. In this respect, it's not a mere rejection; it's an *outright rejection*, leaving little to no room for negotiation. This description draws our attention to the behavior that leads Dan to worry that Stu slows things down more than necessary (see Tables 8.2 and 8.3).

In the next step, Dan meets Stu's rejection and raises him one: "Why not?" he asks, before asserting, "He has to be adult about his decision." Although short, this two-pronged move is quite complicated. On the one hand, we might call it a question, because he starts off by asking why not. On the other hand, he doesn't wait for an answer but instead goes on to pronounce, "(Hal) has to be adult about his decision." It's this latter statement that makes the move so complicated, because it implies, "If you [Stu] believe that adults have to be adult about their decisions, then you would do what I propose." Since most of us believe that adults should be adults, it suggests that only unreasonable people would not do what Dan is proposing. In this way, Dan's move—the kind of move a

157

debater might make—*challenges Stu to account for his resistance*, as if his resistance is, on the face of it, unreasonable.

This appears to frustrate Stu who, like most of us, probably believes that adults should act like adults, yet he still doesn't want to do what Dan suggests. And so he exclaims, "Dan, Dan," as if to stop him before going on to say, "I don't have the same degree of certainty you do that there are going to be shares." In this statement, Stu explains why he's rejecting Dan's suggestion, in effect saying, "I'll tell you why not. You're certain about something I'm not at all certain about." Here we might simply say that Stu is *explaining his concerns* or *raising a concern* about offering shares. But also notice what he's *not* doing: *He's not asking Dan to address his concerns.* He doesn't say, for example, "You have more certainty than I have about the shares. If I understood why, I might feel more comfortable doing what you suggest. What leads you to be so confident?" Instead Stu *raises a concern without asking Dan to address it.*

This last description, unlike the first two, describes not only what Stu *is* doing (raising a concern) but also what he's *not* doing (not asking Dan to address the concern). This kind of description is always tricky, because there are any number of things he's *not* doing: he's not checking his voice mail; he's not pacing the room; he's not yelling at Dan. How can we possibly know how to focus our attention? Once again, the answer is to rely on their initial assessments, where we discovered that Stu wants Dan to stop debating and start advising, and Dan wants Stu to move faster and to overreact less (see Tables 8.2 and 8.3). As with all people, it's not just what they do that gets in the way of what they want; it's also what they don't do. And here's a great example. By not inviting Dan to address what troubles Stu about the idea, Stu gives Dan no room to put his troubles to rest, which requires Stu to persist to get Dan to address his concerns. But this only leads Dan to think that Stu is overreacting, which requires Stu to persist further. And so on.

In the next step of the interaction, Dan responds by asking, "Why wouldn't you be [as certain as I am], Stu?" Here, you could say that Dan is asking a question. But that wouldn't say much about the *kind* of question he's asking, nor would it explain how the two get stuck. After all, Dan isn't asking just any question. He's asking *why Stu isn't already as certain as he is.*

That question is quite different from the more open-ended question, "What leads you to be uncertain, Stu?" If anything, Dan's question assumes that his level of certainty is the right standard, and it implies that Stu must justify why he isn't meeting it. In this sense, Dan's question doesn't open up an inquiry as much as it launches a debate, in which Dan is *debating the legitimacy of Stu's concerns.* This more nuanced description of Dan's question helps explain exactly how their interaction breaks down and what leads them to feel frustrated and worried.

Although the three of us continued to make our way through their interaction, by now you probably get the gist of what we did: we described their interaction in ways that helped us understand what behaviors gave rise to their concerns. Let's move on to how you can pull these descriptions together into a map that captures the pattern underlying their interaction.[9]

Mapping the Pattern

Mapping is a technique that helps you understand patterns of interaction that produce outcomes that neither person in a relationship consciously wants or intends. By using the template in Figure 8.1, you can portray in graphic form *how each person's actions help to elicit reactions that produce the next step in the sequence that makes up the interaction.*[10] This helps people see how their actions and reactions interlock to form an identifiable pattern, allowing them to step outside the pattern, see how it works, and imagine how it might work differently.

Figure 8.1 The Act-React Template.

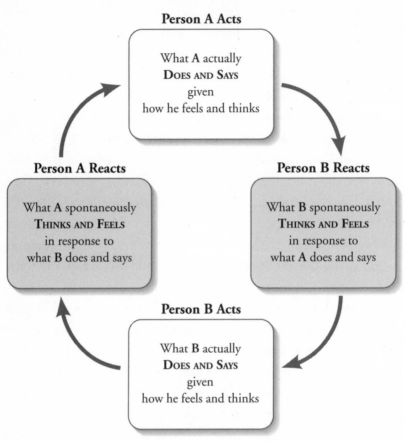

Person A Acts

What **A** actually
Does and Says
given
how he feels and thinks

Person A Reacts

What **A** spontaneously
Thinks and Feels
in response to
what **B** does and says

Person B Reacts

What **B** spontaneously
Thinks and Feels
in response to
what **A** does and says

Person B Acts

What **B** actually
Does and Says
given
how he feels and thinks

The map in Figure 8.2 uses this template to pull together and add to what we've learned so far. Included in the white boxes, labeled "Dan Acts" and "Stu Acts," are descriptions of what Dan and Stu did. Each action is described so that Dan and Stu can see what they're actually doing to give rise to the other's concerns. All of this is pretty straightforward.

The next step—adding their reactions—is trickier. We don't yet know what Dan and Stu are thinking or feeling. And even if they told us, we couldn't be sure if what they said was entirely

Figure 8.2 Mapping Dan and Stu's Interactions.

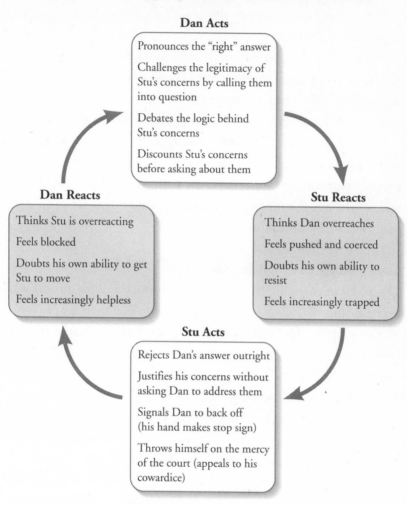

Dan Acts

Pronounces the "right" answer

Challenges the legitimacy of Stu's concerns by calling them into question

Debates the logic behind Stu's concerns

Discounts Stu's concerns before asking about them

Dan Reacts

Thinks Stu is overreacting

Feels blocked

Doubts his own ability to get Stu to move

Feels increasingly helpless

Stu Reacts

Thinks Dan overreaches

Feels pushed and coerced

Doubts his own ability to resist

Feels increasingly trapped

Stu Acts

Rejects Dan's answer outright

Justifies his concerns without asking Dan to address them

Signals Dan to back off (his hand makes stop sign)

Throws himself on the mercy of the court (appeals to his cowardice)

valid.[11] Only in cartoons do people have bubbles over their heads. In real life, all that thinking and feeling is going on inside people's heads, where we can't see what's happening. That's why the React boxes are shaded in gray: to remind us to hold loosely whatever we put in those boxes, because they lie in a gray zone. At the same time, we can't ignore reactions just because they're difficult to get at. Reactions are the connective tissue that holds an interaction together, tying one action to the next. That means we have to find some way to get at them.

In everyday life, we rely on three approaches to get at people's reactions: asking, speculating, or predicting what someone is feeling or thinking. While none of these approaches is 100 percent reliable, some work better than others, especially when implemented in better or worse ways. As Table 8.4 suggests, the more you move down or to the right, the more you run the risk of distorting people's reactions.[12] Conversely, the more you stay toward the top and to the left, the more you're likely to find out what people are *really* feeling and thinking.

Calibrating Your Understanding

The point of mapping isn't to nail down, once and for all, the way a relationship works. It's to map a pattern well enough for purposes of changing it. The test of a good map, then, isn't whether it's right or wrong, but whether it's good enough to serve change. To calibrate whether that's the case, you need to discuss maps in light of data from other meetings, adding to and modifying the map until everyone thinks it's good enough to inform change.

Sometimes in calibrating a map, people will differ over how best to describe an action or a reaction. When that happens, it's tempting to get into an argument over who's right. Like the old beer commercial, one person argues, "Less filling!" while the other claims, "Tastes great!" One person sees and appreciates one aspect of what happened; the other sees and appreciates another.

For illustrative purposes, let's say that after seeing the map, Dan disagrees with the characterization of his opening move as "pronouncing the right answer." Let's say he thinks we should call it "an effort to help." Instead of getting into an argument, we're better off paying attention to what he's seeing that we don't.

Table 8.4   Getting at People's Reactions.

	Better Ways	Worse Ways
Ask	Stop the action and ask an open-ended question, such as, "What's your reaction?"	Later on, ask a leading question that is based on how *you* would feel, "Did you feel anxious last week when Dan persisted?"
Speculate	On the basis of what people have said about their reactions in similar situations, hypothesize what they *might* be feeling or thinking in this one. For example, "Given what Dan and Stu said in their assessments, Dan *may* think Stu is overreacting and slowing things down, and Stu *may* think Dan is trying to win a debate. Let me ask if that's the case here."	On the basis of *your* reactions to similar situations, make assumptions about what these people *must* be thinking or feeling in this one. For example, "If I were Dan, I'd think Stu was acting immaturely, and it would piss me off. Dan *must* be pissed off. If I were Stu, I'd think Dan was being unfair, making me do things I don't want to do, and that would piss me off too. Stu *must* be pissed off."
Predict	On the basis of a relatively developed theory about how people tend to react to different behaviors, make predictions about how these people *might* be reacting here. For example, "Under these circumstances, many people might feel blocked or pushed. Let me test to see if that's the case here."	On the basis of a relatively simplistic grasp of people's motivations derived exclusively from *your* experience, make predictions about how people in this situation *must* be reacting. For example, "Dan cares only about control; he *must* be livid that he can't get his way. Stu only cares about protecting himself; he *must* be scared to death by what Dan's doing."

And what might he be seeing? The word *effort* is a tip-off, as would be such words as *trying, intending,* or *hoping.* In calling his move an "effort to help," Dan is turning our attention to what he was *trying to do* as opposed to what he *was actually doing.* He's pointing to his *intentions* or *motives* instead of *his actions.* And at that level, chances are, he's right; he probably was trying to help. At the same time, his *actions* suggest that his way of helping is to pronounce the "right" answer. If that's the case, then both descriptions are true: the map focuses on his actions, and Dan focuses on his intentions while taking those actions. While it's true that other intentions may also be at play—he may be trying to convince Stu, or hoping to get Stu to do things his way—that doesn't mean he isn't also trying to help. People rarely have one intention or purpose in mind when acting.

By taking into account what Dan sees, we can more quickly turn his attention to what he doesn't see: the way he pursued his intentions and the results of his efforts. After all, the data are pretty compelling: Dan's actions didn't leave Stu feeling helped, and Stu certainly didn't budge. So if Dan was trying to help—and we have no data to assume otherwise—he may need to reconsider his approach. He'll be much more likely to do so if we don't argue with him over what he was or was not *trying* to do.

Besides, we'll never know for sure what was going on inside Dan's head or Stu's or anyone's for that matter. When it comes to what people feel, think, or intend, we're forever hampered by *asymmetric access.* As observers, all we have to go on are clues—what actors say or do, their tones of voice, their body language—to glean what they might be thinking, feeling, or intending.[13] Indeed, an overwhelming amount of research demonstrates that our interpretations of others' intentions are more often wrong than right.[14] Only those acting have direct access to what they're feeling and thinking, and even they can't say for sure what's going on.[15]

While this asymmetric access can never be eliminated, it can serve as a constant reminder that we should be forever humble about what's going on in the hearts and minds of those whom we observe. The best we can do is make it as easy as possible for people to tell us what they're feeling, thinking, and intending as accurately as they can.[16]

This means demonstrating—not just espousing—a genuine interest in what people have to say. Only then will they have a genuine interest in telling you. And remember: people will watch what you do closely. When you ask questions, they'll notice whether you're trying to understand them ("What's going on?") or lambaste them ("Why on earth would you do that?"). And when you listen, they'll look to see if you're capturing what they're saying accurately or simply caricaturing it. These things matter, and they'll be on the lookout for them.

Once people map the pattern underlying repetitious inter-actions, they can see what they're each doing to contribute to that pattern, putting them in a much better position to alter it. With the aid of that map, Dan can see that his debating con-tributes to Stu's "overreactions," and Stu can see how his outright rejections increase the odds of Dan debating. With one person debating and the other rejecting, it's easy to see why it's taking so long to communicate. By putting familiar problems (taking a long time to communicate) in unfamiliar light (what each person is doing to slow things down), maps produce what some writers call a "shock of recognition," engaging people's emotions as well as their intellects.

TAKING ACTION
How to Map Patterns of Interaction

Now that you've seen how we mapped Dan and Stu's relationship, here's what you can do to map yours.

- Identify one or two interactions that illustrate the concerns raised in your relationship assessment from Step 1.

- Capture the interaction by taping or taking close notes on what you each said and did and on what you each felt and thought at the time.

- Describe in concrete terms what you each did (and did not do); do not speculate about what you were trying to do or intending to do.

- Describe your reactions (what you were actually thinking and feeling at the time); do not justify, interpret, or explain them.

- Organize your description into a map that shows how each of your actions contributed to reactions that make the other's actions more understandable.

- Calibrate your map by modifying or adding to it on the basis of what happened in other interactions.

If, on the basis of the map, you both want to invest further, proceed to Step 3. If you had trouble taking Step 2, get help first.

Step 3: Design Action Experiments

Many of us figure, "If I try harder and harder to change some pattern of interaction and it doesn't change, it must not be changeable." But this overlooks another possibility: that we're trying the wrong things. In fact, our efforts may be part of the problem. Oftentimes the problem isn't *how hard* we try; it's *what* we try.

	STEPS TOWARD CHANGE
Stage 1: Disrupt	Assess the Relationship
	Map Patterns of Interaction
	Design Action Experiments
Stage 2: Reframe	Freeze Frame
	Invent New Frames
	Design Frame Experiments
Stage 3: Revise	Revisit Past Events
	Restructure Outdated Knowledge
	Return to the Future

To change patterns, you have to throw a monkey wrench into the works by thinking—and then acting—outside the pattern.[17] If you find that difficult to imagine, let alone do, you've got lots of company. That's why it's best not to take this step until you've mapped the pattern that concerns you. Maps give you the understanding and distance you need to think outside the box. With map in hand, you're no longer *in* the pattern; you're *outside*, looking back at it. From this perspective, you are in a much better position to invent action experiments—experiments designed to disrupt the pattern and make it more amenable to change.[18]

The first step in any action experiment is to go back and look at the interlocking actions and reactions depicted in a map and to ask the question, *What actions can I take to make it hard for the other person to react the way he or she does?* Usually this question will require you to invent actions that are "counterintuitive"—actions that lie outside of your intuitive way of seeing and doing things. For this reason, the perspective of a skilled third party often helps, because he or she can imagine options, as I do below, that those in the pattern can't:

DIANA: Stu, let me suggest something counterintuitive. When Dan says, "I think you ought to do this, this, and this," instead of rejecting him outright, put him to work. Tell him what you need to feel more comfortable and ask him to make it more concrete for you. That way you're less likely to get Dan the debater and more likely to get Dan at his best—a fine teacher. And Dan, when Stu rejects what you're saying and blocks, I'd slow down and ask him what he needs to be more comfortable, then I'd go back and help him see what leads you to be comfortable already.

In making these suggestions, I had the map in mind. That map alerted me to how trapped Stu felt and how helpless Dan felt. I predicted that these two moves—Stu putting Dan to work, and Dan helping Stu—would disrupt the pattern. If Stu can put Dan to work, perhaps he won't feel so trapped that he has to reject Dan's views outright; and if Dan is given the space to explain his views, perhaps he won't feel so helpless that he has to debate Stu's concerns before understanding them. He might even *want* to understand them, as a good teacher does.

Suggestions like these, although simple, go against the grain of people's behavioral repertoires. Indeed, if they don't, they probably won't disrupt the pattern, because *all patterns are a product of people's intersecting behavioral repertoires.* It's only reasonable, then, that people will worry about trying out a new action. That's why I wasn't surprised or offended when Dan reacted to my suggestion by saying, "I hear what you're saying, but we're in implementation mode on a number of key points here. I don't think we can postpone thinking about this one." Instead of discounting or debating his concern, I use it to encourage him to try something new:

DIANA: Let me stay with this for a second. I'm sympathetic to the worry that time is running out. So my advice for you is as counterintuitive as it is for Stu. If you're in such a hurry, then the last thing you want to do is have Stu kick you out of the conversation, which is exactly what he's doing.

Right now, your speeding up isn't saving time; it's slowing things down. He'll listen more, and listen more efficiently, if you slow down, ask him about his concerns, then go back to the basics on ownership in addressing them.

It's not as obvious to him as it is to you why he won't get into trouble. In fact, he's really worried about it, so there's already static in the system. Don't add more.

This line of thinking made sense to Dan, and he agreed to give it a try. The next few weeks provided several opportunities for them to experiment with new actions. While they were a bit clumsy in their execution, Dan and Stu saw that these actions allowed them to conduct their business more swiftly. No longer debating or blocking quite as much, they were able to get more done, *and* they felt better about themselves and each other.

The old pattern was disrupted. Yet even had the experiment "failed," as many initial experiments do,[19] that too would have been okay. It would have given us the information we needed to go back to the drawing board and design another experiment.

TAKING ACTION
How to Design an Action Experiment

Now that you've seen how we designed Dan and Stu's action experiment, here's what you can do to design your own.

- Use the map you created in Step 2 to move outside the pattern that concerns you, so you can look back at it and see how it works.

- Ask yourselves, *What actions can I take to make it hard for the other person to continue acting and reacting the way he or she now does?*

- Invent actions that lie outside the box defined by the patterns—actions that might put a monkey wrench in the way it works.

- Even if the new actions look like the cure that makes the illness worse, try them. Right now, you just want to shake the pattern up and make it more amenable to change.

If, following the experiment, you both want to invest further, proceed to Stage 2. If you had difficulty with Stage 1, get help first.

Stage 1 Results

This last step launched Dan and Stu's relationship into a state of flux, making it more amenable to change. With the old pattern disrupted, they could no longer rely on mindless routines. They had to pay closer attention to what they were each doing, leading them to notice and puzzle over things they'd previously taken for granted. What's more, once their action experiments succeeded in disrupting the pattern, they saw that their actions did make a difference, and they found themselves reacting somewhat differently to each other. As a result, by the end of Stage 1, Dan and Stu were able to

- Imagine a significantly better state of affairs
- Demonstrate a greater ability and willingness to try new things
- Feel and express more hope for the relationship

Even so, Dan and Stu continued to struggle from time to time. When things got especially tough, they'd revert back to old behaviors, feeling neither comfortable nor confident enough to use the behaviors they were learning. And for good reason: they weren't very good at them yet. Under stress, Dan would grit his teeth and sound impatient every time he asked Stu about his concerns, while Stu would screw up his face and look pained every time he resisted the urge to block Dan.

While all this is to be expected, it creates a dilemma:

- On the one hand, the only way to disrupt a pattern is to try out new actions.
- On the other hand, these new actions will at first look clumsy, awkward, or insincere, leading people to become anything from annoyed to suspicious.

Left unaddressed, this dilemma can slow change down by breeding mistrust and annoyance. But if people understand that this dilemma is a necessary by-product of this stage, they can use it to catapult them into the next stage of change. This is because the dilemma's resolution depends on people becoming so adept at taking new actions that those actions feel natural to them and genuine to others. Yet as the next chapter shows, the only way people can do this is to alter the way they see themselves in relation to each other. That's the core task of the next stage of change, and accomplishing it allows new patterns of interaction to emerge.

NINE

Reframing Each Other

I'm not sure what to do.
I don't want to go into the pool until it's warm,
but it won't be warm until I go in.

——MY GOOD FRIEND MAX SOSSA, EIGHT YEARS OLD AT THE TIME

All too often and much to our dismay, frustrating patterns of interaction persist despite our efforts to change them. The reason is simple: we give short shrift to the interpretations that keep them going. Left to their own devices, these interpretations have a nasty habit of getting stuck in one gear. No matter what someone does, we see him or her the same way. Soon our emotional reactions get caught in a rut, and our interactions start spinning their wheels. From this point on, we're trapped.

As long as Dan sees Stu's blocking as irrational, and Stu sees Dan's lecturing as an effort to impose his will, they'll continue to reenact the same push-block pattern day in and day out. While new actions might disrupt the pattern briefly, the only way they can create a significantly new pattern is by transforming the way the two see each other. In this second stage, Dan and Stu do just that by taking three steps:

Step 1: Freeze Frame
Step 2: Invent New Frames
Step 3: Design Frame Experiments

To complete these steps successfully, Dan and Stu will have to tackle the central paradox of this stage: *they will have to act as if they believe to be true interpretations they "know" to be false.* As the saying goes, seeing is believing. People will shift frames only if they believe it's warranted, and they will believe it's warranted only if they see evidence to that effect. It's not enough, then, simply to imagine a different way of seeing. People must try—through their actions—to *create* experiences that make a new way of seeing come true.

That's why each step in this stage is designed to build just enough confidence for Dan and Stu to *act*—not merely think— outside the box. Only by seeing things differently will they be able to create a new pattern. Let's see how they fare.

Step 1: Freeze Frame

No matter how complex a situation gets, we're rarely at a loss (see Chapter Five). Our minds are sense-making engines, spitting out one interpretation after another so we can put to rest whatever anxiety, confusion, or puzzlement we feel. By the time that mental engine's done selecting, labeling, weighing, and organizing thousands of little data points into one big interpretation, we can't imagine seeing things any other way. Yet if asked, we'd be hard-pressed to say why, because all that interpretive activity takes place outside our awareness—under the hood, so to speak.

STEPS TOWARD CHANGE	
Stage 1: Disrupt	Assess the Relationship
	Map Patterns of Interaction
	Design Action Experiments
Stage 2: Reframe	Freeze Frame
	Invent New Frames
	Design Frame Experiments
Stage 3: Revise	Revisit Past Events
	Restructure Outdated Knowledge
	Return to the Future

This is a big problem. While reactions tend to vary from pattern to pattern within a relationship, the interpretations embedded in those reactions tend to grow more stable with time. As Figure 9.1 depicts, these more stable interpretations—what I call frames—turn patterns of interaction into more enduring relationship structures *without our even realizing it.* Once these frame-based structures take hold, they determine the range and quality of patterns a relationship has at its disposal. By shifting frames—first with effort, then automatically—you shift the structure underlying a relationship, increasing the range and quality of its patterns.

In this first step of Stage 2, we use Dan and Stu's reactions to freeze frame—that is, to bring their frames into the foreground. That allows us to see how, under stress, their frames are pulling them back into old patterns and preventing new ones from emerging (see Figure 9.1).

We did three things to freeze frame. First, we used emotionally charged moments to uncover their reactions; second, we named the frames embedded in those reactions; and finally, we mapped the way their frames intersected to maintain troubling patterns.

175

*"Oh, and your feelings have been trying
to get in touch with you."*

Using Emotionally Charged Moments

People's reactions are much easier to access in the heat of the moment when they're bubbling close to the surface.[1] Like all of us, Dan and Stu had a number of such moments. But an especially hot one occurred while they were discussing how Stu's business unit, Focuspoint, would interact with Merrimac's core business.

Minutes into the discussion, everyone in the room could feel the tension. Looking more and more agitated, Dan spoke faster and faster in an increasingly contemptuous tone of voice about why Stu's view was wrong, layering one reason on top of another. And while Stu said very little—only a sighing "I know, Dan"—his body spoke volumes: he squirmed in his seat; he pushed back his chair; he grimaced; he pulled his chair forward; he grimaced again.

Figure 9.1   Freeze Frame.

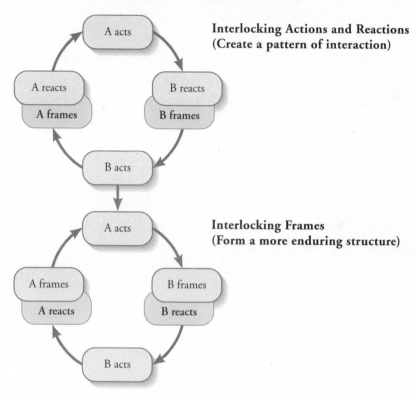

Interlocking Actions and Reactions
(Create a pattern of interaction)

Interlocking Frames
(Form a more enduring structure)

While I could see they were upset, I couldn't see why. To find out, I interrupted them and asked them to describe, as best they could, what they were thinking and feeling. They said the following:[2]

DAN: I'm thinking this is a *really* important issue, and I've got a deep conviction Stu's going in the wrong direction. I feel like I've got to get through to him, but I can't figure out a way to get him off the direction he's headed. So now I'm convinced there's going to be a train wreck, and he's gonna get killed and Focuspoint along with him. So I feel this overwhelming sense of helplessness *and* obligation, at which point I panic.

177

STU: Dan keeps pushing me to do things that make me feel exposed. Today he keeps lecturing me on things I already know, which makes me feel like he thinks I'm stupid! Last week, when I didn't get what he was saying, I figured, "Geez, I really *must* be stupid!" What he was saying wasn't at all obvious to me, even though it was sounding awfully obvious to him—at which point I don't have a clue what to do. Then, I *really* feel exposed, so I just freeze.

These accounts of what was going on inside their heads helped us see how they were reacting to each other in the heat of the moment. While such accounts can never tell us the whole truth and nothing but the truth, they're far better than conjecture alone, and they gave us enough fodder to explore how they were framing each other when upset.[3]

Naming That Frame

With these accounts in hand, we took up three questions:

- How are they seeing (or framing) the situation? What do they think it's about?
- How are they seeing themselves in relation to each other?
- What goals or purposes are they setting for themselves as a result?

In each case, we grounded our search in what was happening in the moment, repeatedly asking, *Given the way Dan and Stu are reacting and acting right now, how must they be framing things?* In searching for an answer, we paid close attention to the language they used, especially to the metaphors, because they reveal a lot about how people frame things. Stu's account, for instance, speaks of Dan *pushing* him, of *making* him feel *stupid* and *exposed*, at which point he *doesn't have a clue what to do,* leading him to *freeze.* Dan's account speaks of Stu *going in the wrong direction,* of the *train wreck* that's coming, of his *overwhelming sense of helplessness and obligation,* leading him to *panic.* In this language, I can discern the broad outlines of their interlocking frames, which I capture in the map that follows.[4]

Mapping Interlocking Frames

As Dan and Stu's frames came into sharper focus, I mapped how they intersected to keep Dan and Stu stuck in the same repetitious pattern despite a mutual desire to break free (see Figure 9.2). Looking at the map, they could see that it really wasn't the other guy who was getting in their way; it was their interlocking frames.

As the map illustrates, Dan and Stu's frames fit together perfectly to keep them stuck. Convinced that Stu is blind to the dangers around him, Dan casts himself in the role of his protector, leading him to work frantically and helplessly to avert a train wreck (he pronounces the "right" answer; he challenges, debates, and discounts Stu's views). Though these actions all follow naturally from his frame, they lead Stu to see himself as the proverbial deer in the headlights—powerless, stupid, and exposed—with an aggressive driver bearing down on him. With no clue what to do, he freezes (he forms a stop sign with his hand to get Dan to back off; he appeals to his vulnerabilities). Like Dan, Stu's actions follow naturally from his framing, but they only reinforce Dan's "deep conviction" that Stu needs his protection.

The point is, as long as their interlocking frames remain intact, Dan and Stu won't be able to create a fundamentally new pattern—no matter how much they want to or how hard they try.

TAKING ACTION
How to Freeze Frame

Now that you've seen how Dan and Stu explored their frames, here's how you can get started on doing the same.

- Stop in the heat of the moment and capture your partner's reactions (and your own) by asking an open-ended question such as, "What's going on?"

- No matter how tempting, don't react to what you hear. You can't tell what your reactions—or your partner's reactions—are saying about you, him, or the relationship. Think of them as "data," and use them to uncover your frames.

- To uncover your frames, ask yourselves, *Given the way I'm reacting, how must I be seeing myself, my partner, the situation, and my purpose in it?*

- Take a few moments to write down your answers before discussing them with each other. Then go back over them to make sure they're connected to what you felt, thought, and did.

- Discuss what you've learned with each other *without justifying your reactions or your frames.* Stay focused on exploring and mapping how your frames intersect to maintain the interlocking actions you mapped in Stage 1.

If, based on your new map, you both want to invest further, proceed to Step 2. If you had trouble taking Step 1, get help before proceeding.

Figure 9.2   Mapping Interlocking Frames.

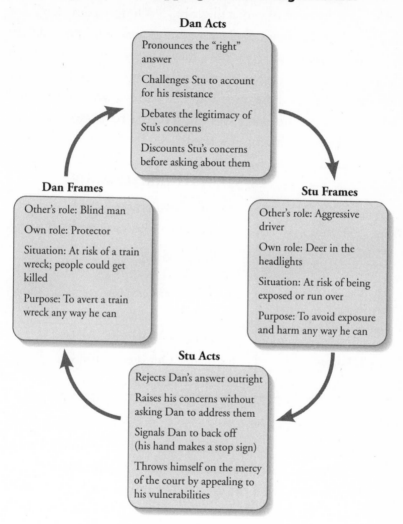

Dan Acts

Pronounces the "right" answer

Challenges Stu to account for his resistance

Debates the legitimacy of Stu's concerns

Discounts Stu's concerns before asking about them

Dan Frames

Other's role: Blind man

Own role: Protector

Situation: At risk of a train wreck; people could get killed

Purpose: To avert a train wreck any way he can

Stu Frames

Other's role: Aggressive driver

Own role: Deer in the headlights

Situation: At risk of being exposed or run over

Purpose: To avoid exposure and harm any way he can

Stu Acts

Rejects Dan's answer outright

Raises his concerns without asking Dan to address them

Signals Dan to back off (his hand makes a stop sign)

Throws himself on the mercy of the court by appealing to his vulnerabilities

Step 2: Invent New Frames

With their map in hand, Dan and Stu could see that their patterns of interaction were a product of their own making, even if they felt those patterns were out of their control. This new awareness opens up new possibilities: perhaps Stu's freezing and blocking is just his way of avoiding exposure, and perhaps Dan's lecturing and debating is his way of protecting Stu. No longer convinced that the way they see things is the way things are, they can entertain new ways of seeing. But right now, they can only see things through their frames. This is when third parties come in handy, because they can see things those caught up in a pattern can't. In Dan and Stu's case, that third party was me. For the next few weeks, we worked together to invent new frames.

	STEPS TOWARD CHANGE		
Stage 1: Disrupt	Assess the Relationship
	Map Patterns of Interaction
	Design Action Experiments
Stage 2: Reframe	Freeze Frame
	Invent New Frames
	Design Frame Experiments
Stage 3: Revise	Revisit Past Events
	Restructure Outdated Knowledge
	Return to the Future

Stu: Reframing Dan

When we began our work together, Dan and Stu said they wanted to create a more reciprocal relationship. Toward that end, Stu suggested that he and Dan do a better job of "containing their reactions." That way, Dan's annoyance and Stu's fears wouldn't conspire to put Stu in a one-down position. On the face of it, his suggestion makes good sense. But containing reactions can only take people so far. Given the way Dan and Stu see each other when they're upset, their reactions are likely to get so intense that they'll flood whatever dam they build.

To set a new pattern in motion, Dan and Stu will need to do something other than contain their reactions. *They will need to reframe how they see themselves in relation to each other, so they don't have those reactions in the first place—or not so intensely.*

But just how is Stu supposed to do *that?* I suggest that before he does anything, he stop and say to himself, "Wait a second. Maybe Dan doesn't think I'm stupid. Maybe he isn't making me feel exposed. Maybe he's just feeling helpless or anxious. Maybe he needs my help." This mental reminder, informed by the map, takes Dan out of the driver's seat and puts Stu in it, where he stands a much better chance of turning their one-way pattern of interaction on its head.

After making the suggestion, I listen carefully to see whether Stu picks up on it, especially since it goes against the grain of his framing *and* more widely shared assumptions about authority relations. Much to my surprise, far from resisting my suggestion, Stu runs with it, saying, "So when I'm feeling lectured and trying to get him to stop, instead I might listen to him and try to help him." "That's right," I tell him. "And when he listens," I add, "he's going to have to listen with a different ear." Stu suggests he understands this, when he goes on to say the following:

STU: So, when I hear that professorial tone of voice, and I feel criticized and exposed, that has to be a sign for me that something is happening with him, independent of me, and I have to stop and find out what's going on with Dan.

At this point, Dan joins the conversation to acknowledge his tone and to clarify what it means:

DAN: I recognize the tone you're describing. It's very censorious. It's like, "Who the hell are you kidding, you stupid idiot." But usually that's a sign that I'm feeling anxious. Unlike you, in those moments, I don't freeze. I just sound critical or angry.

This acknowledgment hits Stu hard. For the first time, he can see that Dan really does need his help, and he readies himself to give it. What Dan does next makes it easier to do.

Dan: Reframing Stu

Despite Dan's formal power, he spends a lot of time feeling helpless. The idea that a CEO feels helpless always comes as a surprise to people lower down in organizations. Most people fantasize that CEOs have endless levers at their disposal with which to make things happen—especially if they, not their CEO, were pulling them. Most people can't see or imagine the constraints under which CEOs operate, and those who do often underestimate their effect. What's more, conventional wisdom is adamant about the role of CEOs. Never show your vulnerabilities. Exude confidence and power. Absorb the anxieties of your subordinates. Never let 'em see you sweat. If you want a friend, get a dog.

In Dan's relationship with Stu, he has an unprecedented opportunity to reframe his role related to subordinates. Right now he's convinced that his subordinates' success depends heavily on his constantly "protecting" them by motivating, pushing, lecturing, inspiring, or cajoling them. Within the confines of this role, he believes it's inappropriate to share his burdens or to ask for emotional support.

When I make this observation, Dan agrees, then offers his own more understated observation in a subdued, almost cynical tone of voice. "I'd say I'm rather conservative when assessing the probability that I'd ever get [emotional support]."

This puts Dan in a terrible position. Convinced that his followers will get hurt without his protection, he must continuously scan his surroundings for signs of danger. Equally convinced that he can't rely on anyone for support, he ends up feeling isolated and burdened. When I suggest as much to Dan, he exclaims, "Exactly!

This job's fairly solitary. There are any number of things I can get agitated about and very few people I can talk to about them."

When I suggest that he might talk to Stu and ask for his help, he takes to the idea, at first haltingly, then with more conviction. "You know, you're right," he says, sounding somewhat surprised. "Stu *can* help. I think I can talk about what I'm feeling fairly freely with Stu, and I know I'd find it helpful." Though a modest idea on the surface, it reflects a new way of seeing: maybe Dan can get help, even from those he's felt compelled to protect.

Dan's ready to take the next step.

TAKING ACTION
How to Invent New Frames

Now that you've seen how Dan and Stu invented new frames, here's what you can do to reframe yourself in relation to others.

- Look at the map created in Step 1, depicting how your frames interlock to keep old patterns in place.

- Consider the self-reinforcing nature of your frames— that is, how your frames lead you to act in ways that reinforce the other's frame of you, and so on.

- Help each other invent frames that will create a new pattern. The best frames are those that make it easier for both of you to be at your best.

- Come up with things that you can say to yourself in the heat of the moment to bring the new frame to mind.

If, on the basis of what you invent, you both want to invest further, proceed to Step 3. If you had any trouble taking Step 2, get help first.

Step 3: Design Frame Experiments

Thinking outside the box—or, better yet, *acting* outside the box—is critical to relationships. Things change, people grow. As a result, opportunities come and go; demands go up and down. In the case of Dan and Stu, the firm's new strategy gives them an opportunity to work more closely together—an opportunity that demands greater interdependence. To take advantage of this opportunity and meet its demands, Dan and Stu want to create a more reciprocal relationship. Toward that end Dan and Stu have already taken two steps: mapping the interlocking frames that put reciprocity out of reach, and inventing frames that promise more give and take. These two steps give them enough conviction to try out new actions. In the third step, they use this conviction to devise *frame experiments*—experiments designed to create experiences that alter their frames, allowing new patterns to emerge.

	STEPS TOWARD CHANGE
	Assess the Relationship
Stage 1: Disrupt	Map Patterns of Interaction
	Design Action Experiments
	Freeze Frame
Stage 2: Reframe	Invent New Frames
	Design Frame Experiments
	Revisit Past Events
Stage 3: Revise	Restructure Outdated Knowledge
	Return to the Future

Taking Small Steps to Make a Big Difference

People often assume that big changes require big moves. But nothing could be farther from the truth. Most people are so fearful of making big moves they do nothing. When it comes to making big changes, all people really need to do is take a series of small steps, each one generating the data and the confidence they need to keep going until bigger changes result.

In Dan and Stu's case, all Dan needs to do—at least at this point—is protect Stu less by censoring himself less; all Stu needs to do is ask Dan what's going on. These two moves will initiate subtle shifts in the informal distribution of burdens and power that defines their relationship. These shifts, while small at first, will invite further moves, eventually creating a pattern with a new look (comrades-in-arms instead of aggressive boss lecturing submissive subordinate), a new feel (less anxious, more connected), and a new function (mutual support instead of unilateral protection).

Though easier to imagine, even the smallest moves can be hard to take, especially if they go against the grain of people's behavioral repertoires or the larger culture. Dan's tendency to lecture and debate in a denigrating tone of voice is deeply ingrained in him *and* shared by many a CEO in our culture. Similarly, Stu's tendency to block anything that might expose his vulnerabilities is also deeply ingrained in him *and* shared by many a subordinate in our culture. To see if we can alter tendencies that are both deeply ingrained and highly shared, we design a frame experiment for Dan and Stu each to try in the hope of creating a new pattern.

Designing Stu's Experiment

By the time we reach this third step, Dan and Stu are ready to try something different. But they're having difficulty imagining what that something might look like, because they're so used to seeing each other in a particular light. This dilemma prompts a perplexed Stu to ask me if there's "some routine" he can use to create a new pattern, something that tells him what to do when Dan raises his voice. He then adds, "I'll figure out how to deal with the emotions

187

once I've got the behavior down, but it would help to have some kind of routine to try."

This comment suggests that Stu intuitively grasps the paradox of this stage. *He's going to have to act his way into feeling differently, not feel his way into acting differently.*[5] When I go on to suggest two routines, we have a short but telling exchange:

DIANA: One routine is to tell yourself, "Oops, Dan is in trouble." But you'll have to say that to yourself whether you believe it or not [chuckling].

STU: [Also chuckling] That's the point. I don't have to believe it. I'm not looking for something I have to believe yet.

DIANA: The next thing is to say out loud, "Dan, what's going on?" That's all. Nothing else.

STU: Okay, I'll give it a try.

Stu is one step ahead of me here. He understands that he doesn't have to believe Dan's in trouble. He simply has to act *as if* he believes it. While Stu's ready to give it a try, I suspect he's more apt to succeed if he can connect the new move to the pattern we're trying to change. With this in mind, I make another observation:

DIANA: When you freeze and say, "Dan, I'm stuck," or "Dan, stop!" you keep the pattern the way it's always been: Dan helping you get unstuck and you responding to all that "help." You completely change that pattern by saying "Dan, what's going on?" and then listening to him. With that one move, you'll learn a lot about how he ticks, and he'll be much more able to recoup.

Like all frame experiments, this one is designed to create experiences that his old framing can't. Up until now, it hadn't occurred to Stu to ask Dan how he's feeling. This made it impossible for him to see Dan's vulnerabilities or to help him. By asking Dan what's going on, Stu will act *as if* Dan needs help, leading him to discover that Dan often feels as anxious as he does, and to see that he (Stu) has the power to help Dan handle his anxieties more effectively. *Once Stu sees and experiences these things for himself, his old frame will shift, leading him to feel and do things differently— without having to think about it. It will just come naturally.*

Designing Dan's Experiment

Dan would be the first to argue that people need an appropriate amount of autonomy and control to succeed. But when pressures mount, he has trouble figuring out how much (or what kind) of control and autonomy is appropriate. Like many CEOs, he often finds himself erring between two extremes. Sometimes he exerts too much control, other times too little. Sometimes he gives people too much autonomy, other times too little. Sometimes these differences reflect a conscious choice; other times—too many times— he feels compelled to do one or the other, because like many CEOs, he feels trapped in a dilemma that goes something like this:

- If I give people more autonomy and exert less control, they're more likely to fail, get hurt, harm others or the business, and ultimately blame me.
- Yet if I give people less autonomy and exert more control, they're more likely to *feel* like a failure, get hurt, harm others or the business, and ultimately blame me.

Caught between two equally troubling options, Dan often finds himself in a no-win situation. The best he can do is bounce back and forth between the two, dissatisfied with the results each option produces. Going forward, any experiment we design will have to address this dilemma and address it better than his current oscillating approach does.

We have our first chance to design such an experiment during a business meeting in which Stu presents some ideas for Focuspoint's new website. Excited by the new technology, Dan jumps in to build on Stu's ideas. Stu, who rebuffs Dan, says his suggestions are too complicated to implement. When Dan asks why, Stu cites imperfections in Merrimac's current accounting system, saying they make Dan's suggestions impractical. Upset that Stu would accept such imperfections, Dan challenges and debates Stu's argument in the same way he has in the past.

Only this time things turn out differently. Before the argument can spin out of control, we stop the action and design a frame experiment for Dan to try. The exchange below begins after I ask Dan how he's hearing Stu, so I can see how he's framing things:

DAN: I hear him putting forth what are to me two equally absurd possibilities. One possibility is that we're going to be *completely* incompetent for the rest of our lives and *never* learn how to keep track of time. I think the financial accounting system *is completely* unacceptable. But it's not going to stay that way, full stop! So if someone can't keep track of time, fire 'em!

DIANA: Tell me the second thing you hear that's "absurd."

DAN: He thinks I'm suggesting that we keep track of every thirty minutes we spend [explains why he's not saying that]. I don't think what I'm suggesting is an enormously complex system. But what Stu's proposing *is* complicated. It will *never* be understood by *anybody* and, since they won't understand it, *they won't buy it.*

DIANA: Let me ask you a question—

DAN: [Interrupting]—I don't understand what the *BIG* problem is—

DIANA: [Interrupting]—And you'll never understand as long as you ask it that way!

DAN: [Laughing] Probably. But I thought you were going to say, "as long as I live."

STU: [Also laughing] I'll tape your mouth shut; maybe then you'll understand!

Dan's hyperbolic statements alone indicate he's *very* upset: "We're going to be *completely* incompetent for the rest of our lives," "It will *never* be understood by *anybody*," "If someone can't keep track of time, fire 'em!" It's easy to see from these cascading exclamations, each one delivered in a contemptuous tone, that Dan's button is pushed. But we can't yet see what that button is or how Stu pushed it.

That's why, when he disdainfully concludes, "I don't understand what the *BIG* problem is" I counter with, "And you'll never understand as long as you ask it that way!" This unexpected response stops Dan in his tracks, and he laughs at himself: "I thought you were going to say, 'as long as I live.'" The tension broken, Stu can now poke fun at Dan ("I'll tape your mouth shut"), while I can use the moment to ask him what he's feeling, prompting him to reflect:

DAN: At first, I felt excited about what Stu was doing and the ideas I had about how he might go about it. Then there was a very short period of genuine mystification, because I didn't understand what the big problem was with what I was suggesting. Then there was a period of, "Oh my God, maybe he's really saying"—and this is the real nightmare scenario—"I, Stu, designed this system around a structural failure of the company," which will only preserve the structural failure of the company. So I'm thinking, "That's not an option." That's a real hot button for me.

191

STU: Yeah, you clearly got mad about something, and I couldn't figure out what it was.

DAN: It was all the stuff about, "I don't trust us to be competent. Maybe in the year 2020, but not now."

STU: I understand. But I don't get mad about stuff like that. So I didn't quite know what you were reacting to or what to react to myself, so it just spiraled until all of a sudden, I felt, "I can't even talk about this now." That's when I shut down. Still, there was a little voice saying, "Why am I shutting down?" Now I can see: it's because of the anger!

From this exchange we learn two things. First, we learn that Stu's comment inadvertently activated Dan's nightmare scenario: the firm's imperfections will persist because people like Stu will design around them, forever dooming the firm to mediocrity. Within the confines of this framing, Dan sees Stu putting the firm at risk, which obligates him to grab the wheel from Stu, so he can put himself in the driver's seat, as he's done in the past. Second, we learn that while Stu can see that Dan's upset, he can't fathom why. All he knows is that Dan is bearing down on him, talking faster and louder with each passing second. And so Stu freezes, as he has in the past.

Only, this time Stu's got this "little voice"—this more reflective voice—asking him why he's shutting down, as if it might not be the only response possible. And this time, Dan turns on a dime, switching from a highly agitated state of mind to a highly reflective one.

In a matter of seconds, we're able to convert a bad moment into an opportunity to deepen our understanding of Dan and Stu's relationship. Dan, who can now talk more freely, can recount with much greater clarity how his feelings went from excitement to mystification to anxiety and anger. He can also name the button

Stu pushed—his "nightmare scenario"—and he can put his finger on what pushed it: Stu's comment about the accounting system.

This gives Stu a much better understanding of Dan. He can now see that Dan's reactions say something not just about him but about Dan: what triggers him and how he reacts. What's more, Stu can see why he shuts down in those moments: "It's because of the anger!" That anger—and the uncertainty about its source—is just too much for him.

With these insights under our belts, we turn to design Dan's frame experiment. No longer caught up in his reactions, Stu steps in to help, offering a suggestion that Dan then builds on:

STU: If you said something like, "People say that all the time around here, and it drives me crazy," I would have said, "Huh. It kind of drives me crazy too, although I don't get that mad about it."

DAN: I was actually trying to do that in the moment, but I couldn't because it took me a while to figure out what I was mad about. Sometimes, I know what I'm mad about but not today.

STU: Yes, I've seen that.

DAN: Maybe it would change the pattern if I just said, "Let me think out loud for a moment," or "Stu, are you saying we have to keep these bad systems until 2020? If you are, what you're saying is making me nervous, because in my mind, you're speaking to something very fundamental."

By helping Dan design his frame experiment, Stu conducts his own. Throughout this exchange, he's helping Dan, not blocking him, which allows him to find out more about what makes Dan tick. He discovers that Dan gets mad about things that don't trouble Stu that much, making it easier for Stu to help Dan in those moments. In the end they come up with something new for

Dan to try: *Say what's going on with you, not what's wrong with others* and *Ask for help if you don't know what's going on with you.*

If Dan makes these moves, he will see for himself that people like Stu can be of help, at least some of the time, and that he

---

TAKING ACTION
How to Design a Frame Experiment

Now that you've seen how we designed Dan and Stu's frame experiments, here's how you can design your own.

- Look at the frames you invented at the beginning of this stage and ask the question, *If I thought this frame was true, what would I say and do?*
- Let your partner know when you're experimenting and ask for his or her help in interpreting the results.
- When interpreting the results, don't look to confirm old frames; look for even subtle shifts—either in what happened or in your experience.
- If you can't find any, look at the actions you took and see if they really do follow from the new frame. If they do, reconsider the frame you invented to see if it really is new or just a slight variation on an old theme.
- Depending on what you learn, either stay the course or go back and redesign the experiment.

If, on the basis of the experiment, you both want to invest further, proceed to Stage 3. If you had difficulty with Stage 2, get help before proceeding.

---

doesn't need to protect them, at least not all of the time. And once Dan sees that, his frame will shift, leading him to relax more and worry less.

Dan and Stu's ability to recoup in this meeting is encouraging, as is their ability to learn from what happened. It indicates that they're ready to recast the way they see themselves in relation to each other and equally ready to conduct experiments to see if they can make that recasting come true. Over the next few months, Stu made a point of asking Dan what was going on when he seemed irritated or impatient, and Dan responded by telling him directly what he was feeling and reflecting with Stu on what those feelings said about the two of them and their relationship. These experiments gradually gave rise to a more reciprocal pattern—one with less protection and more give and take. As a result, they no longer felt as constrained as they had in the past, allowing them to pick up the pace with which Focuspoint got up and running.

Stage 2 Results

By the end of this stage, Dan and Stu's frame experiments lead them to reframe how they see themselves in relation to each other. Stu now sees that when Dan starts debating and lecturing, he's usually feeling helpless and anxious, prompting him to help Dan rather than freeze or block. This leads Dan to revise his view that Stu needs a lot of protection, and it opens up the possibility of getting emotional support from Stu. This relaxes Dan and makes it easier for him to talk about his anxieties directly, which makes them less mystifying and troubling for Stu.

These experiences—experiences they couldn't create within the confines of their old frames—give rise to new ways of seeing and set in motion a more virtuous cycle of interaction.

By the end of this stage, Dan and Stu are able to do several things they couldn't do before:

- Use upsetting moments to learn, so they can change themselves and their interactions more quickly and effectively
- Make progress on controversial tasks more quickly and effectively
- Operate more freely within the relationship (less walking on eggshells) *and* with a greater sense of connection (more camaraderie, less adversity)

As a result, when Dan and Stu differ on substantive matters, they're less likely to get bogged down, and if they do, they're more able to recoup. At the same time, they continue to get into trouble when they're under intense pressure, because this second stage of change poses a dilemma:

- On the one hand, the only way people can reframe one another is to say how they see and feel about each other when they're upset.
- On the other hand, saying how they see and feel about each other when they're upset runs the risk of pushing the other person's buttons and resurrecting into old patterns.

Left unresolved, this dilemma can slow down the pace of change or bring it to a halt. Efforts to resolve it, however, catapult people into the next stage of change. During that stage, people explore what their reactions say about them and how they view the world, *independent* of the other person. As we'll see with Dan and Stu, this exploration prompts them to reexamine and restructure the experiential knowledge they use to frame each other, strengthening their relationship and enhancing their leadership.

TEN

Revising What You Know

If it's hysterical, it's probably historical.

—MICHELLE CONLIN[1]

Dan and Stu came by their quirks honestly: they learned them. Over the years—as they grew up at home, went off to school, and took up careers at work—they converted one experience after another into knowledge about how to handle different people and situations. When they first met, they drew on this *experiential knowledge* to set the structural foundation of their relationship. Now it is only by restructuring that knowledge that they can reset it. This brings us to the third and last paradox of change: *to move forward, they must go back and revisit the knowledge they bring to their relationship.* This chapter shows how Dan and Stu do this by taking three steps:

Step 1: Revisit Past Events
Step 2: Restructure Outdated Knowledge
Step 3: Return to the Future

By revisiting historical events in the context of their relationship, Dan and Stu are able to create new knowledge out of current

197

events. By the end of this stage, they're able to use this knowledge to accelerate their growth and the growth of the firm.

Step 1: Revisit Past Events

Dan and Stu have already traveled a long distance. By the time they reach this last stage of change, they've not only succeeded in disrupting a highly entrenched pattern, they've set a more flexible one in motion. Still, when pressure mounts and time dwindles, they continue to get caught in the old pattern, and they will continue to do so until the newer, more flexible pattern takes hold—that is, when it becomes a more enduring structure. To convert an unstable pattern into a more stable structure, we first explore the events[2] and capture the knowledge that prevent new patterns from taking hold.[3] For continuity's sake, I start with Stu, then turn to Dan.

	STEPS TOWARD CHANGE
	Assess the Relationship
Stage 1: Disrupt	Map Patterns of Interaction
	Design Action Experiments
	Freeze Frame
Stage 2: Reframe	Invent New Frames
	Design Frame Experiments
	Revisit Past Events
Stage 3: Revise	Restructure Outdated Knowledge
	Return to the Future

Stu: Avoiding the Limelight

Like all of us, Stu has a large stock of experiential knowledge at his disposal, only a fraction of which comes into play with Dan. Our attention, then, is focused only on that knowledge he used first to form, then to build the structure underlying his relationship with Dan. Within this structure, you might recall, Stu is prone to view Dan as if he's an aggressive driver relentlessly bearing down on him, while viewing himself as the proverbial deer in the headlights with no means of defending himself. Seeing things this way, Stu feels his only options are to freeze and block or to duck and cover whenever Dan begins to debate or lecture.

To alter this structure, we have to understand what leads Stu to see things this way and not another. After all, while many senior leaders at Merrimac find it difficult to deal with Dan in his worst moments, not everyone views him the way Stu does, nor do they interact with him in the same way. To get at Stu's part in the structure, we need to figure out what Stu brings to the relationship independently of Dan.

What he brings, we discover, is his own history. We got our first glimpse of this history when Dan made what he assumed was a benign suggestion—namely, that Stu hire a "chief of staff" to help him manage his expanding responsibilities. Much to our surprise, the idea horrified Stu, who saw in it everything he dreads about advancing as a leader. In the course of exploring his reactions, we discovered the source of Stu's dread, and along with it, the historical origins of his reactions to Dan and other leaders at Merrimac. We launched our exploration right after Stu made fun of his trepidation:

DIANA: I know you're joking, but what's the trepidation?

STU: It makes me feel overexposed, more important than I am—all the things I don't like: being onstage, being noticed, and being different. I can't just stand up and do what Dan did the other day: give a terrific speech off the top of his head. That stuff just doesn't come naturally to me. I don't know what to do, I know I'm going to look silly, and I know it shows. All my emotions are perfectly visible, and I feel as if everyone's looking at me and laughing at me and I get very nervous.

DIANA: I think *you* start looking at you.

STU: I do!

Stu's account told us a lot about what he does and doesn't "know" when he's onstage, either figuratively or literally: he *knows* he's going to look silly, he *knows* it's going to show, and he doesn't have a clue what to do about it. In his mind every one of his emotions, which he now feels acutely, is there for everyone to see and ridicule. Stu's anxieties start to mount, he starts to fumble, and his worst fears are realized.

A few minutes later, Stu connected his fears to a voice mail he sent Dan earlier in the week, giving us an opportunity to trace their origins.

STU: As I reflect on this fear of being laughed at, something else just popped up, which is that incredibly intemperate voice mail I sent to you, Dan, about my work on New Product. That voice mail is connected to this. You took something that I had a suspicion wasn't going to be very good, and you exposed it to three people who can devastate me. I just made a connection to why I went through the roof. So what led me to go off like that? It's obviously tapping into something that's very close to the surface.

Stu's language is revealing: he feels *exposed* when his *not very good work* is given to people who can *devastate* him, sending him *through the roof.* This way of capturing his experience reveals two things: the theme implicated in his reactions—exposure—and how close to the surface the events are that gave rise to that theme, as his answer to my next question confirms:

DIANA: So what do you imagine is going to happen when they look at your work?

STU: I'll get laughed at. Get rejected. I spent a lot of time having that happen as a kid. Up until I was about thirteen years old, I lived in a neighborhood where everybody had been in the same neighborhood for a long time, and we all went to the same elementary school together. I was a pretty oddball kid, and I wasn't particularly good at athletics, so the other kids would laugh at me and run away. And then there was the classic joke, "Invite Stu over and then not be there." (After a pause) You know, it's funny. I haven't thought about this for years. When you asked why I had a really hard time, my first reaction was, "I don't know why. It just is." But then it came to me: I'm afraid somebody's going to laugh at me just like they did when I was a kid.

Many of us underestimate the residual effects of childhood events like these. But these kinds of events—no matter what they are or why they matter—live on well into adulthood, shaping how we see ourselves and the people around us. While the events themselves may fade into the fog of memory, the feelings they generate often remain as sharp as the moment they occurred, as Stu suggested when he went on to say the following:

STU: I don't remember everything that happened exactly, but I do remember the humiliation and the anger, and I have a very keen sense of the degree to which children are, for the most part, immensely cruel creatures. I hated childhood. I was always an outcast.

You can see in these two remarks what Stu took from his childhood: that he's an oddball, an outcast, while his peers are immensely cruel creatures. This conception of himself in relation to others lives on into the present despite his becoming a highly respected and well-liked head of a successful business unit. Had Stu not eventually learned how to navigate his childhood circumstances successfully, he wouldn't have made it that far. But he did. In fact, by the time he was seventeen, he'd managed to transform himself from an outcast into a popular success, working on the school paper, getting good grades, and winning wrestling matches. "All of a sudden, I was worth talking to," he says with a note of disdain, then adds the following:

STU: That whole experience, combined with staying out of trouble with my father, led me to think, "Don't get noticed. If you get noticed, somebody's going to laugh at you, especially if you make a mistake or you look weird." I still have this intense dislike of being laughed at, and I still have a huge amount of contempt for these people.

Stu's intense dislike of being laughed at is matched only by his equally intense conviction that it's inevitable, and that some people—those who resemble his peers at school or his father at home—have the power to devastate him. That conviction is directly connected to his relationship with Dan and to his current model of success as a leader:

STU: My model for success is, "Never let anyone see you coming." When I ended up at the top of my class in college, people were literally saying, "Where did *he* come from?" That's just fine with me. I like coming up from behind. It feels safer. I work hard, I keep my head down, I don't bother people, and I show up at the top. I hate being out front. I hate it viscerally.

You can see in Stu's account how the theme of exposure emerged. You can also see how this theme, once it had taken hold, activated intense emotions—fear, anger, contempt—all of which acted like Velcro, both attracting and attaching to it:

- *Stories:* When I was a kid, other kids invited me over, then wouldn't be there.
- *Propositions:* If you get noticed, somebody will laugh at you, and if you work hard, keep your head down, and don't bother people, you will show up at the top.
- *Moral Values:* Looking more important than you are is bad, coming up from behind is good, mistakes are bad, success is good.
- *Action Strategies:* Stay out of trouble and don't get noticed.

This stock of knowledge may have served Stu well in the past, but it was interfering with his relationships and with his development as a leader now. Understanding this, Stu was eager to see if he could restructure this knowledge. But before illustrating how he did so, let's first look at the events that shaped Dan's life, what he made of those events, and their effect on his relationship with Stu.

Dan: Protecting Against Catastrophic Loss

In turning to Dan, we set out to understand where his debating and lecturing behavior came from. We could see that Stu's freezing and blocking triggered these behaviors, but we couldn't see what led Dan to respond this way and not another. And while we now understood that Dan's anger was rooted in anxiety, we didn't understand where that anxiety came from. We knew Dan worried about people getting hurt and perhaps blaming him, but what led him to worry about that and not something else? And what led him to convert his worry into those contemptuous lectures tailor-made to push Stu's buttons?

Until we understood this, Dan was apt to revert to old patterns under stress. We got our first chance to explore these questions during a meeting in which I broached my puzzlement:

DIANA: This sensitivity to people getting hurt—and this feeling compelled to do something about it—you have to ask yourself the question, What did you learn such that you're left with this idea that people will get hurt and that only you can do something about it?

In turning to this question, Dan recounted not a single event but two streams of events, each one raising the specter of loss and the need to rely on himself, unprotected by others. The first set of events took place when he was a child living with his family in a Third World country:

DAN: When I was a little kid, I mostly worried—not that something bad would happen *from* my parents—but that something bad would happen *to* my parents. If I got a "D" on my report card, yes, I was worried on that day about their reaction. But my big fear was that my parents would get killed and I'd be left without them. My first memory of life—any memory I have—is of dead bodies. I can date it almost to the day. I was two years old.

Dan went on to recount how his family had traveled that day from the country's capital to a summer resort, accompanied by a military convoy due to recent fighting between the government and communist guerrillas. A few hours into the drive, the convoy came to a halt:

DAN: Everyone was sitting there in these clanking jeeps armed with machine guns. It was horribly hot. Finally, a guy came down the line, tapping on the windows, telling us, "We'll be here for awhile. You can get out." As we got out, on the ground were six to nine people lying there, stretched out like in Vietnam-style pictures, all of them dead, one of them with a bullet in his head. We all looked at them for a while, then drove away. That's the first memory I have.

After saying "the whole thing was much more interesting than scary," he went on:

DAN: The searing memories—the ones that are terrifying—aren't actually of dead people, because they're already dead. It's these horribly deformed people—the people with flies all over their suppurating stumps. I remember walking on these sidewalks. You'd know it's coming. They're on the sidewalk, and they're begging. You're going to have to walk right by them, and you're going to be two feet away, although when you're a kid, you're even closer. Half the time the adults are in some chitchat, and you're not sure they even notice. Even now, I get the willies a little bit when I think about it, although not really. Now there are the shades that come down over my eyes.

But before those shades descended, what did he make of this, and how did he feel about it?

DAN: You worried. You're in a part of the world where you see dead bodies, and you aren't really sure what your parents are doing. They'd simply go out, and you'd stay home. I spent a lot of time worrying about whether my parents would come home, whether something might happen to them. I was always very glad they got home.

After months of making his way around suppurating stumps and the occasional dead body, Dan concluded that the world is a pretty dangerous place. This conclusion—coupled with the specter of losing his parents—left Dan worried. He couldn't help but imagine the worst. He may even have believed that by imagining the worst, he could stop the worst from happening. After all, whenever he worried, his parents came home.

Small wonder Dan entered adulthood with a nonstop engine of anxiety. But where and how did he learn to convert that anxiety into contempt? Later on in the same meeting, we got the beginnings of an answer when Dan recounted a second stream of events:

DAN: I always felt loved by my parents. But as far back as I can remember my father could be very caustic and emotional in his criticism. I don't know whether I ever consciously worried I would lose his love, but I sure as hell wanted his respect, and I *knew* I could lose that, especially when he'd say that bewildered, "How could you think *that*?!"

The tone with which Dan mimicked his father was uncanny, almost eerie: it's the very tone he uses when *he's* anxious. When I pointed this out, Dan stopped in his tracks. "I guess I *am* my father at times," he told me. "While I hate and fear the idea, I also feel a great sense of relief. It's like, 'Oh, is that what it is?' At least now I can think about it." In thinking about it, we went on to explore what led Dan to adopt his father's voice as his own, piecing together the account paraphrased here:

Early on, like most sons, Dan cherished his relationship with his father and felt secure in his affections. He spoke with tenderness about how his dad, a warm and emotional man, would hold his hand as they walked down the street, giving each other a quick squeeze—their secret way of saying "I love you." When it came to his respect, however, things felt more tenuous.

Throughout Dan's childhood, his dad held him to exacting standards, expected exceptional performance at school, and demanded compliance through example and critique.

His dad, who treated people graciously no matter their social status, elicited admiration and respect everywhere he went. As a parent, he expected no less of his kids, and he let them know it whenever they fell short. Dan, ever anxious to secure his dad's respect, worked hard to live up to his expectations and dreaded his admonishments, especially when they were delivered in that slightly bewildered, contemptuous tone of voice he used when disappointed.

As Dan grew older, he grew tired of his dad's caustic comments, and like many teenagers, felt they were unfair and unreasonable. No longer willing to take it, Dan started to fight back. Figuring the best defense was a good offense, he started to lash out at his dad with the same caustic, contemptuous tone his dad used with him. Much to Dan's surprise, his father backed down. Soon Dan found himself winning arguments he used to lose, making it harder and harder for his dad to assert his authority.

During this same time, his father got increasingly caught up in his own midlife troubles. He seemed more interested in his own happiness than in his children's welfare—at least in Dan's eyes—and Dan felt abandoned and let down. Outraged by his dad's apparent selfishness, Dan stopped seeing his father as the loving dad with whom he'd held hands. Now all he saw was an unreliable, self-indulgent kid masquerading as an adult. At this point, as far as Dan was concerned, his dad was gone; he could no longer rely on him.

The specter of loss in a dangerous land, combined with the loss of his father, had a profound effect on Dan, eventually giving rise to the twin themes of loss and reliability. Now any time circumstances activate these themes, Dan experiences anxiety, which he instantly converts into the anger and contempt he first saw in his father, then adopted as his own. As was the case with Stu, these emotions act like Velcro, simultaneously attracting and attaching to his themes a rich stock of knowledge, including the following:

- *Stories:* When I was a kid, I lived amid suffering and violence, where my parents were at risk of getting killed any time they went out.
- *Propositions:* If you want to win an argument or protect your esteem, discount and denigrate others before they discount and denigrate you. If you constantly imagine the worst, you can prevent it from happening. And, if you want someone to rely on, get a dog; people will just let you down.
- *Moral Values:* People in power who act like self-sufficient adults are good; those who act like self-indulgent kids are bad. Depending on oneself is good; depending on others is bad. Taking care of others is good; taking care of yourself is selfish.
- *Action Strategies:* Never rely on anyone if you can avoid it, especially men. Take care of unreliable others as you wish they'd take care of you. Anticipate how others will let you down and inoculate yourself against any disappointment.

This stock of knowledge may have served Dan well in the past, but as Merrimac grew—and along with it, Dan's need to rely on others—it was breaking down. It was time to see if he could restructure this knowledge in the context of his relationship with Stu and others at Merrimac.

TAKING ACTION
How to Revisit Past Events

Now that you've seen what Dan and Stu did to revisit past events and to capture their experiential knowledge, here's how you can take this step:

- Figure out what kind of help you need to make the most of this step and be sure to get it.

- With that help, identify the historical events that most remind you of this relationship.

- Write down what happened in those earlier moments and what you took or learned from them. Put aside what you wrote for twenty-four hours.

- Go back and read what you wrote; then extract from your account any stories, propositions, values, and practical strategies you see, as I did here.

- Explore how the knowledge you've built out of past experience is affecting your development and your relationships, including this one.

If you think your past is jeopardizing your success or the success of key relationships, proceed to Step 2—but only after lining up the help you'll need to make the most of it.

Step 2: Restructure Outdated Knowledge

Now that we had a better window onto the knowledge Dan and Stu used to form their relationship, we were ready to take the next step: resetting the basis of their relationship by restructuring the experiential knowledge they bring to it. To help Dan and Stu take this step, I created several documents that were based on what you've just read. With these documents in hand, we were able to consider two questions: where is their experiential knowledge breaking down, and how can we restructure it so that it better fits their current circumstances and abilities? The following pages recount where these questions led us.

	STEPS TOWARD CHANGE	
Stage 1: Disrupt	Assess the Relationship	
	Map Patterns of Interaction	
	Design Action Experiments	
Stage 2: Reframe	Freeze Frame	
	Invent New Frames	
	Design Frame Experiments	
Stage 3: Revise	Revisit Past Events	
	Restructure Outdated Knowledge	
	Return to the Future	

Stu: Turning the Light on Others

We started out by asking how Stu's knowledge was holding up. Not so well, we quickly discovered. Indeed, this became glaringly obvious as soon as Stu connected what he'd learned so far to his long-standing difficulties with George Quipsalot, another leader at Merrimac.

STU: This is why I have so much trouble with George: he can make fun of me in a way that makes me feel defenseless. I don't think he intends to be cruel, and I don't think he has a clue that he makes my skin crawl. But when he gets really sarcastic, he's my worst nightmare from high school: popular, always has something to say, never at a loss. Completely my opposite.

210

In Stu's nightmarish way of seeing things, he and George *are* complete opposites: George is popular, Stu's an outcast; George is never at a loss, Stu's always at a loss; George always has something to say, Stu never has anything to say. So even though you'd be hard-pressed to find a more popular leader at Merrimac, or one who had more to say, Stu still sees himself as that oddball kid surrounded by people all too ready to make fun of him.

This example, fresh in Stu's mind, gave us our first opportunity to entertain three possibilities that had never occurred to Stu. First, Stu's "come from behind" theory, while serving him well in the past, was now breaking down under the pressures of a role that required him to go onstage and to look important—in short, to be exposed. Second, the behavior Stu saw as evidence of George's cruelty might just as easily be viewed as evidence of his vulnerabilities. Third, although Stu may have been defenseless as a kid, he was far from defenseless now. In point of fact, he was a man of many talents with a remarkable intellect and a good deal of social and political capital.

Stu readily accepted the first two ideas: that his "come from behind" theory wouldn't work in his new role and that sarcasm could indicate vulnerability as much as cruelty. But he had trouble accepting the notion that he (Stu) wasn't defenseless. "The only way I know how to defend myself," he told us, "is to put up an impenetrable shield."

Dan disagreed. "I wouldn't underestimate the degree to which people see you as a pretty formidable debater," he told him. "When you're in your comfort zone, the other person has to watch out, or he may lose." He then drove the point home by returning to George:

DAN: Sometimes when George gets sarcastic, it's like one of those classic tricks: he's losing the game, and so he knocks the table over. In an argument with you, it's, "Say something sarcastic about Stu, so he'll dissolve and leave me alone." I'm not saying he does it consciously, but I think he's got great antennae, and he'll do the "Hey, look at that bird!" as a way of distracting you while he regroups and tries to figure out what to do next.

STU: [After a brief pause] What you just said clicked seriously.

By placing George in a one-down position relative to Stu, Dan not only gave Stu another way of seeing George, he gave him another way of seeing himself relative to George: it was Stu, not George, who was winning the game! What's more, Stu's arguments were so powerful that the other guy—in this case, George—had to resort to card tricks to regain the upper hand. The implication was clear. It was no longer, "If you want to win the game, keep your head down and stay out of trouble." It was more like, "If you want to win the game, don't fall for the card trick." This time, the recasting worked: what Dan said "clicked seriously."

Stu now saw that his success as a leader would, in part, depend on his putting the past where it belonged: in the past. This made his relationship with Dan critical, because that relationship was slowly but surely helping him restructure how he saw himself in relation to people in power, as he illustrated a few weeks later with the following story:

STU: Last week I got into a tough discussion with Jack Gregory, a very smart CEO who's very much a debater. We'd been debating whether he should buy another company, and for a whole host of reasons, I thought it was a bad idea and told him so, at which point, he turned to me and said, "If the answer isn't buying another company to get bigger, what are we supposed to do? You haven't proved that what you suggest will work or is feasible." At first, I broke out in a sweat. But then

I said to myself, "No, this guy's struggling with something. He doesn't know he's putting me in a box by asking me to prove something that can't be proved. Maybe if I find out what he's worried about, we start to get out of the box."

What's notable about this vignette isn't so much that Stu found a way out of an adversarial dynamic, although he did. It's that he was able to shift his attention away from his vulnerabilities and onto the other guy's struggles. From this new vantage point, he could see a way out of the box: he didn't have to erect an impenetrable shield; he could ask what was worrying the CEO.

Out of this experience and others like it, Stu gradually restructured his concept of himself in relationship to others. In each case, he revised outdated knowledge and built new knowledge about how to conduct himself as a leader in relationship to others. No longer seeing either his peers or his superiors as the cruel or all-powerful bullies from his childhood, he understood that people like Dan, George, and Jack have their own vulnerabilities. More important, he came to see that he was neither defenseless nor at a loss for words, but someone capable of talking his way out of boxes and even helping others when *they're* at a loss.

As this suggests, Stu was able to generalize from his relationship with Dan to other relationships like those with Jack and George. In the next step, this process of generalization accelerates and deepens. But before seeing how, let's take a look at what Dan did to restructure the knowledge he'd built around the theme of reliability.

Dan: Learning to Rely on Others

For twenty years Merrimac has been growing quickly in size and complexity, putting more and more pressure on Dan's role at the center of the firm. From a structural perspective the problem was as simple as it was hard to solve: too many people were looking to him for too much, while he was looking to too few people for too little. The balance of trade—that delicate exchange of give-and-take—is out of whack, and it's putting a ceiling on the growth of the firm and its leaders, including Dan. Like most problems of this kind, it has many causes. But one of the most important ones is the implicit premise that *it's dangerous to rely on people,* along with the associated strategy to *always be on guard to make sure really bad things don't happen.* Dan talked about this early on:

DAN: You have to be suspicious of the people you rely on. It's dangerous not to be, because people have weaknesses. Even strong people have weaknesses.... If I were to hold forth on whether you should be intimate as a leader, I'd say, "Look. One of the things you can't do is be unilaterally intimate with people. As a leader, that's not going to work, because you're either going to put stuff on them they can't deal with, and, despite their best efforts, they will become unproductive, or they will take what you have given them and abuse someone with it. On average, they'll not be able to handle it. You have to be selective."

Most people would agree that you have to be selective. The trouble is, when assessing someone's reliability, many people make two mistakes. The first is to compare the other person's weaknesses to their strengths, making the person *look* a lot less reliable. The second and less-detectable mistake is to act in ways that bring out the worst in the other person, as Dan did with Stu, making the other person *act* less reliably.

Having observed Dan make both errors, I might have suggested, as I initially did, that he discuss his doubts and concerns more openly with people to sort through any biases he might have and to put some of his worries to rest. But given the state of his relationships—and his concept of his role relative to others—such advice, by itself, wasn't very practical, as Dan demonstrated:

DAN: I *know* what's going to happen. They'll probably cave in and collapse. They'll say, "Dan thinks so little of me" or "I'm so hapless" or "I can't get this. I'm going to give up." "I'm going to go somewhere else." "I'm going to go off in a corner and die."

Notice his line of thinking here. If he tells people what he really thinks, he *knows* what's going to happen. Either they'll "die," as he worried his parents might, or they'll "cave in and collapse," as his father did. Either way, he can't rely on them. This makes talking openly about doubts, concerns, and criticisms a very weighty matter, as Dan himself goes on to explain:

DAN: Deciding whether to proceed is a very heavy decision. It's like the judge who's thinking about whether to sign a death sentence: do I really want to do that? A lot of these people will leave, and for some of them, it's absolutely the wrong thing to do. They're better off here. What you want is for them to accept something as real that they don't want to face. What you don't want is for them to blow their brains out. But you can make them do that pretty easily. I've seen it happen frequently.

Dan talks here as if he has the power, as judge, to determine whether someone lives or dies. If he tells people the truth, they'll leave, which is the equivalent of blowing their brains out. Since he's seen it "happen frequently," he's trapped. And since he can "make them do it pretty easily," he can't get out of that trap without killing someone.

To free himself, Dan was going to have to see that the problem, which he located exclusively outside of himself, also resided inside

215

his head—that is, in the knowledge he'd built out of experience. This knowledge primed him to see himself (as a leader), his followers, and stressful situations in a particularly lethal and anxiety-producing light *and* to act accordingly, signaling to people that they could rely on him while telling himself he couldn't rely on them. Given the lopsided nature of this implicit contract, Dan found exactly what he expected to find: people looking to him for reassurance or motivation, people getting upset when he doesn't provide it, and people blaming him for the upset. No surprise that by the time we began our work together, Dan couldn't count on most of the people around him.

This reality, which is partly of Dan's making, poses a dilemma. If I simply tell him to rely more on others, I'll be doing to Dan what everyone else is doing: relying on him to bear a disproportionate share of the burden for solving the problem.

This is why the work with Stu is so important, and why it's so important that Stu take the lead even though he's the nominal follower. Here's someone who's ready to challenge Dan's way of thinking while remaining open to challenge himself. The fact that Stu can still get anxious and upset from time to time is all for the better, because—despite his imperfections—he doesn't leave and he doesn't collapse, nor does he die or kill anyone else. He simply hangs in there, earning Dan's respect and the right to challenge the way Dan thinks:

STU: I think you expect certain things of leaders and you get particularly mad when people don't act that way.

DAN: That's probably true, but I'm trying to figure out who you've got in mind versus who I have in mind when you say that.

STU: [Lists the names of people] Including me, on occasion, although not much until recently, given I was coming up from behind [laughing].

Dan: [Also laughing] That's helpful. That's a very important group of people.

Stu: The interesting thing for me is that you start out cutting these people a lot of slack, but then it tips, and you don't cut them *any* slack *at all.* Oftentimes it's unclear where your tipping point is [goes on to give an example].

Observations like these, coming from Stu, are much more powerful than any I can make, because they communicate two messages simultaneously. First, they tell Dan that he can count on Stu to tell him the truth without complaining or blaming him. Thus the medium is the message: Stu's matter-of-fact but warm tone, neither condemning nor softening what he sees and says, commands Dan's attention and respect. Second, the observations themselves focus on Dan's "expectations" and on Dan's "tipping point," putting a spotlight on Dan's internal workings for the first time. This combination of messages—*you can rely on me* and *let's take a look at you*—turn Dan's attention to what goes on inside his head.

In shifting to what goes on inside Dan's head, we discussed three documents, in which I reconstructed the experiential knowledge Dan had built around the theme of reliability. The first document, based on the data you see in this chapter, captured Dan's personal narrative around reliability. According to this narrative, the only way Dan can ensure a happy ending is to do all he can to protect people whose character flaws blind them to the dangers around them. In reality, things don't turn out so well. Once enacted, all this narrative leaves Dan feeling is burdened, resentful, and trapped at the center of the Merrimac universe.

Still, as soon as someone's reliability is called into question, Dan fills in the blanks of this skeletal narrative with specific names and circumstances, making old sense of current events. No matter how problematic the consequences—and they are quite problematic—Dan will resist change until he sees that it isn't the situation alone that dictates his choices and his actions; it's his personal narrative. *That narrative, and the knowledge he's built on it, governs what he can and cannot see in situations and what he can and cannot make out of them as a result.*

Seeing the narrative on paper, Dan paused to reconsider his experience as a leader: perhaps the results he gets aren't inevitable; perhaps they're partly of his making. This possibility provided Dan the impetus to explore the same questions we asked of Stu:

- In what ways, if any, is this narrative breaking down and under what circumstances?
- What results would other narratives create, if he acted upon them as if they were true?

To answer the first question, we didn't need to look very far. Dan's mounting sense of frustration was enough to tell him that, under the pressure of growth, his character in the narrative was struggling. At the same time, our work with Stu and other senior leaders provided compelling evidence that he could in fact rely not on everyone for everything but on a select number of people for different things and that the deathly consequences he imagined were highly unlikely.

Dan had no difficulty seeing all of this. But the second question—the question of alternatives—is far trickier, because here we run into Dan's *implicit theory of learning.* For years Dan has gone beyond the call of duty in his efforts to develop people, investing more in people's learning than any CEO I've ever met. These efforts, partly driven by the firm's need for more leaders, were informed by a widely shared and highly problematic cultural belief that learners are empty vessels in need of filling. According to this belief, all you have to do when developing someone—figuratively speaking, anyway—is pry open their heads and pour in what you know. This makes endless lectures not only reasonable but downright necessary.[4]

Upon this cultural belief, Dan built his own unique theory of learning, using his narrative about reliability to give that belief its own peculiar twist. As a result, when people fail to act like empty vessels—say, by raising doubts or by differing with him—he views them through the lens of his narrative, imagining them to be self-indulgent kids, too blind or too full of hubris to learn quickly. If you want to speed up learning, says his implicit theory, you have to work harder and harder—and faster and faster—to *get* people to see this or that, lecturing them here, debating them there. Before you know it, learning becomes a life-or-death struggle, in which Dan feels compelled to cajole or subtly coerce people into adopting his view. Once in the grip of this theory, Dan doesn't realize that far from speeding up development, he is slowing it down.

This second document, which drove home the downside of his theory, made Dan eager to try an alternative. But he was so trapped in his informal role—and in the self-fulfilling prophecies it created—he was at a loss. What could he actually *do* differently, he asked, to work his way out of his current role as a leader? A third document addressed this question by suggesting what Dan might do to transform the narratives and theories that undermined his leadership and his relationships (see Table 10.1). On the left side is his current way of operating when his reliability button is pushed. On the right is an alternative based on a different narrative and theory. By giving Dan practical suggestions for what he might do when his button is pushed, the document helped him revisit and revise what he "knew" to be true in those moments.

Table 10.1   Action Sequences.

Current Action Sequence	Alternative Action Sequence
You get a small snippet of data that someone may not be learning fast or well enough, getting himself, you, or the firm into trouble as a result.	You get a small snippet of data that someone may not be learning fast or well enough, getting himself, you, or the firm into trouble as a result.

Current Action Sequence:

- You start interpreting these data, using your narrative about reliability to fill in the gaps and to imagine a disastrous ending.
- Your hypervigilant radar now turned on, you start looking for evidence that suggests the ending you fear most will come to pass.
- The more evidence you see and the less counterevidence you notice, the more your anxiety mounts.
- The more your anxiety mounts, the more people look like the two-dimensional characters in your narrative: self-indulgent kids incapable of taking care of themselves or anyone else.
- To save the day, as your character in the narrative dictates, you work behind the scenes to protect the firm, others, and yourself from harm.

Alternative Action Sequence:

- You discuss what you're seeing—and any worries it creates—with people who will neither collude with your view nor dismiss it outright.
- You ask people for evidence that might moderate your concerns, not just confirm them, helping you develop a more nuanced view of the person.
- The more nuanced your view, the more able you are to discuss your concerns productively with that person.
- The more productively you discuss your concerns, the more clearly you each see what those concerns are saying about you and what they're saying about the other person.
- No longer seeing the other person as a problem you must solve, you're able to work together to address any concerns you have about each other.

(continued)

Table 10.1 *(Continued)*

Current Action Sequence	Alternative Action Sequence
• When others continue grimly on in blind oblivion, you feel less respect for them and the need to speak the truth mounts.	• As you work together to address your respective concerns, you take increasing responsibility for helping each other address them.
• When you are finally compelled to speak, weeks or months of pent-up anxiety and frustration leak or blurt out.	• No longer feeling compelled to speak or not speak, you're free to address things as they arise.
• Caught unaware, the other person gets very upset, confirming your view they can't take the "truth," and resigning you to the inevitability of a deadly crash.	• More aware and less constrained, you feel more connected to each other and more confident that you can create a good outcome together.

By focusing on Dan and Stu's relationship, and not on Dan alone, Dan learned that he could in fact rely on Stu, whose own changes made that reliance tenable.[5] With each person's progress now accelerating the other's, Dan came to see Stu and other members of his team in a new light. Eighteen months later, Dan told me in a somewhat surprised tone of voice that he no longer felt anxious or mad about other people's shortcomings or limits. "I just don't have the same emotional agita," he said. "Even when people make mistakes, I'm not annoyed. In fact, I'm sitting here asking myself, 'Why aren't I mad about this?' Well, I'm just not." His next set of reflections suggest why:

DAN: My relationship with these guys has moved from a source of worry to a source of satisfaction, partly because I talk with them more and understand them better, but partly because objectively, they're in a better place. I used to feel in the classic lifeguard situation where you're trying to save people who are trying to pull you under. That feeling just no longer exists. I no longer feel that they have to be saved or that I have to save them.

By focusing on Dan's relationship, and not on Dan alone, we get this felicitous mixture of others getting better and his understanding of them getting better—all of it freeing Dan up to restructure the knowledge that's been telling him for years, *You've got to save these guys.* No longer compelled to save people—and no longer mad or anxious that he can't—he can reset his relationships on a more flexible basis. Freer to respond to them in any number of ways, he's able to derive satisfaction from his relationships and the greater mutuality they afford.

"Sir, the following paradigm shifts occurred while you were out."

TAKING ACTION

How to Restructure Experiential Knowledge

Now that you've seen what Dan and Stu did to restructure their experiential knowledge, here's how you can do the same:

- Figure out what kind of help you need to make the most of these steps, and be sure to get it.
- Ask yourself, In what ways are my circumstances and relationships different now from what I experienced earlier in life?
- Ask yourself, In what ways am I different today than I was earlier in life (aside from my waistline)?
- Review the stories, propositions, values, and strategies you wrote down in Step 1.
- Ask yourself, How would I revise my stories, propositions, values, and strategies so they better fit my relationships and circumstances today?
- Write down what you would like to do differently in your most important relationships as a result of what you've learned.

    Proceed to the next and last step to consolidate the changes you've made so far and to redefine your relationship on a new basis.

Step 3: Return to the Future

To sustain progress without my help, Dan must continue to rely on others, and Stu must continue to brave the limelight, *even when events press long and hard on old experiential knowledge.* This third step addresses the question of sustainability under pressure by turning our attention back to the future. Here we consolidate the gains we've made, define new objectives, anticipate new challenges, and set the terms of a new relationship.

	STEPS TOWARD CHANGE
Stage 1: Disrupt	Assess the Relationship
	Map Patterns of Interaction
	Design Action Experiments
Stage 2: Reframe	Freeze Frame
	Invent New Frames
	Design Frame Experiments
Stage 3: Revise	Revisit Past Events
	Restructure Outdated Knowledge
	Return to the Future

Consolidating Gains

Eighteen months into our work together, I put together a notebook that showed how far Stu and Dan had come. On the business front, it catalogued their various accomplishments: Stu successfully launching his own business; Dan making good headway on the group strategy; the two of them demonstrating to others how they could launch their own business quickly and well. On the relationship front, it used transcripts to illustrate the greater reciprocity characterizing their relationship: Stu seeking to help Dan while challenging him more productively; Dan seeking to understand Stu's concerns while offering counsel Stu could use.

All these data suggested to us that their investment was paying off. The pattern of interaction that occasionally derailed them—Dan lecturing and debating, Stu blocking and hiding—was no longer wielding the same power. Both Dan and Stu were now able to see, interrupt, and alter the pattern before it wreaked havoc. More important, they were able to help each other put a more satisfying pattern in motion. At this point, their relationship would never be the same. Built on a commitment to learning, and no longer on a foundation of protection, it could only grow stronger with time.

Defining New Objectives and Anticipating Future Challenges

Despite these gains—perhaps because of them—Dan and Stu still had their work cut out for them. Even the best relationships confront setbacks, upsets, and failures. Besides, nothing stays the same. As long as Merrimac continued to grow and change, they'd have to as well.

That's why, far from bringing things to a close, this last step launched the work yet to be done. In taking this step, Dan and Stu defined new objectives and identified the challenges they'd face as they tried to achieve them. Dan went first, saying he wanted to gradually extricate himself from the center of the firm and transfer more leadership to others. Stu said he wanted to play a more central role in the firm, taking on leadership within the group, not just his unit.

Both objectives are developmentally appropriate. At this point in Dan's life and in the life of the firm, Dan *should* be looking to extricate himself from the center of Merrimac's universe. Similarly, Stu should be looking to step up and take more leadership. What's more, the two objectives go hand-in-hand: Stu's stepping up making it easier for Dan to extricate himself, and Dan's extricating himself making it easier for Stu to step up.

But nothing in real life is ever as easy as it looks on paper. Getting from here to there will undoubtedly pose challenges. Best to anticipate what those are, we reckoned, so we could figure out ahead of time how Dan and Stu might handle them. In thinking together, we anticipated that Dan would face some version of the following challenges:

- Given that Dan had operated at the center of the Merrimac universe since its inception, most people would continue to expect him to deliver the goods—whether those goods took the form of a pep talk, a prized resource, much-needed protection, or special mentoring. As frustrated as people might have been with the bottlenecks caused by Dan's centrality, they would be even more frustrated when they could no longer count on it.

- If people reacted poorly to the changes Dan was making in his role—and some inevitably would—they could easily resurrect his implicit premise (*It's dangerous to rely on people*) and his implicit strategy (*Always be on guard to make sure really bad things don't happen*), luring him back into the center where he would feel trapped once again.

- If Dan started to feel trapped, his natural affection and respect for people would come under threat, and he'd find it harder to build the kind of collegial relationships that he wanted and that a growing professional firm needed to succeed.

In turning to Stu, we thought he'd have to master some version of the following challenges:

- As Focuspoint became more important to the group, Stu would face substantive business challenges and a related set of relationship challenges. On the business front, he'd need to figure out where the most promising synergies lay within the group and how best to exploit them; on the relationship front, he'd need to keep key relationships on a synergistic track, even when feeling exposed or ridiculed.

- For Stu, this would be tricky at best. As "the poster child" for building new entities within the group, Stu now had a great deal of visibility with key people in the company, putting him right smack in the middle of powerful, fast-talking people. If these people ridiculed Stu out of their own insecurities, it could easily resurrect Stu's implicit premise that he should avoid the limelight, because there lies nothing but ridicule and sorrow.

- If Stu started to feel caught in other people's headlights, his desire and ability to take leadership at a group level would plummet, as would his partnership with Dan.

Setting the Terms of a New Relationship

Far from discouraging them, these challenges strengthened Dan and Stu's resolve to continue working on their relationship. To give ballast to that resolve, they made a series of commitments that defined how they wanted their informal relationship to look going forward. Among these commitments were the following:

- Instead of a one-way relationship in which Dan pronounced and Stu denounced, they would take mutual responsibility for creating a two-way dynamic.
- To create that two-way dynamic, they would join together to find solutions that work for both of them (instead of Dan's pushing and Stu's blocking).
- To move forward together, they would challenge each other to grow *while* providing each other the support they would need to sustain that growth under pressure.
- To challenge and support each other, they would acknowledge and reflect on their reactions while helping each other handle them more constructively.

Undoubtedly, they would need help from time to time. But by this point, they would be able to find that help in each other.

TAKING ACTION
How to Return to the Future

Now that you've seen how Dan and Stu turned to consider the future, here's how you can do the same.

- Capture the progress you've made to date—both on the business front and on the relationship front.

- Take stock of what you've accomplished and figure out a way to celebrate together.

- Identify the objectives you would each like to achieve in the future and anticipate the challenges those objectives will pose for your relationship.

- Set the terms of your new relationship by making explicit commitments to each other.

- Make sure the commitments specify what you will actually do to sustain the changes you've made and to master future challenges.

- Make sure the commitments specify how you will help each other when you need it.

- Going forward, look to each other for help when either of you falls short of your commitments or finds them hard to meet.

Stage 3 Results

By any of our original measures, Dan and Stu are in a very different place (see Table 8.2). Far from going stale, their relationship now serves as a model for others. Their old one-way structure—with Dan pushing and Stu blocking—has been replaced by a reciprocal structure that allows for greater mutuality and flexibility. Within this new structure, Dan is gradually learning how to rely on others, while Stu is learning how to brave the limelight. As a result, they're able to keep growing, while tackling controversial issues—each time with a little less anxiety, a little more confidence. By the time we end our work together,

- They respond more flexibly to each other and more effectively to the demands around them. No longer trapped by their knee-jerk reactions to each other, they are able to make decisions more quickly and effectively together.
- They treat their relationship as a context for growth. No longer so intent on protecting themselves or each other, they are able to explore their anxieties, beliefs, and interests openly, so they don't unknowingly affect what they decide or how they decide it.
- They recoup quickly when they get into trouble. Even their hottest conflicts strengthen rather than damage their relationship, because they are able to cool down together and use what happened to learn.

In short, Dan and Stu have developed enough resilience to continue building even more resilience in the future. With our initial mission accomplished—by their metrics and my own—we might simply declare victory and go home. But just as the first two stages end with a dilemma, so does this one. That dilemma goes something like this:

- To secure whatever changes you've made, you need to solidify them—internalizing what you've learned and perhaps institutionalizing it.
- Yet the more you internalize and institutionalize change, the harder it can be to make new changes, reducing flexibility and making adaptation more difficult.

Engaging this dilemma head-on catapults people right back to the beginning of Stage 1, where they start all over again, only this time on their own. From here on in, Dan and Stu must stand ready to disrupt any patterns that start limiting their growth or the growth of the firm. Looking back now, five years after the fact, I can tell you this: that's exactly what they did.

APPENDIX A

A Guide to Behavioral Repertoires

Experience is a great teacher, except when it isn't. What we make of experience—and whether it serves us or harms us—depends on the knowledge we build out of it. And make no mistake: we're all master knowledge-builders, able to turn the most random events into knowledge about the world and how to operate in it. Much of this knowledge—what I call *experiential knowledge*—lies outside our awareness, where it's difficult to see or assess. Worse yet, the *interpretive strategies* we use to build that knowledge also lie outside our awareness, making it hard to update and revise what we know as our circumstances change and we ourselves grow.

This guide offers a brief overview of the experiential knowledge and interpretive strategies that define our *behavioral repertoires*: the characteristic ways we respond to people.[1] I used this guide to map the experiential knowledge that Chris and Peter brought to their relationship (Chapter Five) and that Dan and Stu brought to theirs (Chapter Ten). You can use it to reflect on your own experiential knowledge and on how you're building and revising it.

Experiential Knowledge

For decades, social scientists have been studying the knowledge people use to make sense of the world and to take action in it. Some focus on the culturally shared knowledge we acquire as we're socialized into some group; others on the more variable, personal knowledge we fashion out of the unique experiences that shape our lives (see Table A.1, far left column).[2]

Among these folks, some look at the narratives we weave out of events; some study the theories and beliefs we use to explain and predict them; others explore the value systems we evolve over time, while still others catalogue the practical strategies, scripts, and routines we follow (see Table A.1, top row). Let's take a brief look at each type of knowledge—at how it's built and deployed—then consider how each one works with the others to form the more or less coherent whole that governs how we interact with others.

Narrative Knowledge

As children, we're forever turning events into narratives, then storing those narratives in our more or less conscious minds. Once we're adults, we draw on those narratives to interpret people and situations, to assume and assign roles, to imagine how events might

Table A.1   Different Types of Experiential Knowledge.

	Narrative	Analytic	Moral	Practical
Personal (Highly variable)	Stories, personae, characters	Implicit theories, explanations, constructs	Principles, moral logic	Personal action strategies
Cultural (Highly shared)	Scenes, roles, and stereotypes	Implicit theories, beliefs, or assumptions	Norms and values	Cultural routines and scripts[3]

unfold, and to envision what a more or less happy ending might look like.[4]

Some narratives are culturally shared; others vary from person to person. At a cultural level, narratives include *scenes, roles,* and *stereotypes.* These are especially handy in culturally familiar situations: going to a restaurant, attending a funeral, talking with colleagues at a cocktail party, buying a rug at a bazaar. Although each situation is different, none requires much thought. We're able to recognize them immediately, because we have a large stock of *scenes* in our heads that correspond to them. We can also recognize the people in each scene: the rude patron at the restaurant, the bereaved widow at the funeral, the bon vivant at the cocktail party, the haggler at the bazaar. They're all cultural *stereotypes.* All of this makes it easy for us to assume an appropriate *role* in relation to others: the patient patron at the restaurant, the sympathetic friend at the funeral, and so on.

These energy-saving cultural narratives work terrifically well as long as people or circumstances don't go beyond what any one-dimensional stereotype, bare-boned scene, or socially conscripted role can handle. But what if that rude patron at the restaurant turns around and you discover, much to your horror, that it's no stranger but your Uncle Harry! Then, even more stunning, you notice he's wearing a rumpled suit and launching into an agitated recitation of the Bill of Rights! Search as you might, you can't find a cultural scene, stereotype, or role that corresponds well enough to this turn of events to lend it enough meaning to respond.

To handle moments like this, you have to rely on your own private stock of *personal narratives,* picking up where cultural narratives leave off. Fortunately, all of us have plenty of such narratives at our disposal, whether they be cautionary tales, psychological thrillers, or melodramas. Built out of unsettling events, these narratives help

233

us understand and put to rest—without much, if any, conscious thought—whatever disquiet some inchoate event evokes.

Once you find a narrative that fits well enough—one that allows you to turn Uncle Harry into a more or less sympathetic *character* and to assume a *persona* that will allow you to redeem the situation, if not for Uncle Harry, at least for yourself—some responses will seem obvious, while others will never occur to you. Either way, once wrapped in this narrative blanket, whatever disquiet you feel will start to abate.

Analytic Knowledge

Out of our narratives, we build thousands of generalizations about what causes what. This type of knowledge, which in its purest form says, "if this, then that," helps us explain and predict everyday events and behavior.

At a cultural level, people acquire through experience and socialization a large number of *implicit theories, beliefs,* and *assumptions*—relatively rudimentary propositions that allow some group or society to understand the social world similarly enough to take collective action. The common belief that people's behavior is caused by their disposition rather than situational pressures is one well-researched example.[5] That's why most people seeing Uncle Harry would assume he's simply nuts and not consider the possibility that he may be responding to a set of situational factors we as observers don't see.

At a more personal level, analytic knowledge also comes in the form of implicit theories, beliefs, and assumptions, but these vary much more widely among people. They include our own *personal explanations,* complete with associated *constructs,* all of it built out of our own unique experience.[6] This knowledge allows us—in ways that are more personally meaningful—to identify and sort events, things, and people and to explain and predict their occurrence.

Take Uncle Harry. As soon as you see Uncle Harry reciting the Bill of Rights, you recognize his behavior as crazy, because you have instantaneously sorted it into a *construct* or *category*—a kind of mental file folder—called "crazy behavior." But to predict what Uncle Harry might do next, you still have to find an *explanation* for the crazy behavior, one that fits with past experience. All of a sudden, it "comes" to you: given your family history and what you know about mental illness, your uncle must be suffering from bipolar disorder, just as your grandfather did. This personally meaningful explanation is tailor-made to explain what your Uncle Harry is doing. It fits. Now you can be relatively confident that he won't turn around next and act completely normal. In fact, you may have to do something about your Uncle Harry.

Moral Knowledge

Out of our narrative and analytic knowledge, we build knowledge that tells us what's good and bad, and what's right and wrong. When people act differently than our theories predict or our stories anticipate, it not only surprises us, it offends our sensibilities: they've violated our sense of what's supposed to happen, our sense of what's right.

Some moral knowledge is culturally shared. As we grow up, we internalize *cultural values* that inform the way people behave and a related set of *cultural norms* that set people's expectations for behavior. Both values and norms are reflected in and reinforced by our cultural beliefs and assumptions. For example, the belief that dispositions, not situations, cause behavior reflects and reinforces a cultural value of individual responsibility and a cultural norm of holding people accountable. Such values and beliefs are so deeply held and highly shared that when someone violates them, it can threaten our collective identity, motivating us to punish or ostracize the "offending" party to ensure our sense of well-being.

235

At a more personal level, we select from a cultural menu of values and norms those we want to incorporate into our own personal value system, developing that system to a greater or lesser degree. This more or less complex system provides the *moral logic* we need to reason our way through difficult moral dilemmas. Although this logic may be more or less developed,[7] its *content* consists of *principles* that reflect and reinforce our narratives and theories. So while I might condemn Uncle Harry as an irresponsible ne'er-do-well who's never worked a day in his morally bankrupt life, you might defend him, calling him a victim of circumstance, who's never hurt a soul in his life and persevered despite a string of bad luck.

Practical Knowledge

As the term implies, this knowledge offers practical strategies for coping with different situations, telling us, "Do this, don't do that." Only by doing what this knowledge tells us to do can we act on what we see. Some practical knowledge—politeness scripts and face-saving routines—is highly shared. All you have to do is violate one to see just how shared.[8]

Out of these scripts and routines people fashion *personal action strategies* through an ongoing process of selection, improvisation, and elaboration. We rely on these more variable strategies to improvise our way through the situations we confront given our unique life circumstances. These action strategies allow us to negotiate even the most complicated situations, as our narrative, analytic, and moral knowledge lead us to see them.

Going back to our example of Uncle Harry, let's say in your role as a sympathetic niece or nephew, you become quite anxious about your uncle's welfare and your own; after all, it's an awkward situation and you're not quite sure what Harry might do next. To address both anxieties, you need to find a strategy that will allow you to protect Harry *and* yourself, while staying true to your role as the sympathetic family member. Again, without having to give it much conscious thought, it just "comes" to you: call for help without intervening yourself. Someone else—someone who saw Harry differently—might just as automatically enact a different strategy, either taking Uncle Harry by the hand or abandoning him altogether.

When our personal strategies backfire, we must reboot. If, as you step outside to call for help, Harry grabs your arm and hollers— "And where do you think you're going?!"—like it or not, you will have to find a new way to respond. And if no response currently exists in your repertoire, well, then you'll have to cobble together a new response out of existing ones, expanding your repertoire over time.

Cultural and Personal Knowledge

Both cultural and personal knowledge have their advantages and disadvantages. Cultural knowledge makes it possible for people to act in concert. The risk is that we apply old cultural knowledge when new knowledge or more personal knowledge might do better. The problem is that cultural knowledge is so highly shared that it takes on a sense of validity it rarely warrants, making it difficult to explore or discover its limits.[9]

Unlike cultural knowledge, personal knowledge gives us especially meaningful ways of understanding novel or upsetting situations. At the same time, because this knowledge is built out of unsettling events, we tend to call on it when we're under similar stress, whether or not it applies. This can lead us to repeat history again and again instead of creating a better future.

This brings us to the interpretive strategies we use to build and deploy knowledge. How well we draw on—and how quickly we revise or develop—our stock of experiential knowledge depends on the depth and breadth of our *interpretive strategies.*

Table A.2 Interpretive Strategies.

Strategy	Views Knowledge	Connects Knowledge	Defends Knowledge	Renews Knowledge
Test	As a hypothesis	To what you see (the observable "facts" of the situation)	By debating: make a case based on what you see	By exploring: examine hypotheses in light of data or what others see
Sense	As an intuition	To your feelings about the situation	By pleading: appeal to your feelings; claim a right to them	By sharing: share your feelings, and ask others to do the same
Negotiate	As a perspective	To how others see, think, and feel about a situation relative to you	By bargaining: grant the other this, if they grant you that By agreeing to disagree	By creating: invent new insights out of each other's perspectives

Interpretive Strategies

When we differ with others, we reveal through our behavior the interpretive strategies we use to deploy, defend, and renew our experiential knowledge (see Table A.2). In my clinical research, I've identified three distinct strategies. Each has its own way of viewing knowledge, connecting knowledge to events, defending knowledge, and renewing knowledge.

The broader and deeper your repertoire of interpretive strategies, the greater your interpretive freedom will be, allowing you to revise old knowledge and develop new knowledge more quickly. The question in terms of depth is whether you can explore what you know with people who rely on different strategies. The question in terms of breadth is whether you can *connect*, *defend*, and *renew* what you know. Let's consider each in turn.

Strategic Depth

The more shallow your repertoire, the more problematic differences become. People get so hung up on *how* they discuss their differences they can't resolve them. One person is talking feelings, another is talking facts, and yet another is endlessly comparing and contrasting different points of view. By dismissing a strategy outright, all you do is limit what you can learn.

Each strategy offers something the others lack. Take people who rely on their sense of things to read situations. They will focus primarily on people's feelings. Since feelings play such a pivotal role in relationships, this strategy provides an important window onto how a relationship is going and where it's getting into trouble. Those who prefer to test their views in light of observable facts help us see dynamics we might otherwise miss—namely, the external circumstances people are up against and what people are actually doing or saying. Finally, those who take multiple perspectives into account will ensure that we look at things from different points of view.

Each strategy, deployed well, has an important role to play, whether we play it ourselves or rely on others to play it for us. People who are able to take advantage of the full range of strategies fare better in relationships than those who don't.

Strategic Breadth

How well a strategy is deployed is another matter. That depends on the breadth of a repertoire—that is, on how well you connect, defend, and renew what you know. Some people have trouble *connecting* what they know to anything. People who prefer testing can't say what data would refute their view; people who prefer sensing can't say what led them to feel a certain way; and people who prefer negotiating can't say what their perspective is or how it relates to others or connects to a specific situation.

Others are so quick to *defend* what they know that they don't explore whether the knowledge they're applying fits a particular case, making them slow to revise old knowledge and even slower to create new knowledge. Still others—although a minority—tend to *renew* their knowledge so quickly that they don't ever defend it, making it difficult for them to articulate a clear and consistent point of view or to develop a reliable moral compass.

When it comes to developing enough flexibility to handle a wide range of relationships, renewal is by far the most important interpretive strategy. All of us experience *slippage* from time to time—a gap between what we see and what we know that creates a zone of uncertainty or dissonance. Some people view this slippage as a portal of discovery, offering an opportunity to renew their knowledge by revising or adding to it. For those people, the discomfort caused by uncertainty is minimal and their sense of urgency about closing the gap manageable. In contrast, others view even the slightest slippage as a gaping hole, intensifying their discomfort and amplifying their sense of urgency about closing the gap.

Those people who are able to connect, defend, and renew what they know fare better in relationships than those who don't.

The Three R's

Knowledge-building goes best when people follow the three R's: *reflecting* and *reframing* in the context of *relationships.* Continually reflecting with others on what we "know" reduces the odds of fooling ourselves and increases the odds that we'll discover interesting new things—that we'll reframe.

This is especially true when the quality of reflection is high; that is, when it's conducted not in the abstract (where it's divorced from action) but in light of specific situations and what you and others are actually feeling, thinking, and doing in them. By grounding reflection in the world of action, you're much more likely to create knowledge that's useful in action. More important, you're much more likely to stay alive mentally and emotionally and to grow alongside those who matter the most to you. Appendix B offers a tool that will help you ground your reflections so you can use them to learn and change with others.

APPENDIX B

The Ladder of Reflection

Ever since organizational learning pioneers Chris Argyris and Donald Schön introduced a tool called the Ladder of Inference, countless people have appropriated it for their own purposes, calling it everything from the Ladder of Influence (a Freudian slip perhaps?) to the Ladder of Interpretation (by my sights, a bit more apt).[1]

One reason the tool is so popular is that it opens a window onto how your mind works when you make sense of situations. And once you see how your mind works, you can never quite see things the same way again. All of a sudden you realize that what you see isn't necessarily the way things are, and what you take to be matters of fact are actually matters of interpretation—and pretty abstract interpretation at that.

In this book, I put the Ladder of Inference to yet another use: reflecting on interactions for the purpose of mapping them. And I rename it yet again, calling it the Ladder of Reflection.

Using the Ladder of Reflection to Observe and Map Interactions

Whenever you map interactions, you need some way of ensuring (1) that you're not deluding yourself and (2) that people can use the map to understand and change the pattern it captures. You can use the ladder in Figure B.1 to reflect on interactions, starting with what people are actually saying and doing and ending with your conclusions about what it all means.

By reflecting on interactions a step at a time, you're much less likely to jump to premature conclusions and much more likely to see gaps in your views or to see alternative interpretations, especially when you reflect with other people who are also taking it a step at a time.

Figure B.1   The Ladder of Reflection.

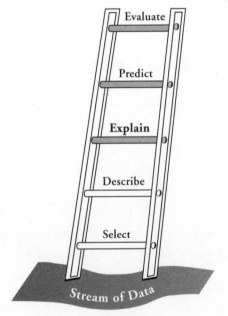

For the purpose of mapping, I've given my ladder five rungs: select, describe, explain, predict, and evaluate.[2] The first two steps include our *observations*, the last three our *conclusions*. I've put all three *conclusion rungs* in gray as a reminder to stop and take a closer look before proceeding, because this is where people get into the most trouble, especially if they can't climb back down the ladder to say how they moved from the bottom to the top. Unable to say what leads to their conclusions, they don't have a leg (or a ladder) to stand on.

When mapping interactions, you can use this ladder to

- Go from some behavior you observe to your conclusions about that behavior
- Connect any conclusions you reach to the behaviors you see
- Examine your conclusions to see if you're missing things that might alter your view
- Discuss with others the steps you took to arrive at your conclusions
- Explore any differences in what you and others see
- Look at the same behavior from different angles
- Inquire into any behavior that puzzles or surprises you
- Consider what each person's conclusions reveal and conceal

Going Up the Ladder a Step at a Time

In this section I take a close look at each step on the ladder, using a simple example to illustrate. Next to that example, I offer a counterexample to illustrate common mistakes I see people make. Underlying each of these mistakes is the tendency to think that our most abstract conclusions are concrete facts. As you'll see, they're not.

Select

Any time you observe an interaction—whether you're in it yourself or just watching—you can't possibly pay attention to everything that's happening. There's just too much going on. You have to select something. For the purpose of mapping, you want to select those behaviors that might be implicated in some pattern, even if you can't yet name the pattern or explain it very well. You've got to start somewhere, and the best place to start is with what people are actually saying and doing in *here-we-go-again* moments—moments that are easy to recognize but hard to understand or alter. To do this, *select* from your notes (or a tape recording) what people said and did during those moments.

Example of Selected Behavior

Dick said, "See Spot! Look at Spot run!" Jane said, "Run, Spot, run!"

Counterexample of a Common Mistake

Dick vied for Jane's affections by showing her something he believed she'd find interesting. She pretended to show her affection by looking at what he showed her.

Where the first example simply reports what Dick and Jane said, the counterexample skips a few steps on the ladder and rushes to judgment about what their words mean. Anytime you hear such words as *vie, believe,* or *pretend,* you'll know you skipped this step. These are not behaviors but explanations for behaviors, as the next section shows.

Describe

Once you've selected behaviors, you can *describe* them in relatively observable terms *without* speculating about motives, feelings, intentions, frames, or the like. At this step, it's vital that you stick to what you see or hear. This makes it easier for people to point out behavior you might have missed or to understand which behavior you think needs to change. Either way it's the single most important step in mapping—and the one most people skip.

Example of Described Behavior

Dick directed Jane's attention to the running dog. Jane looked at it and exclaimed.

Counterexample of a Common Mistake

Hoping to gain Jane's favor, Dick tried to get her attention by showing her something he believed she'd find interesting. He thought he succeeded when Jane joined in the fun, but Jane was just trying to appease Dick, who was acting like a chauvinist by dominating her attention.

As with the first step, be on the lookout for such words in your description as *try, intend, hope, want, fear, worry, believe,* and the like. Each of these words refers to what's going on inside of people (which you can't directly see), not to what they're doing (which you can directly see). In this respect, they're not descriptions as much as they are explanations for the behavior you have yet to describe.

Explain

If the previous step is the most important, this one is the trickiest, which is why it appears in bold. Having selected and described those behaviors you think contribute to some pattern, you must now explain what causes those behaviors by drawing on some theory. In this book I relied on the Anatomy Framework to explain behaviors (see Figure 3.1). In everyday life, we rely on our largely unconscious experiential knowledge. While this knowledge gets the job of framing done quickly and effortlessly, if not always effectively, it isn't up to the job of mapping—at least not as long as it stays unconscious. To be useful and reliable, explanations must be conscious enough that you can state them so others can consider them and help you see things you might have missed.

Since it's widely accepted that observed behavior is caused by both internal and external factors, most theories of human behavior refer to both (such external contexts as immediate situations or triggering events *and* such internal mental states as intentions, purposes, goals, beliefs, assumptions, or frames). To use these theories well, you need more than just observed behavior; you need a window onto the external and internal factors that might be causing that behavior. Without them, all you can do is speculate. And who's to say whether your speculations apply in this case? Not a very solid basis for understanding behavior—and certainly not for changing it.

So far, in our example, we don't have a clue what Dick and Jane are feeling or thinking, nor do we have any idea what external factors might be at play. Thus the behavior we've selected could be explained very differently depending on the external context (whether it's occurring in the midst of a dog fight or on a playground at school) *and* depending on Dick and Jane's internal thoughts and feelings (whether they're feeling warmly or resentful toward each other).

To illustrate, let's say that Dick and Jane are on an elementary school playground during recess, and let's say that Dick tells us that he likes Jane very much, that he was excited to see his own dog Spot running onto the playground, and that he was thinking to himself, "Jane likes dogs. Jane will certainly want to see my dog." Now let's say that Jane tells us that she also likes Dick, that she does indeed like dogs very much, but that when she turned to see the dog, she saw what she believed to be a coyote running after it, leading her to fear for the dog and to think to herself, "If Spot doesn't run faster, he'll surely get eaten!"

Example of Explained Behavior

Because Dick liked Jane and thought that Jane liked dogs, he directed Jane's attention to his dog Spot when he ran onto the school playground. *Because* Jane likes Dick as well as dogs, she looked where Dick directed her attention. And *because* she then saw what she thought was a coyote running after the dog, she feared for the dog's life. This caused her to exclaim, telling the dog to run.

Counterexample of a Common Mistake

Because Dick is a chauvinist, he made Jane look at his dog. *Because* Jane is a member of a submissive class, she felt compelled to go along. *Because* she identified with the dog—being chased as it was by a coyote, who reminded her vaguely of Dick—she tried to protect the dog from being eaten.

As silly as the counterexample seems, I've seen sillier in everyday life, and I bet you have too. The point is, we can make almost anything out of the behavior we see; people do it all the time, and they get away with it. Most of us are too polite to point out that it's beyond our comprehension how others reached the conclusions they reached.

In the first example, by contrast, you can connect the explanation to the description that preceded it and to the data on what Dick and Jane were feeling, thinking, and doing. This is what makes it relatively easy for you to see how someone might reach this conclusion, whether or not you agree with it. Similarly, if you look at any of the conclusions I reached about Dan and Stu (see Chapters Eight through Ten), you can see how I arrived at them and judge for yourself whether they make sense. In the case of our counterexample, you'd be at a loss.

Predict

Like the previous step, this fourth step involves thinking through what causes what. Only, in this case, you're not thinking about what caused the behavior you see, but what the behavior you see causes—the consequences that behavior creates or at least contributes to. That's why, to take this step, you again need some kind of theory that can tell you what causes what. Just as I used the Anatomy Framework throughout the book to explain what caused behavior, I also used it to predict the consequences that behavior might cause. What's more, I focused my predictions on outcomes people cared about, and I formulated them in ways that helped people avoid outcomes they didn't like and achieve outcomes they did. But to stay with our example here, consider these predictions:

Example of a Prediction

By directing Jane's attention to his dog Spot, Dick makes it more likely that Jane will turn and see Spot. By listening to Dick and turning toward Spot, Jane will be more able to see Spot and the other animal chasing him. This will make it possible for her to do something to try and save Spot's life. If Dick and Jane continue to interact this way, they will likely continue to be good friends; they may even save a few dogs.

Counterexample of a Prediction

By imposing his will on Jane, Dick will perpetuate the power dynamics that characterize the male-dominated playground so prevalent in Western society. By following Dick's unilateral directions, Jane will never learn to be self-directed and will continue to be victimized by society's paternalistic social order. Because of people like Dick, that paternalistic social order will continue to stifle seven-year-old women like Jane, and many a sentient dog like Spot will get eaten because only those Dick points out will get saved.

As these two examples illustrate, not all theories are equal. The more abstract, unconscious, or disconnected your theory is, the harder it is to scrutinize the predictions you make. This makes it more likely that your predictions won't come to pass because they're wrong or won't help much because they're so disconnected from what's happening that people can't do anything about them. Conversely, the more conscious and connectable a theory is, the easier it is to revise predictions (making them more powerful) and to alter the outcomes it predicts (making them more useful).

Evaluate
This last step draws on all the others to assess whether you like what you see. Just as the previous two steps required a theory, so does this one. But it requires something else too, something that's not always so easy to see: our values. It's not by chance that the word *evaluation* has the word *value* at its core.

In this last step, you look back at your explanations and predictions and say whether some behavior is "good" or "bad"—or, in business parlance, whether it's effective or ineffective, whether it's value-added or not. Whatever words you use, you're sizing behavior up relative to some value or criterion. If you value profits above all else, then you'll consider a hard-driving rainmaker who only sees his or her kids twice a month to be effective. If you value a balanced life or family above all else, then you'll deem the same person deficient. It's all relative, depending on what you're looking at *and* the values you use to assess what you see.

To avoid getting caught in an endless loop of relativity, perhaps even to find common ground, you need to take into account not just your values, but the values of others, and you need to search for values that are more universally shared—say, justice or a sense of security.[3] Equally important, you must use the ladder to connect these values to what you now see and to what you'd prefer to see in yourself, another person, or in the world.

Example of an Evaluation

Dick and Jane's interaction illustrates an effective way of connecting, having fun, and helping out a dog in need.

Counterexample of an Evaluation

Dick's behavior—boorish in the extreme—illustrates just how badly boys can behave and the difficult position in which they put good girls like Jane.

As you can see, the second example is even sillier than the first, and that's saying something. What adds to the second example's silliness is the blanket value judgment that gets woven out of a single thread of behavior, and a small thread at that. All these blanket value judgments do is smother any chance of learning or finding common ground.

Implications

Though truth and accuracy are the first casualties of sloppy reflection, they're not the only ones. Change and growth also get killed, usually in their wake. The problem with our counterexamples isn't that there's no truth to them. There *is* inequality in the world; boys do dominate girls at times. The question is whether that's the best way of understanding what's happening here. Unlikely. The leaps of abstraction taken right from the start make it hard to know whether the reflections apply in this case, and if they did, what any of us would do about it.

On Ladders, Labels, and Frameworks

The Dick and Jane example has the benefit of being simple. But if you look throughout the book, you'll see more complex examples, including Jobs and Sculley, Chris and Peter, Stu and Dan, and so on. In each case I used the ladder to analyze the interactions between these pairs and to explore how they gave rise to relationships that had a characteristic structure. In each case, you can see how I go from some "data"—what these folks were thinking, feeling, saying, or doing—to my conclusions about them and their relationships.

Though it takes time and practice, once you master the ladder, it's easier to imagine different ways of seeing the "same" behaviors and easier to see behaviors you or others might miss, because each of you will be giving the other a window onto how you climbed the ladder. Equally important, once you and others are able to connect your more abstract insights to what someone is actually feeling, thinking, doing, or saying, you'll be more able to help each other alter what you see.

Ultimately this will give you far more traction than tossing around labels or characterizations (he's passive-aggressive, she's a wimp, he's a control freak, she's too aggressive, he's a monster, she's a jerk). While any of these labels may be directionally true, they're not especially useful. Most of the time, they exacerbate the very behaviors they label, as people feel compelled to defend themselves and to attack back.

Even nontoxic labels such as those used in the Myers-Briggs assessment can get bandied around in ways that cut off the curiosity and empathy you're going to need to help each other change.

Though the assessment is designed to help people appreciate difference, many people only end up thinking, she's *simply* an ISTJ (introverted, sensing, thinking, judging); he's *simply* an ENFP (extroverted, intuition, feeling, perceiving). That explains *everything*!

In this case, the problem isn't so much the labels as the labelers. Most people slap them on and give no more thought to what they see. This not only cuts off the potential for growth ("I am what I am," as Popeye said); it also lops off a person's underlying complexity—making it harder for you to more fully understand them or to spot toeholds for change. *The point is, no set of labels can explain everything, even when they're based on solid theory and evidence. All have a range of usefulness beyond which they're more trouble than they're worth.*

Even so, we can't live without them. Labels are here to stay. It's the way the mind works. But nothing about the mind requires us to use bad labels, to apply them mindlessly, or to think you've figured everything out once you've applied them. All that's up to you. The Ladder of Reflection gives you a way to connect labels to behavior and to use frameworks like the Anatomy Framework to see what no label can help you see: how something works.

As the father of renowned physicist Richard Feynman advised his son, as they puzzled together over a bird that was busily at work pecking at its feathers: "You can know the name of that bird in all the languages of the world, but when you're finished you'll know absolutely nothing whatever about the bird. You'll only know about humans in different places, and what they call the bird. Let's look at the bird and see what it's *doing*—that's what counts."

Feynman later said of this impromptu lesson, "I learned very early the difference between knowing the name of something and knowing something."[4]

NOTES

Part 1

1. Clothier, *Bones Would Rain from the Sky*, 49.

Chapter 1

1. Kahney, "Being Steve Jobs' Boss."
2. Morrow, "Steve Jobs Oral History," 12.
3. Jobs, Stanford University commencement address.
4. Kahney.
5. Kouzes and Posner, *Leadership Challenge*, 24–25.
6. Heifetz and Linsky, *Leadership on the Line*, 75.
7. Daniel Goleman's colleagues include Richard Boyatzis and Annie McKee. See, for example, Boyatzis and McGee, *Resonant Leadership*, 104.
8. See Goleman, *Emotional Intelligence*. Also see Goleman, *Working with Emotional Intelligence*.
9. Goleman and Boyatzis, "Social Intelligence," 76.
10. Other leadership scholars also speak to the importance of relationships, for example, those studying team member exchange (see Tse, Dasborough, and Ashkanasy, "Multi-Level Analysis of Team Climate"), coworker member exchange (Sherony and Green, "Coworker Exchange"), toxic supervisor-subordinate relationships (Harris, Kacmar, and Zivnuska, "Investigation of Abusive Supervision"), dyadic relationships in groups (Moreland, "Are Dyads Really Groups"; Wu, Tsui, and Kinicki, "Consequences of

Differentiated Leadership"), the nature and implications of a leader's relationship network (Balkundi and Kilduff, "The Ties That Lead"), and authenticity in relationships (Ilies, Morgeson, and Nahrgang, "Authentic Leadership and Eudaemonic Well-Being"). Still other leadership experts such as Ram Charan speak of relationships in terms of interactions and dialogue: "The primary instrument at (a leader's) disposal is the human interaction—the dialogues through which assumptions are challenged or go unchallenged, information is shared or not shared, disagreements are brought to the surface or papered over. Dialogue is the basic unit of work in organizations." (Charan, "Conquering a Culture of Indecision," 2). Even Warren Bennis, who believes leaders are self-directed, says that "learning and understanding are the keys to self-direction, and it is in our relationships with others that we learn about ourselves" (Bennis, *On Becoming a Leader*, 35). Despite all this interest in relationships, there is a relative paucity of research on relationships in the fields of leadership and organizational behavior. In a 2010 book (Nohria and Khurana, *Handbook of Leadership Theory and Practice*), Glynn and DeJordy's chapter says that only 18 percent of articles published in top organizational journals since their inception focus on the dyadic or relational aspects of leadership.

11. Goleman and Boyatzis, "Social Intelligence," 76.

12. These include studies on (a) attraction; (b) self-presentation, cognition, and communication; (c) sexual desire and behavior; (d) attachment style and individual differences; (e) interdependency and social exchange; (f) conflict and betrayal; (g) satisfaction, social support, and health; and (h) maintenance and repair. When it comes to the last—maintenance and repair—many couples turn to the aid of professionals to help them analyze and repair their relationships. See Miller and Perlman, *Intimate Relationships*. The main types of couples counseling are behavioral couple therapy, cognitive-behavioral couple therapy, integrative behavioral couple therapy, emotionally focused therapy, and insight-oriented couple therapy.

13. David Kantor is another rare and important exception. In his book with William Lehr, *Inside the Family*, Kantor presents his findings, which are based on tape-recorded observations of different

families. Also see "Critical Identity Image," "Couples Therapy, Crisis Induction, and Change," and *My Lover, Myself.* As with Gottman, Kantor's insights are much more connected to what people actually do. In fact, family therapists in general are more descriptive and prescriptive about relationships, but their ideas don't always transfer easily to organizations. See, for example, Watzlawick and Weakland, *The Interactional View.* For a discussion of the transfer challenge, see Hirschhorn and Gilmore, "The Application of Family Therapy Concepts."

14.   Gottman, *Why Marriages Succeed or Fail.* Also see Gottman and DeClaire, *The Relationship Cure.*

15.   In one longitudinal study, the researchers used videotapes of just the first three minutes of a marital conflict discussion to predict with 83 percent accuracy which couples would be divorced six years later (Gottman and Carrere, "Predicting Divorce Among Newlyweds."). On the basis of his research findings, Gottman has also built an approach to helping couples: (a) build love maps by mapping each individual's inner psychological world; (b) share fondness and admiration by expressing affection and respect for each other; (c) turn toward each other by stating needs and responding to those expressed by the partner; (d) take a positive perspective to problem solving and repair attempts; (e) manage conflict by handling solvable problems; (f) make life dreams come true by encouraging each person to talk about their hopes, values, convictions, and aspirations; and (g) create shared meaning by understanding important visions, narratives, myths, and metaphors about the relationship. His institute also serves as a training center for other couples therapists interested in using his method.

16.   Historically, the earliest research on leadership focused on traits (the so-called Great Man theory of leadership) or behaviors and styles independent of context. Then, as today's more turbulent, interconnected world began to take shape in the 1960s, scholars gradually shifted from static notions of leadership to ones that embraced environmental instability and its associated need for continual organizational learning and change. To succeed in this world, leadership scholars argued, leaders must be able to adapt to shifting circumstances; learn and lead in the face of uncertainty;

and motivate their followers to continually learn, grow, and change. Small surprise that against this backdrop we find scholars taking a more situational view of leadership and making distinctions that are based on the kinds of relationships leaders form with their followers—most notably, whether they are transformational or transactional in nature. More recently, a small number of researchers have begun to study how leaders develop, maintain, and repair relationships with their subordinates. In 2006, one of the most influential members of this group, Mary Uhl-Bien, knitted previous work together to propose what she calls a relational leadership theory—an overarching framework for the study of leadership as a social-influence process through which coordination and change are constructed and produced. See Uhl-Bien, "Rational Leadership Theory."

17. To clarify my use of the term *relationship*, let me make two points. First, even when you use the term *relationship* to include relationships among groups or organizations, you're ultimately referring to relationships among the human beings who represent them—human beings who have "emotions, deeply held values, and different backgrounds and viewpoints" (See Fisher, Ury, and Patton, *Getting to Yes*, 19). Second, all two-person relationships within an organization exist within a larger web of relationships within some organizational context. So even if you focus primarily on two-person relationships, as I do here, it's important to remember that other people and relationships are always lurking in the background, impinging on how the people in any two-person relationship regard and behave toward each other.

18. My clinical research is based on tape-recorded observations of leaders conducted over many years. Those tape recordings are then transcribed and analyzed. The frameworks presented in this book emerged out of those analyses, and those analyses were in turn guided by the work of many people, most important, Chris Argyris (*Theory in Practice*, written with Donald Schön), Donald Schön (*The Reflective Practitioner*), David Kantor (*Inside the Family*, written with William Lehr), Karl Weick (*The Social Psychology of Organizing*), Berger and Luckman (*The Social Construction of Reality*), Bennis, Van Maanen, Schein, and Steele (*Essays in Interpersonal Dynamics*), Paul Watzlawick (*Pragmatics of Human Communication* with Bavelas and Jackson), Fisher, Ury, and Patton,

Getting to Yes, and others studying how social realities of one type or another are created, negotiated, perpetuated, defended, and changed.

19. See Ross, "Intuitive Psychologist and His Shortcomings." Also see Nisbett and Ross, *Human Inference.*

Chapter 2

1. Sedaris, "Old Faithful."

2. See, for example, Hertzfeld, *Revolution in the Valley,* 267: "The weak sales were beginning to put pressure on the relationship between Steve Jobs and John Sculley for the very first time. They had gotten along fine when everything was going well, but hitherto. they had never had to deal with much adversity."

3. This account shows how Jobs and Sculley's relationship had an adverse effect on Apple's performance. I'm not suggesting that other factors, such as the decision not to open their platform, didn't also have an adverse affect.

4. I rely heavily on two sources for the case material on Sculley and Jobs's relationship. The first is Frank Rose's account in *West of Eden,* written in the wake of the relationship's demise. Rose based his book on extensive interviews with Apple's executive staff, as well as solid historical research on the computer industry and the emergence of Silicon Valley. The other major source is John Sculley's memoir, *Odyssey,* which offers a relatively direct account of what he and Jobs said and did with each other, as well as direct data on what he was thinking and feeling at the time. I use Sculley's account to look at his interactions with Jobs and at his (Sculley's) reactions to those interactions, not Jobs's. For direct data on Jobs's reactions I relied on a 1995 *Smithsonian* interview (see Morrow, "Steve Jobs Oral History") and his 2005 Stanford commencement address (see Jobs, Stanford University commencement address). In addition, I rely on Rose's account, which is supported by other accounts in the public domain, including one by a core member of the Macintosh team; see Hertzfeld, *Revolution in the Valley.*

5. Rose, *West of Eden,* 16.

6. Ibid., 15–16.

7. Ibid., 70.

8. Ibid., 75.

9. In 1981, two years before Sculley joined the firm, Mike Markkula stepped down as chairman and assumed the position of CEO. At that time, Jobs took Markkula's job as chairman. All this occurred after Markkula's friend from his semiconductor days, Mike Scott, got pushed out as CEO after launching a round of firings that came to be called Black Wednesday. Scott's survival probably wasn't served by his decision to appoint John Couch, not Jobs, to lead the highly desirable Lisa division. This left Jobs to take over a small, experimental project called Macintosh. By this point, Wozniak—Jobs's original partner in founding Apple—had decided to take a break from Apple after a plane crash that affected his short-term memory and a series of disagreements with Jobs.

10. Rose, 71.

11. Ibid.

12. Ibid., 79.

13. Ibid., 108.

14. Sculley, *Odyssey,* 200.

15. Rose, 109.

16. Sculley, 157.

17. Rose, 71.

18. For more on behavioral repertoires, see the sidebar "About the Anatomy Framework" in Chapter Five, under "Step 4: Behavioral Repertoires." Also see Appendix A: "A Guide to Behavioral Repertoires."

19. See Gladwell, *Blink.* Gladwell cites psychologist John Gottman's research on marital relationships to explain how "a distinctive pattern, a kind of marital DNA, ... surfaces in any kind of meaningful interaction" (Gladwell, 26). According to Gottman, this pattern shows up soon after people meet. Gladwell also cites research that suggests that when you first meet someone, your initial impressions emphasize some tacit criteria and overlook others. Later on, subsequent events will bring other characteristics into the foreground, activating other criteria and changing your initial impression (Gladwell, 67). I am suggesting here the mechanism by which all this occurs: when characteristics (say, powerfulness) are thematic, they become especially salient, unconsciously activating the tacit criteria associated with them. With this one criterion activated and others quiescent, you overlook other characteristics

(Sculley's need for control; Jobs's rebellious streak) that may fall short relative to other tacit criteria. As a result, you fail to see how much the person as a whole departs from what you want (Gladwell, 76).

20. See Kahney, "Being Steve Jobs' Boss." In this 2010 *BusinessWeek* interview, Sculley says, "the thing that connected Steve and me was industrial design." It's probably true that it was their shared love of design that brought the two men together, but it was more likely their shared love of power that sealed the deal.

21. Gladwell, 78.

22. Sculley, 90. During their courtship, Jobs asked Sculley, "Do you want to sell sugared water for the rest of your life, or do you want a chance to change the world?" Sculley later wrote of that moment, "It was as if someone had reached up and delivered a stiff blow to my stomach. . . . It simply knocked the wind out of me."

23. Rose tells many stories of Jobs's disdain for and ridicule of institutional authority, starting in high school with the Buck Fry Club—a transposition designed to rankle the principal, Mr. Bryald (Rose, 27). Years later, Apple's motto "one person—one computer" captured in one pithy expression Jobs's complex and long-standing desire to alter the balance of power between the individual and the institution (Rose, 38).

24. In one account, Rose says, "Sculley had more definite ideas about how things should be done, and he expected his managers to try them out. The organization he was creating was one in which decisions came down from above. That was a corollary to the hierarchy he was constructing" (Rose, 167). Also, in *Odyssey* Sculley often refers to his fears of losing control and his efforts at gaining better control.

25. Rose, 139.

26. Ibid.

27. According to Rose, most of Sculley's design decisions reflected a preference for rational order and greater control. Early on, for example, after hanging an organizational chart on his wall, he turned his attention to the network of stores that sold Apple products to the public, deciding that Apple should have its own sales force. As Rose says of that decision: "(Sculley) wasn't happy with the way some of the rep organizations were performing, he

thought it was time that Apple had the prestige of its own sales organization—the prestige and control" (Rose, 166–167).

28. Sculley, 240. It was only much later, after the consequences of the decision had played out, that it seemed so misguided. At the time, Sculley thought giving Jobs more operational responsibility made good sense, so much so that he changed his title from vice president to executive vice president.

29. Ibid., 167.

30. Ibid., 198.

31. Sculley decided to fold Lisa into the Macintosh group so they would have only two lines of business: Apple II and Macintosh. This decision, which upset both those working on Lisa *and* those working on Macintosh, made the Macintosh division more powerful than the Apple II division.

32. Sculley, 199.

33. Jobs's disrespect first emerged during a meeting at Xerox PARC a couple of years earlier. As far as Jobs could tell, no one at Xerox appreciated the dazzling technology they had right under their noses or the brilliant engineers they had working on it, some of whom Apple later recruited. In that moment, Xerox must have struck Jobs as a glaring example of the almost criminal stupidity of big institutions.

34. Sculley, 205–206. My brackets identifying Adams and Glavin.

35. For a detailed account of the impact on Jobs and how he handled it, see Rose, 217–218.

36. Rose, 209.

37. Sculley, 167.

38. Ibid., 166.

39. Ibid., 166–167.

40. Ibid., 167.

41. Ibid.

42. *BusinessWeek*, November 26, 1984. Ironically, the Dynamic Duo label stuck at the very point that their relationship became unglued.

43. Rose, 193–194.

44. Ibid., 211.

45. Sculley, 210.

46. Ibid., 228.
47. Rose, 229.
48. Sculley, 235.
49. Rose, 252.
50. Sculley, 240.
51. Ibid., 238.
52. Rose, 247.
53. Sculley, 236–237.
54. Rose, 259.
55. Sculley, 235.
56. Rose, 254.
57. Ibid., 255.
58. Sculley, 241.
59. Rose, 282.
60. Sculley, 261.
61. Ibid., 240.
62. Ibid., 230–239.
63. Ibid., 252. Also see Morrow, "Steve Jobs Oral History."
64. Sculley, 238.
65. Rose, 282.
66. For a deeper discussion of Jobs and Sculley's post-facto reflections on the aftermath of their collapse, see Chapter One.

Chapter 3

1. Kirn, "I'm OK. You're OK. We're Not OK." This *Time* magazine essay reported on an effort to include "relational disorders" in an updated edition of a psychiatric diagnostic manual.
2. This example also appeared in Edmondson and Smith, "Too Hot to Handle?"
3. And though Naughton uses the language of "we," he implies Bedford, since all this waiting around took place long before he (Naughton) arrived.
4. See especially Argyris and Schön, *Theory in Practice,* on the difference between theories-in-use and espoused theories.
5. Meacham, *Franklin and Winston,* 274.

6. Ibid., 68.

7. Ibid., 45.

8. Sherwood, *Roosevelt and Hopkins*, 363–364. Quoted in Meacham, 108.

9. Meacham, 108-112.

10. Ibid., 116.

11. Ibid., 118.

12. Churchill may have conceded after calculating Britain's political power relative to America's in a post-war and post-colonial world: "It has always been my wish to keep equal," Churchill wrote his wife, Clementine, as the war neared its end, "but how can you do that against so mighty a nation and a population nearly three times your own?" Meacham, 340. Also see Zakaria, "Future of American Power": "In 1945, the United States' GDP was ten times that of Britain. Even then, Britain remained remarkably influential, at least partly because of the almost superhuman energy and ambition of Winston Churchill. Given that the United States was paying most of the Allies' economic costs, and Russia was bearing most of the casualties, it took extraordinary will for Britain to remain one of the three major powers deciding the fate of the postwar world. (The photographs of Franklin Roosevelt, Joseph Stalin, and Churchill at the Yalta Conference in February 1945 are somewhat misleading: there was no 'big three' at Yalta; there was a 'big two' plus one brilliant political entrepreneur who was able to keep himself and his country in the game.)" It may also speak to the underlying pattern, captured best in a comment made by Churchill's daughter Mary Soames: "In love, there is always one who kisses, and one who offers the cheek. Churchill was the suitor, Roosevelt the elusive quarry." Meacham, *xv*.

13. Meacham, 332.

14. Ibid., 270.

15. In a tribute to Roosevelt after he died, Churchill went so far as to praise Roosevelt's "power of gauging the tides and currents of mobile public opinion." Meacham, 353.

16. See Marcus, *Birth of the Mind*.

17. See Begley, "Nature of Nurturing."

18. Reiss, Neiderhiser, Hetherington, and Plomin, *Relationship Code*, 420.
19. Begley, "Nature of Nurturing."
20. Ibid.
21. Marcus, 24.
22. Marcus, 98. Emphasis in original.
23. Marcus, 39. Also see Holloway, "The Mutable Brain," and Kendall, "How Child Abuse and Neglect Damage the Brian." Kendall's article recounts how damage inflicted by abuse and neglect can be reversed by timely interventions. These interventions "help rewire the brain and put psychological development back on track." The article quotes Dr. Bessel van der Kolk, an internationally known expert on psychological trauma from the Trauma Center in Allston, Massachusetts: "Positive experiences that contradict a traumatized child's negative expectations are critical to helping the brain readjust itself. For example, just saying to a child that you are sorry the event happened changes brain chemistry."

Part 2

1. Attributed to Abraham Lincoln, source unknown.

Chapter 4

1. Flood, *Grant and Sherman*, 328. Lincoln's assassination was part of a coordinated plot to kill the leading members of the president's administration, including William Seward and General Ulysses S Grant. Seward was stabbed several times at his home, though not mortally; Grant had decided at the last minute to travel out of Washington, D.C., and thereby averted the plot on his life.
2. Ibid., 329.
3. Goodwin, *Team of Rivals*, 743. The witness was Horace Porter, a brigadier general who served on Ulysses Grant's staff.
4. Donald, *Lincoln*, 186. From William Herndon letters.
5. Thomas and Hyman, *Stanton: The Life and Times*, 120.
6. Sandburg, *Abraham Lincoln: The War Years* i, 447.
7. Pratt, *Stanton: Lincoln's Secretary of War*, 143.

8. See Karney and Bradbury, "Longitudinal Course of Marital Quality." Compare their research on couples.

9. Although this is an actual firm and case, the names are fictional.

10. Dobbs, *One Minute to Midnight*, 6.

11. See Edmondson and Smith, "Too Hot to Handle."

12. High-certainty situations involve present actualities or near-term possibilities that can be illuminated relatively easily through facts and analyses. Low-certainty situations involve more distant or future possibilities for which facts don't yet exist, only inferences.

13. Most topics exist along a continuum, running partly hot, partly cold. But the more a topic grows hot—that is, the more it has the features listed as hot in this table—the harder it is to handle.

14. Metcalfe and Mischel, "A Hot/Cool System Analysis."

15. For example, common cognitive errors such as the actor-observer bias and the fundamental attribution error give rise to and reinforce the individual perspective, while many cultures, especially Western cultures, value individual responsibility in ways that overshadow people's mutual responsibility for creating results and realities no one likes.

16. This strikes me as a worthy hypothesis to pursue—that is, whether by reflecting and reframing in this way, people can cool down and shift perspective more quickly.

17. In reality, I doubt that Luke or Dan had this precise map in their heads, even though they'd discussed it. More likely, they recalled the outlines of the map: its circular quality, the notion that patterns of interaction among people—not people alone—are the problem, and the idea that they each contributed to a pattern they didn't like. While such notions are incomplete and imprecise, they're all you need to stop a hot system from running amok.

18. Also see Smith, "The Muck Stops Here" and McArthur, Putnam, and Smith, "Climbing Out of the Muck."

19. For example, see Myers, *Gifts Differing*.

Chapter 5

1. See Gladwell, *Blink*, 27–29. Also see Note 19 in Chapter Two.

2. Though many details in this story have been modified to protect the confidentiality of the protagonists, most of the data on what

Chris and Peter thought, felt, and said came from case material based on meetings about their relationship.

3. Also see Appendix B, "The Ladder of Reflection," for the tool I used to observe and analyze behavior using this framework.

4. See Berger and Luckmann, *The Social Construction of Reality*, 29. The authors make a similar point when they argue, "'What he is,' therefore, is ongoingly available to me. This availability is continuous and prereflective. On the other hand, 'What I am' is *not* so available. To make it available requires that I stop, arrest the continuous spontaneity of my experience, and deliberately turn my attention back upon myself." Also, see Nisbett and Ross, *Human Inference,* for a good summary of the research on the actor-observer divergence in causal attributions.

5. Theorists from different traditions define and use the term *frame* differently. Cognitive psychologists Daniel Kahneman and Amos Tversky use the term to refer to the more conscious, analytic processes people go through when assessing risk or making choices—such as whether to fly or not to fly, whether to buy one stock or another; see Kahneman and Tversky, "Choice, Values, and Frames." Donald Schön, a philosopher by training and an organizational theorist by trade, uses the term to refer to the process by which professionals reflect on and revise their professional knowledge by framing and reframing their roles. See Schön, *The Reflective Practitioner.* John Van Maanen, an organizational ethnographer, refers to a similar phenomenon when he speaks of "situational definitions," saying that "situational definitions provide an individual with a practical theory for 'what's going on' in concrete situations." See Van Maanen, "On the Understanding of Interpersonal Relations," 64. Although Schön talks in terms of "stories" and Van Maanen of "theories," both refer to the largely tacit or unconscious processes that allow us to make useful sense of situations such that we can act *in the moment* with others. Like Van Maanen and Schön, I use the term to refer to the tacit interpretations we make in the heat of the moment in order to act. But I reserve the term for the more stable interpretations we form about ourselves in relation to others; these more stable interpretations emerge over time out of patterns of interaction and turn those more variable patterns into more stable informal structures.

6. A number of cognitive psychologists claim that we answer these questions in a particular sequence, but little consensus exists as to what that sequence is. Carol Dweck and Ellen Leggett argue that goals come first. See Dweck and Leggett, "A Social-Cognitive Approach to Motivation and Personality." Taking a contrary view, James Shah argues that our representations of others automatically affect the goals we set for ourselves. See Shah, "Automatic for People." While we'll probably never know for sure which comes first, I suspect that goals follow from how we frame situations and ourselves relative to others. Once we've taken that step, some goals naturally spring to mind while others would never occur to us. From the point of view of the actor, however, it doesn't much matter: it feels as if it's all happening at once.

7. See, for example, Lord, Brown, and Freiberg, "Understanding the Dynamics of Leadership." The authors argue that our conception of ourselves is far from monolithic. Rather it's a "confederation of self-schemas derived from past social experiences." Van Maanen makes a similar point when he says, "While the self may be thought of as our most personal and prized possession, it nevertheless resides ultimately in the hands of others who may choose to deny it, confirm it, ignore it, or change it.... We can be mothers, lawyers, socialites, sisters, secret sinners, devout believers, workhorses, aggressive lovers, shy speakers, politicians, game players, and so forth. We can play several roles at the same time, change roles, fake roles, and still we tend to think of ourselves as whole and unique." See Van Maanen, "On the Understanding of Interpersonal Relations," 45. Also, James Shah summarizes evidence that suggests "our complex representations of significant others may come to influence not only how we perceive others, and interact with them, but how we come to perceive and evaluate ourselves." See Shah, "Automatic for People."

8. See Lord, Brown, and Freiberg, "Understanding the Dynamics of Leadership." The authors, who develop the notion of self-schema in the context of leader-follower relationships, distinguish between peripheral and core self-concepts.

9. Nearly everyone agrees that human behavior is purposive—that is, designed with some purpose in mind. But much disagreement exists

as to how to understand purposes and what kind of understanding is most useful for explaining behavior in specific situations. See Dweck and Leggett, "A Social-Cognitive Approach." The authors argue, as I do here, that conceiving of purposes as general motives—say, for power—can't predict specific behavioral consequences. Conceiving of purposes as specific goals solves that problem. Goals are more connectable to specific behavioral patterns and thus a more useful concept for understanding and altering those patterns.

10.   See Shah, "Automatic for People."

Chapter 6

1.   Conlin, "I'm a Bad Boss? Blame My Dad," 60.
2.   Some relationships have a major impact regardless of people's formal roles. Compare Tushman and O'Reilly, *Winning Through Innovation*, 94–97. Note their observation that key leaders are those individuals and their associated networks that have a major impact on outcomes of importance regardless of formal power.
3.   See Henry Mintzberg's thoughts on "mutual adjustment" in *The Structuring of Organizations*.
4.   See Galbraith, *Designing Organizations*.
5.   See Chris Argyris's work, especially *Strategy, Change, and Defensive Routines*.

Part 3

1.   Havel, "The Power of the Powerless," 136.

Chapter 7

1.   Compare Polivy and Herman, "If at First You Don't Succeed."
2.   Another benefit of taking a staged approach is that you can choose to stop at the end of any stage by considering two things: (1) how strong your relationship needs to be and (2) how willing and able you are to continue.
3.   Never poke fun unless you're sure there's no hidden, hostile meaning lurking behind it.
4.   See Masten, "Ordinary Magic."

Chapter 8

1. Johnson, *Where Good Ideas Come From,* 18.

2. As before, the firm and case are actual, although the names are fictional. All data on what Dan and Stu felt, thought, said, and did came from tape recordings and observations of nonverbal behavior.

3. These characteristics—trust, commitment, approach to conflict, results orientation, accountability—correspond to those cited in Lencioni, *The Five Dysfunctions of a Team.* Thinking in these terms, you might conclude that a relationship is functioning well (or badly) at any point in time. Whether a relationship has the ability to sustain a high level of functioning over time and across circumstances is another question. As argued in Chapter Four, that depends on a relationship's cool system. That system determines whether and how quickly people in a relationship can shift perspective in the heat of the moment, allowing them to build relationships that function well over time, even under adverse conditions.

4. The data included in all three tables are taken from meetings with Dan and Stu.

5. Some people worry that they'll be self-conscious about tape-recording or videotaping, but most people forget about it as soon as they get caught up in a conversation. If taping is out of the question, though, take careful notes on what you and others are actually saying—not your descriptions or interpretations of what you're each saying.

6. These data were excerpted from a meeting transcript.

7. For more on "behavioral repertoires," see Chapter Five and Appendix A.

8. By observing and describing behavior closely, as an anthropologist would, and asking open-ended questions, as any good researcher would, you stay curious enough to fully understand interactions and to uncover the factors that lead them to persist, putting you in a better position to alter patterns that get in people's way. Developing the ability to observe closely and to inquire openly depends on three things: using the frameworks and techniques introduced here and in Chapter Five, using the Ladder of Reflection outlined in Appendix B, and adopting the relational perspective described in Chapter Three.

9. At this point, our explanation of their interaction can only be partial, because we do not yet understand all the factors that maintain the pattern, including the themes that predispose them to get triggered and the experiential knowledge they've built around those themes, such that they see things one way and not another. Our explanations become more complete as we move through the stages of change. See Chapters Nine and Ten.

10. This template is derived from the Anatomy Framework and singles out for attention people's interlocking reactions and actions. For more, see Chapter Five.

11. See Nisbett and Wilson, "Telling More Than We Can Know." Also see Argyris, Putnam, and Smith, *Action Science*.

12. There are limits to each of these approaches even when done well. Asking gives you the most direct data but not necessarily the most reliable: people are often unaware of what they think and feel. Speculating on the basis of other things people have said—for instance, in an initial assessment—can help you connect patterns to people's goals and concerns but won't necessarily capture what the person is feeling and thinking in that particular moment. Finally, predicting on the basis of some theory and what people are now doing will open up possibilities people might not have considered, but it's never easy to tell whether that theory (and thus the predictions) apply in this case. This means you have to hold tentatively any statements that wind up in this box, remaining ever ready to revise them.

13. No matter how suspect we might be of actors' abilities to know or to describe what they are thinking or feeling, they can go inside themselves and register some kind of feeling and notice some kind of thought. Putting aside whether this access is accurate, it is indisputably different. Thus actors and observers will tend to see different things in—and make different meanings out of—the "same" behavior.

14. See Nisbett and Ross, *Human Inference*.

15. For an engaging account of the difficulties involved in describing what we are feeling or thinking, see Spence, *Narrative Truth and Historical Truth*.

16. Nothing will close people down faster—or make them more defensive—than telling them what's going on inside their heads or

their hearts. Better to be humble and to defer to their account, at least provisionally. You can always come back later and revise your understanding when everyone is more able and willing to explore and to discuss with each other how they're really feeling.

17. For laugh-out-loud examples of what happens when people throw a monkey wrench into everyday cultural works, see Garfinkel, *Studies in Ethnomethodology.*

18. For more on action experiments, see Argyris, Putnam, and Smith, *Action Science.*

19. Space constraints prevent me from illustrating failed experiments. But they are a valuable part of the change process, because they rule out actions that won't succeed in disrupting the pattern. To reduce the costs of failed experiments, it helps to create a context in which experimentation is rewarded and to test out options under less-threatening conditions—for example, by role-playing what you might actually say or do before trying it under real-life conditions.

Chapter 9

1. To get at people's reactions, it's best to ask open-ended questions such as, "What's going on?" But avoid asking *why* someone did something. It's apt to yield what Paul Johnson calls *reconstructed reasoning* or what Chris Argyris and Don Schön call an *espoused theory*—a plausible explanation or justification that's often disconnected from what the person actually feels, thinks, and does. Instead, ask people to describe what's going through their minds as if they have a tape recorder in there. See Ericsson and Simon, *Protocol Analysis.* This method elicits what Johnson calls *authentic reasoning* and Argyris and Schön call a *theory-in-use.*

2. While I've condensed some excerpts from Dan and Stu's exchanges, I've taken care to preserve the actual language each of them used.

3. We can never know for sure all that Dan and Stu were feeling or thinking; even if we could, our ability to infer the frames embedded in those reactions would always be imperfect. Understanding this, we kept our conclusions open to revision, continually going back and elaborating them as we learned more and built even greater trust.

4. Compare Schön, *The Reflective Practitioner.*

5. See Putnam, "Recipes and Reflective Learning." Also see Weick, *The Social Psychology of Organizing*. Karl Weick argues that you must act before you know what you think.

Chapter 10

1. Conlin, "I'm a Bad Boss? Blame My Dad," 61.
2. People don't ever recount events qua events. As Jerome Bruner points out in "On the Perception of Incongruity," it is the storied version of events that we relay. In terms of our task here, that's not a problem. We're less interested in what actually happened, but in what people made of what happened and how that affects their ability to navigate current circumstances.
3. To capture the experiential knowledge that Stu and Dan brought to their relationship, I relied on "A Guide to Behavioral Repertoires" (see Appendix A).
4. Research on learning suggests that learners are anything but empty vessels. Even young children bring their own naïve theories to learning, leading them to structure and restructure what they hear and see in their own terms. For an excellent discussion of how people learn, see Greeno, "A Perspective on Thinking." Also see Hatano and Inagaki, "Everyday Biology and School Biology."
5. See Kets de Vries and Miller, *The Neurotic Organization*, 111. The authors make a similar argument when they write, "It is important for both superior and subordinate to become aware of the existence of dysfunctional interaction patterns, for awareness is the first step toward dissolving them. Promoting this awareness requires the cooperation of both parties." Here I am arguing that neurotic behaviors create repetitious patterns of interaction, which in turn evoke and maintain more neurotic behavior. By focusing simultaneously on changing individual behaviors and the structures they create, you accelerate the change of both.

Appendix A

1. The ideas presented in this guide are cursory, because space does not permit elaboration. For those interested in learning more, the next note includes references to authors who have explored these ideas in much greater depth. Also, for those more interested in

application, see Chapters Five and Ten, which illustrate how you can use the guide to explore and capture experiential knowledge for reflective purposes.

2. Some students of human behavior focus on the more universal, less variable aspects of behavior, others on the more variable, personal aspects. Since I do both in a somewhat cursory fashion, I include references to both here for those who may wish to delve deeper:

    Personal knowledge: Personal knowledge, like cultural knowledge, takes four different forms: *narrative* (see Roy Schafer, Michael White and David Epston, David Kantor); *analytic* (see George Kelly); *moral* (see Lawrence Kohlberg, Robert Kegan, Carol Gilligan); and *practical* (see Smith). Some scholars, such as Jerome Bruner, straddle the categories by exploring different modes of knowing.

    Cultural knowledge: Cultural knowledge also takes four forms: *narrative* (see Iain Mangham, John Van Maanen); *analytic* (see organization theorists who study shared beliefs, assumptions, and theories: Sonja Sackmann , Ed Schein, John Van Maanen, Peter Drucker, Michael Tushman and David Nadler, John Kotter and James Heskett, Gordon Donaldson and Jay Lorsch; also see psychologists studying social cognition: Richard Nisbett, Lee Ross, Timothy DeCamp Wilson, Carol Dweck and Ellen Leggett, Daniel Kahneman and Amos Tversky, and Robert Lord); *moral* (see George Homans, Ed Schein, Chris Argyris and Donald Schön); *practical* (see Esther N. Goody, Erving Goffman, Roger Schank and Robert Abelson, Michael Cohen, Chris Argyris and Donald Schön). As you can see, a number of scholars cross the artificial but hopefully useful boundaries I create here.

3. I don't include rituals in this cell, because I'm focusing on the less-conscious knowledge people use to make meaning and to take action. While rituals express or manifest that knowledge, they are conscious acts, and their meaning is embedded in visible, audible forms.

4. According to psychologist Jerome Bruner, "If (children) don't catch something in a narrative structure, it doesn't get remembered very well, and it doesn't seem to be accessible for further kinds of

mulling over." Quoted in Frank, "Students Discover Economics." Also see Bruner, *Actual Minds, Possible Worlds.*

5. Those who study everyday social cognition refer to this belief as the "fundamental attribution error."

6. See Kelly, *The Psychology of Personal Constructs,* for an account of how these constructs form and change.

7. See Kohlberg, *Essays on Moral Development,* for a structural view of moral development.

8. See Garfinkel, *Studies in Ethnomethodology.*

9. This is especially true when you try to use cultural scripts to handle important relationships in ambiguous or difficult situations. Bargaining routines may work well when one is haggling over a rug, but they rarely work well in complex negotiations in long-term relationships. See Fisher, Ury, and Patton, *Getting to Yes.*

Appendix B

1. For those who enjoy tracing the history of an idea, academic-turned-politician S. I. Hayakawa introduced a notion similar to the Ladder of Inference in 1939 (Hayakawa and Hayakawa, *Language in Thought and Action*), building on the even earlier work of Alfred Korzybski of "the map is not the territory" fame. Hayakawa's notion, called the Abstraction Ladder, shows how we use language to create increasingly abstract categories from *Bessie the cow* to *livestock* to *farm* to *wealth.* Like the Ladder of Inference, you can use the Abstraction Ladder to analyze communications, understandings, and misunderstandings—though some people, who make finer distinctions, would beg to differ (see, for example, Walls and Walden, "Understanding Unclear Situations"). Anyway, as Steve Stockdale explains on his website, ThisIsNotThat.com, Hayakawa's Abstraction Ladder is especially helpful in "immunizing" against political propaganda of the kind that was running rampant in the 1930s. Stockdale explains, drawing on one of Hayakawa's examples, "a local politician attempts to drum up support by exclaiming, *'Farmer Jones, vote for me to ensure that Schmokum County serves as a beacon of forward-looking growth and prosperity!'* As this exhortation contains no specifics, only generalized, highly abstract references, you could infer that this belongs fairly high up on the Ladder of

Abstractions. And if Farmer Jones recognizes this, he will likely ask the Schmokum County candidate, '*What exactly do you mean, what will you do?*' And when the candidate replies, '*Well, er, Jones, what I mean is, uh . . . we're going to build a new road right across your farm!*' " As this example shows, once we come down the ladder, there can now be no misunderstanding—or at least, a lot less. Farmer Jones now knows exactly what this politician means by "forward-looking growth and prosperity." He means a very specific, and pardon the pun, *concrete* road.

2.   Depending on their purpose, different people have created different ladders, each with a different number of rungs, almost all of them going by different names. To cite a few notable ones: Argyris and his colleagues use a five-rung ladder to reflect on people's reasoning; see, for example, Argyris, Putnam, and Smith, *Action Science*. In a similar vein, my colleagues and I at Action Design offer a three-rung version to help people see how they go from some "data" to their closely held "certainties" about the world; see www.actiondesign.com. In *The Fifth Discipline,* Peter Senge speaks of "leaps of abstraction" in the context of people's mental models, as he does in *The Fifth Discipline Fieldbook,* where he and his colleagues offer their own version of the ladder. In *Difficult Conversations,* Doug Stone, Bruce Patton, and Sheila Heen use a three-rung ladder to explain where people's "stories" come from. Finally, Ted Walls and David Walden's five-step "Reasoning Cycle," which intentionally steers away from the term *ladder,* can be used to analyze "language data."

3.   I'm not claiming that these values are enacted, completely shared, or equally applied. But when it comes to learning and to finding common ground, it's enough that most people hold a value, even if they don't always enact it or apply it to others. It still matters to them, usually a lot. And that can serve as the basis of a conversation that's more likely to produce learning and to discover common ground.

4.   Feynman, *What Do You Care What People Think?* 14.

BIBLIOGRAPHY

Argryis, Chris. *Strategy, Change and Defensive Routines.* Boston: Pitman Publishing, 1985.

Argyris, Chris, and Donald A. Schön. *Theory in Practice: Increasing Professional Effectiveness.* San Francisco: Jossey-Bass, 1974.

Argyris, Chris, and Donald A. Schön. *Organizational Learning II: Theory, Method, and Practice.* Reading, MA: Addison-Wesley, 1996.

Argyris, Chris, Robert Putnam, and Diana McLain Smith. *Action Science: Concepts, Methods, and Skills for Research and Intervention.* San Francisco: Jossey-Bass, 1985.

Balkundi, Prasad, and Martin Kilduff. "The Ties That Lead: A Social Network Approach to Leadership." *The Leadership Quarterly* 17 (2006): 419–439.

Begley, Sharon. "The Nature of Nurturing." *Newsweek,* March 27, 2000. Available online at www.newsweek.com/2000/03/26/the-nature-of-nurturing .html. Accessed December 30, 2010.

Bennis, Warren. *On Becoming a Leader: The Leadership Classic.* Cambridge, MA: Perseus Books, 2003.

Bennis, Warren, John Van Maanen, Edgar Schein, and Fred Steele, eds. *Essays in Interpersonal Dynamics.* Homewood, IL: The Dorsey Press, 1979.

Berger, Peter L., and Thomas Luckmann. *The Social Construction of Reality: A Treatise in the Sociology of Knowledge.* Garden City, NY: Anchor Books, 1966.

Boyzatis, Richard, and Annie McKee. *Resonant Leadership: Renewing Yourself and Connecting with Others Through Mindfulness, Hope, and Compassion.* Boston: Harvard Business School Publishing, 2005.

Bruner, Jerome. *Actual Minds, Possible Worlds*. Cambridge, MA: Harvard University Press, 1987.

Bruner, Jerome S., and Leo Postman. "On the Perception of Incongruity: A Paradigm." *Journal of Personality* 18 (1949): 206–223.

Charan, Ram. "Conquering a Culture of Indecision." *Harvard Business Review*, April 2001, 74–82.

Clothier, Suzanne. *Bones Would Rain from the Sky: Deepening Our Relationship with Dogs*. New York: Warner Books, 2002.

Cohen, Michael D., and Paul Baldayan. "Organizational Routines Are Stored as Procedural Memory: Evidence from a Laboratory Study." *Organization Science* 5, no. 4 (December 1994): 554–568.

Conlin, Michelle. "I'm a Bad Boss? Blame My Dad." *BusinessWeek*, May 10, 2004.

Dobbs, Michael. *One Minute to Midnight: Kennedy, Khrushchev, and Castro on the Brink of Nuclear War*. New York: Alfred A. Knopf, 2008.

Donald, David Herbert. *Lincoln*. New York: Simon & Schuster Paperbacks, 1995.

Donaldson, Gordon A., and Jay W. Lorsch. *Decision-Making at the Top*. New York: Basic Books, 1984.

Drucker, Peter. "The Theory of the Business." *Harvard Business Review*, September 1994, 95–107.

Dweck, Carol. *Mindset: The New Psychology of Success*. New York: Random House, 2006.

Dweck, Carol, and Ellen Leggett. "A Social-Cognitive Approach to Motivation and Personality." *Psychological Review* 95, no. 2 (1988): 256–273.

Edmondson, Amy C., and Diana McLain Smith. "Too Hot to Handle? How to Manage Relationship Conflict." *California Management Review* 49, no. 1 (Fall 2006): 6–31.

Ericsson, K. Anders, and Herbert A. Simon. *Protocol Analysis: Verbal Reports as Data*. Cambridge, MA: MIT Press, 1984.

Feynman, Richard P. *What Do You Care What People Think? Further Adventures of a Curious Character*. New York: Bantam, 1989.

Fisher, Roger, William Ury, and Bruce Patton. *Getting to Yes: Negotiating Agreement Without Giving In*, Second Edition. New York: Penguin Books, 1991.

Flood, Charles Bracelen. *Grant and Sherman: The Friendship That Won the Civil War*. New York: Farrar, Straus and Giroux, 2005.

Frank, Robert H. "Students Discover Economics in Its Natural State." *The New York Times,* September 29, 2005.

Galbraith, Jay. *Designing Complex Organizations.* Reading, MA: Addison-Wesley, 1973.

Galbraith, Jay. *Designing Organizations: An Executive Guide to Strategy, Structure, and Process.* San Francisco: Jossey-Bass, 2002.

Garfinkel, Harold. *Studies in Ethnomethodology.* Englewood Cliffs, NJ: Prentice Hall, 1967.

Gilligan, Carol. *In a Different Voice: Psychological Theory and Women's Development.* Cambridge, MA: Harvard University Press, 1993.

Gladwell, Malcolm. *Blink: The Power of Thinking Without Thinking.* New York: Little, Brown, 2005.

Glynn, Mary Ann, and Rich DeJordy. "Leadership Through an Organization Behavior Lens: A Look at the Last Half-Century of Research." In Nitin Nohria and Rakesh Khurana, *Handbook of Leadership Theory and Practice: A Harvard Business School Centennial Colloquium.* Boston: Harvard Business School Publishing, 2010.

Goffman, Erving. "On Facework: An Analysis of Ritual Elements in Social Interaction." In Adam Jaworski and Nikolas Coupland, eds. *The Discourse Reader.* New York: Routledge, 2006.

Goleman, Daniel. *Emotional Intelligence: Why It Can Matter More Than IQ.* New York: Bantam Books, 1995.

Goleman, Daniel. *Working with Emotional Intelligence.* New York: Bantam Books, 2000.

Goleman, Daniel, and Richard Boyzatis. "Social Intelligence and the Biology of Leadership." *Harvard Business Review* 36, no. 2 (July–September 2008): 74–81.

Goodwin, Doris Kearns. *Team of Rivals: The Political Genius of Abraham Lincoln.* New York: Simon & Schuster, 2005.

Goody, Esther N. "Questions and Politeness: Strategies in Social Interaction." In Esther N. Goody, ed. *Cambridge Papers in Social Anthropology* 8. Cambridge, UK: Cambridge University Press, 1978.

Gottman, John. *Why Marriages Succeed or Fail . . . And How You Can Make Yours Last.* New York: Fireside, 1994.

Gottman, John, and Sybil Carrere. "Predicting Divorce Among Newlyweds from the First Three Minutes of a Marital Conflict Discussion." *Family Process* 38 (1999): 293–301.

Gottman, John M., and Joan DeClaire. *The Relationship Cure: A Five-Step Guide to Strengthening Your Marriage, Family, and Friendships.* New York: Three Rivers Press, 2001.

Greeno, James G. "A Perspective on Thinking." *American Psychologist* 44, no. 2 (February 1989): 134–141.

Harris, Kenneth J., K. M. Kacmar, and S. Zivnuska. "An Investigation of Abusive Supervision as a Predictor of Performance and the Meaning of Work as a Moderator of the Relationship." *The Leadership Quarterly* 18, 252–263.

Hatano, Giyoo, and Kayoko Inagaki. "Everyday Biology and School Biology: How Do They Interact?" *Quarterly Newsletter of the Laboratory of Comparative Human Cognition* 9, no. 4 (October 1987): 120–128.

Václav, Havel. "The Power of the Powerless." In Václav, Havel, *Open Letters: Selected Writings, 1965– 1990.* New York: Vintage Books, 1992.

Hayakawa, Samuel Ichiye, and Alan R. Hayakawa. *Language in Thought and Action,* Fifth Edition. New York: Harcourt, 1991. (First published in 1939).

Heifetz, Ronald A., and Donald L. Laurie. "The Work of Leadership." *Harvard Business Review* 75, no. 1 (January-February 1997): 124–134.

Heifetz, Ronald A., and Marty Linsky. *Leadership on the Line: Staying Alive Through the Dangers of Leading.* Boston: Harvard Business School Publishing, 2002.

Hertzfeld, Andy. *Revolution in the Valley: The Insanely Great Story of How the Mac Was Made.* Sebastopol, CA: O'Reilly Media, 2005.

Hirschhorn, Larry, and Tom Gilmore. "The Application of Family Therapy Concepts to Influencing Organizational Behavior." *Administrative Science Quarterly* 25, no. 1 (March 1980): 18–37.

Holloway, Marguerite. "The Mutable Brain." *Scientific American (Special Issue),* September 2003.

Homans, George. *The Human Group.* New York: Harcourt College Publications, 1950.

Ilies, Remus, Frederick P. Morgeson, and Jennifer D. Nahrgang. "Authentic Leadership and Eudaemonic Well-Being: Understanding Leader-Follower Outcomes." *The Leadership Quarterly* 16, (2005): 373–394.

Jobs, Steve. Stanford University commencement address, delivered June 12, 2005. Available online at http://news.stanford.edu/news/2005/june15/jobs-061505.html.

Johnson, Steve. *Where Good Ideas Come From: The Natural History of Innovation.* New York: Riverhead, 2010.

Kahneman, Daniel, and Amos Tversky. "Choice, Values, and Frames." *American Psychologist* 39 (1984): 341–350.

Kahney, Leander. "Being Steve Jobs' Boss." *BusinessWeek*, October 20, 2010. Available online at http://www.businessweek.com/magazine/content/10_44/b4201096309840.htm

Kantor, David. "Critical Identity Image: A Concept Linking Individual, Couple, and Family Development." In John K. Pearce and Leonard J. Friedman, eds. *Family Therapy: Combining Psychodynamic and Family Systems Approaches*, 137–167. New York: Grune & Stratton, 1980.

Kantor, David. "Couples Therapy, Crisis Induction, and Change." In Alan S. Gurman, ed. *Casebook of Marital Therapy*. New York: The Guilford Press, 1985.

Kantor, David. *My Lover, Myself: Self-Discovery Through Relationship*. New York: Riverhead Books, 1999.

Kantor, David, and William Lehr. *Inside the Family: Toward a Theory of Family Process*. San Francisco: Jossey-Bass, 1975.

Kantor, David, and John Neal. "Integrative Shifts for the Theory and Practice of Family Systems Therapy." *Family Process* 24 (March 1985): 13–29.

Karney, Benjamin R., and Thomas N. Bradbury. "The Longitudinal Course of Marital Quality and Stability: A Review of Theory, Method, and Research." *Psychological Bulletin* 119, no. 1 (1995): 3–34.

Kegan, Robert. *The Evolving Self: Problem and Process in Human Development*. Cambridge, MA: Harvard University Press, 1982.

Kelly, George A. *The Psychology of Personal Constructs*. New York: Routledge, 1955.

Kelly, George A. *Theory of Personality: The Psychology of Personal Constructs*. New York: W. W. Norton, 1963.

Kendall, Josh. "How Child Abuse and Neglect Damage the Brain." *The Boston Globe,* September 24, 2002, C1.

Kets de Vries, Manfred F. R., and Danny Miller. *The Neurotic Organization: Diagnosing and Revitalizing Unhealthy Organizations*. New York: Harper-Collins, 1991.

Kirn, Walter. "I'm OK, You're OK, We're Not OK." *Time*, September 16, 2002.

Kohlberg, Lawrence. *Essays on Moral Development, Volume 1: The Philosophy of Moral Development*. New York: Harper & Row, 1981.

Kohlberg, Lawrence, and Thomas Lickona, ed. "Moral Stages and Moralization: The Cognitive-Developmental Approach." *Moral Development and Behavior: Theory, Research, and Social Issues*. New York: Holt, Rinehart and Winston, 1976.

Kotter, John P., and James Heskett. *Corporate Culture and Performance*. New York: Free Press, 1992.

Kouzes, James M., and Barry Z. Posner. *The Leadership Challenge*, Fourth Edition. San Francisco: Jossey-Bass, 2007.

Lencioni, Patrick. *The Five Dysfunctions of a Team: A Leadership Fable*. San Francisco: Jossey-Bass, 2002.

Lord, Robert, and Douglas J. Brown. *Leadership Processes and Follower Self-Identity*. Mahwah, NJ: Lawrence Erlbaum Associates, 2003.

Lord, Robert, Douglas Brown, and Steve Freiberg. "Understanding the Dynamics of Leadership: The Role of Follower Self-Concepts in the Leader/Follower Relationship." *Organizational Behavior and Human Decision Processes* 78, no. 3 (June 1999): 167–203.

Mangham, Iain L. *Interactions and Interventions in Organizations*. New York: John Wiley & Sons, 1978.

Marcus, Gary. *The Birth of the Mind: How a Tiny Number of Genes Creates the Complexities of Human Thought*. New York: Basic Books, 2004.

Masten, Ann S. "Ordinary Magic: Resilience Processes in Development." *American Psychologist* 56, no. 3 (March 2001): 227–238.

McArthur, Philip, Robert Putnam, and Diana McLain Smith. "Climbing Out of the Muck." In Peter Senge and others, eds. *The Dance of Change*, 120–125. New York: Doubleday, 1999.

Meacham, Jon. *Franklin and Winston: An Intimate Portrait of an Epic Friendship*. New York: Random House, 2003.

Metcalfe, Janet, and Walter Mischel. "A Hot/Cool System Analysis of Delay of Gratification." *Psychological Review* 106, no. 1 (1999): 3–19.

Miller, Rowland S., and Daniel Perlman. *Intimate Relationships*, Fifth Edition. New York: McGraw-Hill, 2008.

Mintzberg, Henry. *The Structuring of Organizations*. Englewood Cliffs, NJ: Prentice Hall, 1979.

Moreland, Richard L. "Are Dyads Really Groups?" *Small Group Research* 41, no. 2 (April 2010): 251–267.

Morrow, Daniel. "Steve Jobs Oral History." ComputerWorld Honors Program International Archives. Transcript of a Video History Interview with Steve Jobs, conducted April 20, 1995. Available online at http://www.cwheroes.org/archives/histories/jobs.pdf.

Myers, Isabel Briggs. *Gifts Differing: Understanding Personality Type* (reprint edition). Mountain View, CA: Davies-Black, 1995.

Nadler, David, and Michael Tushman. *Competing by Design: The Power of Organizational Architecture*. New York: Oxford University Press, 1997.

Nisbett, Richard E., and Lee Ross. *Human Inference: Strategies and Shortcomings of Social Judgment*. Englewood Cliffs, NJ: Prentice Hall, 1980.

Nisbett, Richard E., and Timothy Wilson. "Telling More Than We Can Know: Verbal Reports on Mental Processes." *Psychological Review* 84 (1977): 231–259.

Nohria, Nitin, and Rakesh Khurana. *Handbook of Leadership Theory and Practice: A Harvard Business School Centennial Colloquium*. Boston: Harvard Business School Publishing, 2010.

Polivy, Janet, and Peter Herman. "If at First You Don't Succeed: False Hopes of Self-Change." *American Psychologist* 57, no. 9 (2002): 677–689.

Pratt, Fletcher. *Stanton: Lincoln's Secretary of War*. New York: W. W. Norton, 1953.

Putnam, Robert. "Recipes and Reflective Learning: What Would Prevent You From Saying It That Way?" In Donald Schön, ed. *The Reflective Turn: Case Studies In and On Educational Practice*. New York: Teachers College Press, 1991. Available online at www.actiondesign.com.

Reiss, David, with Jenae M. Neiderhiser, E. Mavis Hetherington, and Robert Plomin. *The Relationship Code: Deciphering Genetic and Social Influences on Adolescent Development*. Cambridge, MA: Harvard University Press, 2000.

Rose, Frank. *West of Eden: The End of Innocence at Apple Computer*. New York: Penguin, 1989.

Ross, Lee. "The Intuitive Psychologist and His Shortcomings: Distortions in the Attribution Process." In Leonard Berkowitz, *Advances in Experimental Social Psychology* 10, 173–220. New York: Academic Press.

Sackmann, Sonja. *Cultural Knowledge in Organizations: Exploring the Collective Mind*. Newbury Park, CA: Sage, 1991.

Sandburg, Carl. *Abraham Lincoln: The War Years in Four Volumes*. New York: Harcourt, Brace & World, 1939.

Schafer, Roy. "Action and Narration in Psychoanalysis." *New Literary History* 12 (1980): 61–85.

Schank, Roger, and Robert Abelson. *Scripts, Plans, Goals, and Understanding*. Mahwah, NJ: Lawrence Erlbaum Associates, 1977.

Schein, Edgar H. *Organizational Culture and Leadership*. San Francisco: Jossey-Bass, 1985.

Schein, Edgar H. *Process Consultation: Its Role in Organization Development, Second Edition*. Englewood Cliffs, NJ: Prentice Hall, 1988.

Schön, Donald. *The Reflective Practitioner: How Professionals Think in Action*. New York: Basic Books, 1982.

Schön, Donald. *Educating the Reflective Practitioner*. San Francisco: Jossey-Bass, 1987.

Sculley, John, and John A. Byrne. *Odyssey: Pepsi to Apple . . . a Journey of Adventure, Ideas and the Future*. New York: Harper & Row, 1987.

Sedaris, David. "Old Faithful." *The New Yorker*, November 29, 2004. Also available at www.newyorker.com.

Senge, Peter. *The Fifth Discipline: The Art and Practice of the Learning Organization*. New York: Currency, 1990.

Senge, Peter, Charlotte Roberts, Richard Ross, Bryan Smith, and Art Kleiner. *The Fifth Discipline Fieldbook*. New York: Doubleday, 1994.

Shah, James. "Automatic for People: How Representations of Significant Others Implicitly Affect Goal Pursuit." *Journal of Personality and Social Psychology* 84, no. 4 (2003): 661–681.

Sherony, Kathryn, and Stephen G. Green. "Coworker Exchange: Relationships Between Coworkers, Leader-Member Exchange, and Work Attitudes." *Journal of Applied Psychology* 87, no. 3 (June (2002): 542–548.

Sherwood, Robert E. *Roosevelt and Hopkins: An Intimate History*. New York: Harper & Brothers, 1948.

Smith, Diana McLain. "The Muck Stops Here." In Peter Senge and others, eds. *The Dance of Change*, 125–128. New York: Doubleday, 1999.

Spence, Donald P. *Narrative Truth and Historical Truth: Meaning and Interpretation in Psychoanalysis*. New York: W. W. Norton, 1982.

Stone, Douglas, Bruce Patton, and Sheila Heen. *Difficult Conversations: How to Discuss What Matters Most*. New York: Viking, 1999.

Thomas, Benjamin P., and Harold M. Hyman. *Stanton: The Life and Times of Lincoln's Secretary of War*. New York: Alfred A. Knopf, 1962.

Tushman, Michael, and Charles A. O'Reilly. *Winning Through Innovation: A Practical Guide to Leading Organizational Change and Renewal*. Boston: Harvard Business School Press, 1997.

Tse, Herman, Marie Dasborough, and Neal Ashkanasy. "A Multi-Level Analysis of Team Climate and Interpersonal Exchange Relationships at Work." *The Leadership Quarterly* 19 (2008): 195–211.

Uhl-Bien, Mary. "Rational Leadership Theory: Exploring the Social Processes of Leadership and Organizing." *The Leadership Quarterly* 17 (2006): 654–676.

Van Maanen, John. "On the Understanding of Interpersonal Relations." In Warren Bennis, John Van Maanen, Edgar Schein, and Fred Steele, eds. *Essays in Interpersonal Dynamics*. Homewood, IL: The Dorsey Press, 1979.

Walls, Ted, and Walden, David, "Understanding Unclear Situations and Each Other Using the Language Processing Method." *Center for Quality of Management Journal* 4, no. 4 (Special Issue, Winter 1995): 29–37.

Watzlawick, Paul, and John H. Weakland, eds. *The Interactional View: Studies at the Mental Research Institute, Palo Alto, 1965–1974*. New York: W. W. Norton, 1977.

Watzlawick, Paul, Janet Beavin Bavelas, and Don D. Jackson. *Pragmatics of Human Communication: A Study of Interactional Patterns, Pathologies, and Paradoxes*. New York: W. W. Norton, 1967.

Weick, Karl. *The Social Psychology of Organizing*. Reading, MA: Addison-Wesley, 1979.

White, Michael, and David Epston. *Narrative Means to Therapeutic Ends*. New York: W. W. Norton, 1990.

Wu, Joshua B., Anne S. Tsui, and Angelo J. Kinicki. "Consequences of Differentiated Leadership in Groups." *Academy of Management Journal* 53, no. 1 (2010): 90–106.

Zakaria, Fareed. "The Future of American Power: How America Can Survive the Rise of the Rest." *Foreign Affairs* 87, no. 3 (May-June 2008): 18–43.

ADDITIONAL READING

Berger, Peter L., and Thomas Luckmann. *The Social Construction of Reality: A Treatise in the Sociology of Knowledge*. Garden City, NY: Anchor Books, 1966.

Burns, James MacGregor. *Leadership*. New York: Perennial/HarperCollins, 1978.

Burns, James MacGregor. *Transforming Leadership: A New Pursuit of Happiness*. New York: Atlantic Monthly Press, 2003.

Edmondson, Amy C. "Psychological Safety and Learning Behavior in Work Teams." *Adminstrative Science Quarterly* 44 (1999): 350–383.

Edmondson, Amy C. "Framing for Learning." *California Management Review* 45, no. 2 (2003): 34–54.

Edmondson, Amy C., Richard Bohmer, and Gary Pisano. "Speeding Up Team Learning." *Harvard Business Review* 79, no. 9 (October 2001): 125–134.

Eisenhardt, Kathleen, Jean L. Kahwajy, and L. J. Bourgeois III. "How Management Teams Can Have a Good Fight." *Harvard Business Review* 75, no. 4 (July-August 1997): 77–85.

Eisner, Elliot W. *The Enlightened Eye: Qualitative Inquiry and the Enhancement of Educational Practice*. Upper Saddle River, NJ: Merrill, 1998.

Fisher, Roger, and Alan Sharp. *Getting It Done: How to Lead When You're Not in Charge*. New York: HarperBusiness, 1999.

Follett, Mary Parker. "Constructive Conflict." In Pauline Graham, ed. *Prophet of Management*. Boston: Harvard Business School Press, 1996.

Gerzon, Mark. *Leading Through Conflict: How Successful Leaders Transform Differences into Opportunities*. Boston: Harvard Business School Press, 2006.

Goleman, Daniel. *Social Intelligence: The Hidden Impact of Relationships*. New York: Bantam Dell, 2006.

Guttman, Howard M. *When Goliaths Clash: Managing Executive Conflict to Build a More Dynamic Organization*. New York: Amacom, 2003.

Higgins, Jamie, and Diana M. Smith. "Some Feedback on Feedback." *Harvard Business Management Update*. 1999.

Hirschhorn, Larry. *The Workplace Within: Psychodynamics of Organizational Life*. Cambridge, MA: MIT Press, 1990.

Hughes, Marcia, L. Bonita Patterson, and James Bradford Terrell. *Emotional Intelligence in Action: Training and Coaching Activities for Leaders and Managers*. San Francisco: Pfeiffer, 2005.

Johnson, Paul E. "What Kind of Expert Should a System Be?" *Journal of Medicine and Philosophy* 8 (1983): 77–97.

Katzenbach, Jon R., and Douglas K. Smith. *The Wisdom of Teams: Creating the High-Performance Organization*. New York: Collins Business Essentials, 2003.

Kohlreiser, George. *Hostage at the Table: How Leaders Can Overcome Conflict, Influence Others, and Raise Performance*. San Francisco: Jossey-Bass, 2006.

Kolb, Deborah M., and Judith Williams. *The Shadow Negotiation: How Women Can Master the Hidden Agendas That Determine Bargaining Success*. New York: Simon & Schuster, 2000.

Lakoff, George, and Mark Johnson. *Metaphors We Live By*. Chicago: The University of Chicago Press, 1980.

Lakoff, George, and Mark Johnson. *Philosophy in the Flesh: The Embodied Mind and Its Challenge to Western Thought*. New York: HarperCollins, 1999.

Lencioni, Patrick. *Overcoming the Five Dysfunctions of a Team: A Field Guide for Leaders, Managers, and Facilitators*. San Francisco: Jossey-Bass, 2005.

Masten, Ann S. "Ordinary Magic: Resilience Processes in Development." *American Psychologist* 56, no. 3 (March 2001): 227–238.

Noonan, William. *Discussing the Undiscussable: A Guide to Overcoming Defensive Routines in the Workplace*. San Francisco: Jossey-Bass, 2007.

Ong, Anthony, Cindy Bergeman, Toni Bisconti, and Kimberly Wallace. "Psychological Resilience, Positive Emotions, and Successful Adaptation to Stress in Later Life." *Journal of Personality and Social Psychology* 91, no. 4 (2006): 730–749.

Perlow, Leslie. *When You Say Yes But Mean No: How Silencing Conflict Wrecks Relationships and Companies . . . And What You Can Do About It*. New York: Crown Business, 2003.

Quinn, Robert E. *Change the World: How Ordinary People Can Accomplish Extraordinary Results*. San Francisco: Jossey-Bass, 2000.

Schwarz, Roger. *The Skilled Facilitator: A Comprehensive Resource for Consultants, Facilitators, Managers, Trainers, and Coaches*. San Francisco: Jossey-Bass, 2002.

Senge, Peter, and Art Kleiner, Charlotte Roberts, Richard Ross, George Roth, and Bryan Smith. *The Dance of Change*. New York: Doubleday, 1994.

Smith, Diana McLain. "Keeping a Strategic Dialogue Moving." In Peggy Simcic Brown and Roberta Wiig, eds. *Corporate Communication: A Strategic Approach to Building Reputation*. Oslo, Norway: Gyldendal Norsk Forlag, 2002. Also available at www.actiondesign.com.

Susskind, Lawrence, and Jeffrey Cruikshank. *Breaking the Impasse: Consensual Approaches to Resolving Public Disputes*. New York: Basic Books, 1987.

Uhl-Bien, Mary, and John M. Maslyn. "Reciprocity in Manager-Subordinate Relationships: Components, Configurations, and Outcomes." *Journal of Management* 29, issue 4 (August 2003): 511–532.

———

For further reading, see *The Action Design Bibliography* at www.actiondesign.com; click on "bibliography."

ACKNOWLEDGMENTS

The ideas in this book stem from a tradition that believes there's nothing so practical as a good theory, and that no theory is much good if you can't put it to use. While that tradition has a long reach, I have had the privilege of working with four people who managed to keep it alive in these inhospitable times: Chris Argyris, Donald Schön, David Kantor, and Roger Fisher. Over the past thirty years, all four have influenced my research, my practice, and my theory-building, and I am grateful to all of them for their guidance, kindness, and insights.

I'm also indebted to three organizations that paved the way for me to write: The Monitor Group, New Profit Inc., and Action Design. At Monitor, I owe special thanks to Joe Fuller, Mark Fuller, Steve Jennings, Bill McClements (now at Integreon), and those who participated in a seminar called *Leading Through Relationships*: Ambar Chowdhury, Jong Lee (now at Conformis), Josh Lee, Doug Marshall, and Bill Miracky. In one way or another, they all supported my efforts to capture what I was learning about how relationships shape the fate of leaders and their firms.

At New Profit, I am especially grateful to Vanessa Kirsch, Kim Syman, Doug Borchard, Liz Riker, Sarah DiToria, Jeff Berndt, Rod McCowen, and Will Reynolds. You'd be hard-pressed to find a better group of leaders or partners anywhere; they and the entire staff at New Profit are proof of what is possible when you invest in relationships.

At Action Design, Bob Putnam and Phil McArthur have served as thought partners for close to thirty years, ever since we first met at Harvard. Over the past few months, Bob's careful readings and constructive critiques of the manuscript have been invaluable, but his many visits to discuss the book and to distract me while I recovered from knee surgery engender the greatest gratitude.

My colleagues Connie Hadley and Stacy McManus helped immensely by scanning and synthesizing the literature on leadership and relationships and by helping me situate my work in this broader context. Along the way, Stacy's sense of humor sustained me, while Connie's remarkably discerning eye helped me tighten my argument.

A number of friends, family, and colleagues were kind enough to read parts of the manuscript and to offer much-needed suggestions and encouragement: Hilary Austen, Iris Bagwell, Amy Edmondson, Kathryn Flynn, Mark Fuller, Katherine Fulton, Jamie Higgins, Bill Noonan, Geneva Smith, Kim Syman, and Bill Underwood.

My friend and editor, Tim Murphy, rose to the occasion yet again with this book, reading and editing different drafts and always handling pressure with grace. My editor at Jossey-Bass, Kathe Sweeney, restored my faith in writing books. Her belief in these ideas was contagious, and she is the single biggest reason they are seeing the light of day.

My husband, Bruce, and my brother, Rob, deserve much more than thanks. My husband not only read, edited, and commented on countless drafts, he also put up with me over the past few months. His kindness when I needed support and his forgiveness when I wasn't there for him are an inspiration to me. Much the same can be said of my brother, Rob, who has supported and forgiven me more times than I can count and who saved me from myself by suggesting a great title for the book. The two of them are the best elephant handlers you'll ever meet, always ready to say what needs to be said when no one else is saying it. I dedicate this book to the two of them, for being there, when it mattered most, no matter what.

THE AUTHOR

Diana McLain Smith is the chief executive partner of New Profit Inc., a national venture philanthropy firm. Diana came to New Profit in 2009 from the Monitor Group, where she was a partner and chair of Human Dynamics and Change at Monitor University. For the past thirty years, Diana has advised leaders around the world on relationship matters related to leadership, rapid growth, and organizational change. She is the author of *Divide or Conquer: How Great Teams Turn Conflict into Strength* (Penguin, 2008), the coauthor (with Chris Argyris and Bob Putnam) of *Action Science*, a leading text on research and change, and the author and coauthor of a wide range of articles and chapters on leadership, conflict, negotiation, and organizational learning and change. She has served as a guest lecturer at Harvard Law School, Harvard Business School's Executive Programs, Columbia's Executive Education Program, and Boston College's Carroll School of Management. Diana received her masters and doctoral degrees in consulting psychology from Harvard University. Diana and her husband, Bruce Patton, live outside of Boston.

INDEX

A

Abstraction, leaps of, 253–254
Action (or practical) experiments: in
    Chris-Peter relationship, 116; designing,
    167–170; dilemma of, 171–172; in
    Gavin-Fine relationship, 167–170;
    learning from failed, 169; for revising
    outdated knowledge, 219–221. *See also*
    Frame experiments
Action strategies. *See* Practical knowledge and
    action strategies
Actions: focus on, *versus* motives, 164–165;
    framing of, 101, 106–107; mapping
    reactions and, 159–162; pattern
    formation derived from, 101, 102–103,
    105, 117, 159–162; reactions interlocked
    with, 101, 102–103, 105, 159–162,
    168–169, 177
Allen, W., 119
Ambitious goals, 135–137
Analytic knowledge: cultural, 234; defined,
    232; personal, 234–235. *See also*
    Experiential knowledge
Anatomy Framework: basic idea of, 13, 14,
    101; in Chris-Peter case example,
    100–116, 117; elements of, 101–102,
    117; explaining interactions with, 247,
    254; mapping relationships with, 89–117
Annie Hall, 119
Apple: Apple II division of, 26, 30, 38, 40; Jobs
    removed from, 41–45; Jobs-Sculley
    relationship at, 3–8, 12, 17–46, 48–49;
    Lisa product line of, 19, 24, 27, 30;

Macintosh division of, Jobs in charge of,
    26–36; Macintosh division of, poor
    results of, 38–42; near demise of, 4–8,
    38–42; Sculley's CEO deal at, 19–22
Argyris, C., 124, 243
Armchair reflection, 86–87, 88
Assessment: of assets and liabilities, 147,
    149–151; of degree of interdependence,
    123–124; of odds for success, 127–129;
    of outside pressures, 145–147; of a
    relationship, 144–151; of relationship
    change, 138
Assets, assessing a relationship's, 147, 149, 150
Asymmetric access, 164–165
Asymmetrical awareness, 104–105

B

"Bedford, T." *See* Naughton-Bedford case
    example
Begley, S., 63
Behavior: evaluation of, 251–252; explanation
    of, 248–250; focus on, *versus* motives,
    156, 164–165; genetic and
    environmental factors in, 62–64; internal
    and external factors in, 248; power of
    relationships to change, 62–64, 65;
    predicting consequences of, 250–251
Behavior change: assessing progress in, 138;
    assessing the likelihood of success for,
    127–129; individual *versus* relationship,
    133, 141, 222; misconceptions about,
    133–135, 141; motives and, 156,
    164–165; power of relationships to

effect, 62–64, 65; small moves toward, 186–187. *See also* Relationship transformation

Behavioral repertoires: breadth of, 238, 240–241; in Chris-Peter relationship, 114–116; defined, 231; depth of, 238–240; expanding, 168–169, 237; guide to, 114, 231–241; intersecting, as basis of patterns, 168–169; relationship formation and, 23; role of, 102, 114; social contexts and, 102, 114; themes of, 114–116; types of, 102, 114, 231. *See also* Experiential knowledge; Interpretive strategies

"Being Steve Jobs' Boss" (Kahney), 6

Beliefs: as analytic knowledge, 234–235; cultural, 235–236; as moral knowledge, 235–236

Birth of the Mind, The (Marcus), 64

Blaming: in Chris-Peter relationship, 115; game of, 12, 65; in individual perspective, 48, 49, 50–54, 62, 65, 82

Body language, 102, 103, 164

Boyatzis, R., 9

Brain: hot and cool systems of, 80, 81–83, 85–86; mutability of, 64

British empire, in World War II, 55–61

BusinessWeek, 38, 120

C

Calibration, of pattern maps, 162, 164–165

Cameron, S., 70

Change efforts, organizational, 135. *See also* Behavior change; Relationship transformation

Characters and caricatures, turning people into, 144, 234

Childhood: power of relationships to shape behavior in, 64; residual effects of, 201–203, 204–208, 209, 211

Chris-Peter relationship: analysis of, 104–105; Anatomy Framework applied to, 100–116, 117; background on, 90–91; frames in, 106–111; improvement of, 116–117; social contexts in, 111–114; stages of, 91–99

Churchill, W., and F. Roosevelt, 55–61

"Clear Inc." case example, 50–54

Clothier, S., 1

Cognitive psychology, 64

Coleman, D., 38, 40

Comic relief, 139–140, 191

Complexity, of people, 254

Conflict: avoidance of, 115; as theme in Chris-Peter relationship, 114–116; upside of, 115; using, to strengthen a relationship, 69–88. *See also* Heat of the moment

Conlin, M., 120, 197

Constraints, assessment of, 145–147

Constructs, built from experiential knowledge, 234–235

Control-autonomy dilemma, 189, 216

Cool system, of brain: defined, 80; shifting into, 81–83, 85–86, 88

Cool topics, 79–80

Coordination, degree of interdependence and, 124

Couples, research on, 11

Cowardice, appealing to, 154–155

Cuban missile crisis, 78–79

Cultural knowledge: advantages and disadvantages of, 237–238; analytic, 234; defined, 232; moral, 235–236; narrative, 233; personal knowledge *versus*, 237–238; practical, 236. *See also* Experiential knowledge

D

"Dan Gavin." *See* Gavin-Fine relationship; Gavin-Turner relationship

"David," 96–97, 98, 104, 113

Dawes, H., 70

Decision making, degree of interdependence in, 124

Defending strategy, 240

Demands, assessment of, 145–147

Description(s): calibration of, 162, 164–165; explanation and, 247, 249; of interactions, 155–159, 162, 164–165, 246–247

Development: assessment of relationship's potential for, 123; implicit theory of, 218–219. *See also* Personal growth

Difficulty of change, assessing, 128

Disney, 8

Dispositions: blaming problems on, 48, 49, 50–54, 62, 65, 82; cultural values and, 235–236; describing, 87; focus on, *versus* relationships, 14–15, 87, 89–90, 253–254; genetics and, 62–64, 65; individual perspective and, 48, 49, 50–54, 62, 65, 82; labels and, 253–254; power of relationships *versus,* 62–64, 65; shifting perspective away from, 82–83, 88

Disruption of patterns: action experiments step in, 167–170; in Chris-Peter relationship, 116; dilemma of, 171–172; in Gavin-Fine relationship, 143–172; mapping patterns step for, 152–166; objectives of, 137, 143–144; relationship assessment step for, 144–151; results of, 137, 170–172; steps in, 137, 144–170; in three-stage model of relationship change, 137, 143–172

E

Edmondson, A., 79
Eisner, M., 8
Elliot, J., 40, 42
Emotional intelligence, 9
Emotional responsibilities, informal negotiation of, 23
Emotional tyrant role, 108
Emotions: dampening of, 115; engaging, through maps, 165; framing and, 106, 175–178; in the heat of the moment, 79, 80, 82–83; from historical events, 203, 208; shifting from hot to cool, 81–83, 88; as theme in Chris-Peter relationship, 114–116; upside of, 115. *See also* Heat of the moment
Entrenchment, 39
Evaluation: description *versus,* 155–156; of interactive behavior, 155–156, 251–252
Expectations: building hope and, 140–141; unrealistic, 134
Experience: genetic predisposition *versus* learning from, 62–64; knowledge-building from, 231
Experiential knowledge: analytic, 232, 234–235; aspects of, 114, 230, 231; childhood events and, 201–203,

204–208, 211; in Chris-Peter relationship, 114–116; cultural, 231, 232–236, 237–238; gaps or slippage in, 240–241; mapping based on, 247–248; moral, 203, 208, 232, 235–236; narrative, 203, 208, 217–218, 232–234; personal, 231, 233–236; personal and cultural, compared, 237–238; practical, 232, 236–237; restructuring of outdated, 209–223; revisiting and revising, 197–230; role of, 102, 114; types of, 232–238; unconscious, 247–248, 251. *See also* Practical knowledge and action strategies; Theories; Values

Explanations: personal, in experiential knowledge, 234–235; step of, in mapping interactions, 247–250

Exposure, fear of, 198–203, 210–213, 226–227

F

Failure. *See* Setbacks and failures
Far Side, The, 6, 53
Feynman, R., 254
"Fine, S." *See* Gavin-Fine relationship
Fiorina, C., 8
Flood, C., 69
Follett, M. P., 69
"Four Horsemen of the Apocalypse, The," 11
Frame experiments, 186–195
Frames and framing: dynamics of, 106, 174–175; freezing, 174–181; of goals, 109–111; implications of, 110–111; interlocking, 106–107, 177, 179, 181; inventing new, 181–185; mapping, 179, 181; naming, 178–179; in relationship development stage, 25–26; role of, in pattern repetition, 101, 106–111, 174–175; of roles relative to others, 108; of the situation, 107; uncovering, through in-the-moment reactions, 107–111, 175–179. *See also* Interpretive strategies; Reframing
Franklin and Winston (Meacham), 55
Fun, in relationship change, 139–141, 191
Fundamental attribution error, individual perspective and, 15, 62, 64

Future: anticipating relationship challenges of the, 225–227; step of returning to the, 223–228

G

Gains, consolidating, 223–224
Game playing: of blame game, 12, 65; in Chris-Peter relationship, 104; in Naughton-Bedford relationship, 53–54; of waiting game, 12, 65, 133
"Gavin, D." *See* Gavin-Fine relationship; Gavin-Turner relationship
Gavin-Fine relationship (Dan and Stu): action experiments step in, 167–169; background on, 143–144; demands and constraints on, 145–147; disruption-of-patterns stage of, 143–172; frame experiments step in, 186–195; freeze frame step in, 174–181; invent-new-frames step in, 181–185; mapping patterns step in, 152–166; reframing stage of, 173–196; relationship assessment step in, 144–151; restructure-outdated-knowledge step in, 209–223; return-to-the-future step in, 223–228; revising stage of, 197–230; revisit-past-events step in, 198–209
Gavin-Turner relationship: background on, 71–78; "flaming" voice mail incident in, 75–77, 82–86; reflecting and reframing in, 82–86
Gaye, M., 47
Genetics, power of relationships *versus*, 62–64, 65
Gladwell, M., 89
Glavin, B., 28
Goals: conflicting, 109–111; framing of, 109–111; for relationship change, scope of, 135–137
"Goldstein, H.," 153
Goleman, D., 9
"Gregory, J.," 212–213
"Guide to Behavioral Repertoires, A," 114, 231–241

H

Havel, V., 131
Heat of the moment: in Cuban missile crisis, 78–79; emotions in, 79, 80; freezing frames in the, 175–179; in Gavin-Turner case example, 71–78, 82–88; hot and cool systems of the brain and, 80, 81–82; in Lincoln-Stanton case example, 69–71; recalling new frames in the, 185; reflecting and reframing in, 81–88, 185, 196; strengthening relationships in times of, 69–88
Heifetz, R., 9
Here-we-go-again moments, 246
Hewlett-Packard, 8
Historical events: restructuring outdated knowledge from, 209–223; revisiting, 197–209
Hitler, A., 55, 57–58
Hobbit, The (Tolkien), 133
Hope, creating, 140–141
Hot system, of brain: defined, 80; shifting out of, 81–83, 88
Hot topics, 79–80, 81
Humility, 165
Humor, 139–140, 191

I

IBM, 28, 34, 38
Ignoring, of inconsequential relationships, 126
"I'm OK. You're OK. We're Not OK," 47
Impact assessment, 127
Individual perspective: assumptions of, 12, 48–55, 65; causes of, 81, 89–90; in "Clear Inc." case example, 50–54; in Jobs-Sculley case example, 48–50; on people or relationships, 49; shifting out of, 81–82; on substance or issues, 49
Inference, ladder of, 243. *See also* Ladder of Reflection
Informal structures: breakdown of, 43–45; definition and elements of, 117; development of, 30–34; evolution of, 34–36; frames and, 101, 106–111. *See also* Patterns of interaction; *Relationship headings*
Information sharing, degree of interdependence and, 123–124
Inside pressures, assessment of, 147, 148
Interactions: act-react template for mapping, 159–162; capturing, 152–155, 246;

describing, 155–159, 246–247; mapping, in Gavin-Fine relationship, 152–166; mapping, with Ladder of Reflection, 152–166, 243–253. *See also* Patterns of interaction

Interdependence: assessing the degree of, 123–124; in coordination, 124; in decision making, 124; in information sharing, 123–124; relationship strategies according to degree of, 124–126

Interpersonal rights, informal negotiation of, 23

Interpersonal takeover, 103–104

Interpretive strategies: action-based *versus* intention-based, 164–165; breadth of, 238–239; 240–241; in Chris-Peter relationship, 114–116; depth of, 238–240; role of, 102, 114, 231, 238; types of, 238–241; unconscious dynamic of, 174–175. *See also* Frames and framing; Reframing

Investment, in relationships: calculating odds for success of, 127–129; costs of dysfunctional relationships and, 134–135; decision making related to, 119–129, 134–135; by degree of interdependence, 123–124; impact assessment and, 127; Investment Matrix for, 120–126; by relative importance, 122–123; segment-specific strategies for, 124–126; Sequencing Matrix for, 126–129; strategy of, 126

Investment Matrix, 120–126

J

Jobs, S.: on Apple's near demise, 4–5; background of, 19; in charge of Macintosh division, 26–36; firing of, 4–5; leadership style of, 22, 25; in meeting with Xerox executives, 28–29, 34; removal of, 41–45; return of, 3, 4. *See also* Jobs-Sculley relationship

Jobs-Sculley relationship: accounts of, 3–8, 12; development stage of, 26–36; end stage of, 37–45; formation stage of, 18–25; individual perspective in, 48–50; informal structure breakdown in, 43–45; informal structure development in, 30–34; informal structure shift in,

34–36; initial meeting in, 19–20; others' explanations of, 17–18; themes in, 24, 25

Johnson, S., 143

K

Kendall, D., 20, 31

Kennedy, J. F., 78–79

Khrushchev, N., 78–79

Knowledge, experiential. *See* Experiential knowledge

Kouzes, J., 9

L

Labels, 253–254

Ladder of Inference, 243

Ladder of Reflection: conclusion rung of, 245, 247–254; description rung of, 155–159, 246–247; explanation rung of, 247–250; in Gavin-Fine relationship, 152–166; in Gavin-Turner case example, 83–86; graphical depiction of, 81, 244; implications of, 252–253; observation rung of, 245, 246–247; origins of, 243; selection rung of, 246; using, to map interactions, 152–166, 243–254; using, to observe and map interactions, 244–253; using, to shift perspective, 81–88; using labels *versus*, 253–254

"Lang, K.," 94, 97, 100, 111, 113

Larson, G., 6, 53

Laughter, 139–140

Leaders: assessing a relationship's impact on, 127; control-autonomy dilemma of, 189, 216; development of, through relationships, 123; dispositional approach to, 14–15; hot topics and, 80; individual perspective in, 12, 48–55, 65; relational perspective in, 12–13, 47–48, 55–62

Leadership: importance of relationships to, 8–12; research on relationships and, 10–11

Leadership Challenge, The (Kouzes and Posner), 9

Leadership on the Line (Heifetz and Linsky), 9

Liabilities, assessing a relationship's, 147, 149–151

Limelight, pattern of avoiding, 198–203, 210–213, 226–227

Lincoln, A., 67; and E. Stanton, 69–71
Linsky, M., 9
Loss, protecting against catastrophic, theme of, 203–208

M

Management, relationship, 126
Mangold, C., 31
Mapping and maps: action experiments designed from, 167–170; Anatomy Framework for, 13, 14, 89–117; calibration of, 162, 164–165; in Chris-Peter case example, 100–116; experiential knowledge and, 247–248; in Gavin-Fine case example, 152–166; of interlocking frames, 179, 181; Ladder of Reflection for, 152–166, 244–253; steps in, summarized, 166
Marcus, G., 64
Markkula, M., 20, 22
McChrystal, S. A., 8
Meacham, J., 55, 59, 60–61
Meaney, M., 63
"Merrimac" case example: background on, 71–73, 143–144; "FastStart" unit of, 74–78; "Focuspoint" product business launch of, 143–144, 153, 176, 190; founding friends of, 71–79; Gavin-Fine relationship in, 143–172, 173–196, 197–230; Gavin-Turner relationship in, 71–78, 82–86. *See also* Gavin-Fine relationship; Gavin-Turner relationship
Moral knowledge: cultural, 235–236; defined, 232; personal, 203, 208, 236. *See also* Experiential knowledge; Values
Moral logic, 236
Motivation, for change, 127
Motives, focus on behavior *versus*, 156, 164–165
Myers-Briggs assessment, 87, 253–254

N

Narrative knowledge, 232–234; culturally shared, 233; personal, 203, 208, 217–218, 233–234. *See also* Experiential knowledge
Naughton-Bedford case example, 50–54
Negotiating strategy, 238, 240

Newsweek, 63
Norms, cultural, 235–236

O

Obama, B., 8
Organizations: assessing a relationship's impact on, 127; change efforts in, 135; developmental relationships in, 123; relationships at fault lines of, 119–120; strategic relationships in, 122; symbolic relationships in, 122
Outside pressures, assessment of, 145–147
Ovitz, M., 8

P

Past events: restructuring outdated knowledge from, 209–223; revisiting, 197–209
Patterns of interaction: action experiments to disrupt, 167–170; act-react template for mapping, 159–162; Anatomy Framework of, 100–117; disruption of, 137, 143–172; formation of, 101, 102–103, 105; frame experiments and, 186–195; frames and repetition of, 101, 106–111, 173–175; mapping, 89–117, 152–166, 243–253; mistakes in changing, 133–135; nonproductive, in case example, 82, 83; persistence of, 173–174, 196, 198; productive, in case example, 85–86; reframing, 173–196; revising knowledge for, 197–230; third-party perspective on, 182. *See also* Disruption of patterns; Interactions
Pearl Harbor, 57, 58
PepsiCo, 19, 20, 24, 25, 26, 31
Persona, assuming a, 234
Personal action strategies. *See* Practical knowledge and action strategies
Personal growth: assessing inside pressures for, 147, 148; relationships as context for, 116–117, 123, 141, 229
Personal histories, revisiting, 197, 198–209
Personality type inventories, 87, 253–254
Perspective(s): frames and, 106–107; hot and cool systems and, 80, 81; shifting, through reflecting and reframing, 69–88; shifting, with revised outdated

knowledge, 213; taking multiple, 239, 240

"Petersen, D.," 94–95

Poland, in World War II, 57–58

Popper, K., 61

Posner, B., 9

Power, shared preoccupation with, 24

Practical experiments. *See* Action experiments

Practical knowledge and action strategies: in Chris-Peter relationship, 114–115; expanding one's, 237; in Gavin-Fine relationship, 203, 208; as part of experiential knowledge, 114, 232, 236–237; use and types of, 236–237. *See also* Experiential knowledge

Prediction: of behavioral consequences, 250–251; to get at people's reactions, 162, 163

Principles, derived from moral knowledge, 236

Professional services firm. *See* "Merrimac" case example

Protection theme, 203–208

Psychological rewards, informal negotiation of, 24

Q

Questioning: debate *versus,* 159; genuine *versus* insincere, 165; to get at people's reactions, 162, 163

"Quipsalot, G.," 210–213

R

Rat behavior, 63

Reactions: action experiments for disrupting, 167–170; actions interlocked with, 101, 102–103, 105, 117, 159–162, 168–169, 177; frame experiments with, 186–195; getting at approaches to, 107–111, 162, 163, 175–178; mapping actions and, 159–162; pattern formation derived from, 101, 102–103, 105, 117; reframing, 181–185

Readiness, for change, 127

Realistic goals, 135–137

Reflection: in Gavin-Turner case example, 81–86; for knowledge-building, 241; in Ladder of Reflection, 81, 244–253; on setbacks and failures, 139; steps in,

244–253; unhelpful "armchair," 86–87, 88

Reframing: dilemma of, 196; frame experiments step in, 186–195; freeze frame step in, 174–181; in Gavin-Fine case example, 173–196; in Gavin-Turner case example, 81–86; invent-new-frames step in, 181–185; for knowledge-building, 241; in Ladder of Reflection, 81; objectives of, 137, 173–174; paradox of, 174, 188; results of, 137, 195–196; of setbacks and failures, 139; steps in, 137, 174–195; in three-stage model of relationship change, 137, 173–196; unhelpful way of, 87

Reiss, D., 62–63

Rejection, in communication, 157–158

Relational capabilities, 13; described, 81–88; in Gavin-Turner case example, 71–78, 82–88; using, in the heat of the moment, 69–88. *See also* Reflection; Reframing

Relational disorders, 47

Relational perspective: assumptions of, 12–13, 48, 55–62, 65; in Franklin-Churchill case example, 55–61; on people or issues, 61; shifting into, 81–86; on substance or issues, 61; taking responsibility in, 47–48, 55

Relationship building: overview of, 13; in times of conflict, 69–88

Relationship change. *See* Relationship transformation

Relationship development stage: dynamics of, 25–36; informal structure development in, 30–36; interpretive frames established in, 25–26; in Jobs-Sculley case example, 26–36

Relationship formation stage: dynamics of, 18–25; informal terms in, understanding the, 18, 22–24; in Jobs-Sculley case example, 19–25; themes and patterns in, 23–25

Relationship strengthening: assessing likelihood of success for, 127–129; investment and sequencing decisions in, 119–129, 134–135; mapping patterns and structures for, 89–117; using the heat of the moment for, 69–88

Relationship transformation: action experiments step in, 167–170; anticipating future challenges in, 225–227; dilemmas inherent in, 171–172, 196, 229–230; disrupting-of-patterns stage of, 137, 143–172; frame experiments step in, 186–195; freeze frame step in, 174–181; in Gavin-Fine relationship, 143–172; how to, 14; having fun with, 139–141, 191; individual change *versus,* 133, 141; invent-new-frames step in, 181–185; key points about, 141; mapping patterns step in, 152–166; metrics for assessing, 138; misconceptions about, 133–135; paradoxes of, 144, 174, 188; possibility of, 14; principles and practices for, 135–141; realistic and ambitious aspirations in, 135–136; reframing stage of, 137, 173–196; relationship assessment step in, 144–151; resilience building for, 138–139, 229; restructure-outdated-knowledge step in, 209–223; return-to-the-future step in, 223–228; revising stage of, 137, 197–230; revisit-past-events step in, 197, 198–209; setbacks in using, 138–139; small moves toward, 186–187; sustaining, 223–228; three-stage model of, 136, 137

Relationship-ending stage: dynamics of, 37–45; informal structure breakdown in, 43–45; in Jobs-Sculley case example, 37–45

Relationships: basic strategies for handling, 13, 124–126; as context for individual growth, 116–117, 123, 141, 229; developmental importance of, 123; *ignore* strategy for, 125; importance of, to leadership, 8–11; *invest* strategy for, 126; *manage* strategy for, 125; managing the costs of, 119–129; power of, to shape behavior, 62–64, 65; scholarship on, 10–11; *separate* strategy for, 125; setting terms of new, 227; stages of, 17–46; as strategic asset *versus* liability, 3–11, 147, 149–151; strategic importance of, 122; symbolic importance of, 122; underestimating the costs of, 134–135

Reliability theme: action sequences for revising, 219–221; in Chris-Peter relationship, 107, 108, 110, 115–116; in Gavin-Fine relationship, 208, 213–222; implicit theories derived from, 214–215; narratives derived from, 217–218

Renewal strategy, 240–241

Resilience: building, 138–139, 229; hope and, 140–141

Responsibility, taking: *versus* blaming others, in individual perspective, 50–54, 62, 65; in relational perspective, 47–48, 55

Revising: dilemma of, 229–230; in Gavin-Fine relationship, 197–230; objectives of, 137, 197–198; restructure-outdated-knowledge step in, 209–223; results of, 137, 228–230; return-to-the-future step in, 223–228; revisit-past-events step in, 198–209; stage of, 137, 197–230; steps in, 137, 197–228

Roles: cultural, 233; framing, in relation to others, 108

Roosevelt, F.: quotation, 3; and W. Churchill, 55–61

Rose, F., 19, 21, 22, 25, 29–30, 39

S

"SafetyNet" case example, 90–99. *See also* Chris-Peter relationship

Sarcasm, 210–213

Scenes, cultural, 233

Schön, D. A., 243

Scott, M., 20

Sculley, J.: on Apple and Jobs, 6–8; Apple board's siding with, 4–5, 42; background of, 19; on decision to remove Jobs, 41–42, 43; fateful decisions of, 30–31; leadership style of, 20, 22, 25; on meeting with Xerox executives, 28–29, 34; path of, to becoming Apple CEO, 19–22; at PepsiCo, 19, 20, 24, 25, 26, 31. *See also* Jobs-Sculley relationship

"Secureware" case example, 90–99, 100–116. *See also* Chris-Peter relationship

Sedaris, D., 17, 45

Selection, of interactions to map, 246

Self-concepts, 108, 110

Self-deprecation, 154–155
Self-fulfilling prophecies, 106, 219
Self-interest, 147
Sensing strategy, 238, 239, 240
Separation, structural, 126
Sequencing Matrix, 120, 126–129
Setbacks and failures: of action experiments, 169; learning from, 138–139, 169
Sherwood, R., 58–59
Shock of recognition, 165
Singapore, 57
Situations: framing, 107; personal *versus* cultural knowledge applied to, 237–238; practical strategies for, 236–237; role assumption and, 108
Slippage, 240–241
Social contexts: behavioral repertoires and, 102, 114; in Chris-Peter relationship, 111–114; elements of, 112; role of, 101, 111; table of, 112, 113–114
Sossa, M., 173
Soviet Union, World War II and, 58, 59–60
Speculation, to get at people's reactions, 162, 163
Stalin, J., 59–60
Stanton, E., and A. Lincoln, 69–71
Stereotypes, cultural, 233
Strategic importance, of a relationship, 122
Strategies. *See* Interpretive strategies; Practical knowledge and action strategies
Structures. *See* Informal structures
"Stu." *See* Gavin-Fine relationship
Summers, L., 8
Sustainability, building: by anticipating future challenges, 225–227; by consolidating gains, 224–225; by defining new objectives, 225; in return-to-the-future step, 223–228; by setting terms of new relationship, 227
Symbolic importance, of a relationship, 122

T

Testing strategy, 238, 240
Themes: in Chris-Peter relationship, 114–116; derived from personal history, 198–209; in relationship formation stage, 23–25

Theories, explicit: mapping interactions with, 248–251; pitfalls in using, 253–254
Theories, implicit: in Chris-Peter relationship, 115–116; derived from childhood events, 203, 208, 211; in Gavin-Fine case example, 218–219; of learning, 218–219; as part of experiential knowledge, 114, 232, 234–235
Thompson, C. R. "Tommy," 59
Threatened-subject role, 108
Three-stage model of relationship change: *disrupt* stage of, 137, 143–172; *reframe* stage of, 137, 173–196; *revise* stage of, 137, 197–230; table of, 137; use of, 136. *See also* Relationship transformation
Time, 47
Tolkien, J.R.R., 133
"Turner, L." *See* Gavin-Turner relationship

U

Undiscussables, 124
United Nations, 59–60
United States, in World War II, 55–61

V

Values: in Chris-Peter relationship, 115–116; cultural, 235–236; for evaluating behavior, 251–252; as part of experiential knowledge, 114, 232, 235–236; personal, 203, 208, 236
Voice, tone of, 110, 183

W

Waiting game, 12, 65, 133
Weaver, R., 38
World War II, Franklin-Churchill relationship and, 55–61
Wozniak, S., 20, 38–39

X

Xerox, 28–29, 34

Y

Yocam, D., 26

This is a continuation of the copyright page.

The cartoons on pages 10, 37, and 155. Copyright © Leo Cullum/The New Yorker Collection/www.cartoon.bank.com

The cartoon on page 99. www.cartoonstock.com

The cartoon on page 72. Copyright © Henry Martin/The New Yorker Collection/www.cartoon.bank.com

The cartoon on page 128. Copyright © Barbara Smaller/The New Yorker Collection/www.cartoon.bank.com

The cartoon on page 140. Copyright © Frank Cotham/The New Yorker Collection/www.cartoon.bank.com

The cartoon on page 176. Copyright © William Hamilton/The New Yorker Collection/www.cartoon.bank.com

The cartoon on page 222. Copyright © Robert Mankoff/The New Yorker Collection/www.cartoon.bank.com